Practical
Blacksmithing and Metalworking
Second Edition

2nd ed.

Practical
Blacksmithing and Metalworking
Second Edition

Percy W. Blandford

TAB Books
Division of McGraw-Hill

New York San Francisco Washington, D.C. Auckland Bogotá
Caracas Lisbon London Madrid Mexico City Milan
Montreal New Delhi San Juan Singapore
Sydney Tokyo Toronto

pbk   19 20 21 DOC/DOC 0 9 8
hc   1 2 3   4   5   6 7 8 9 DOH/DOH 8 9 8

Library of Congress Cataloging-in-Publication Data

Blandford, Percy W.
   Practical blacksmithing and metal-working.

     Rev. ed. of: The practical handbook of blacksmithing
& metalworking. 1st ed. c1980.
    Includes index.
    1. Blacksmithing.   2. Ironwork. I. Blandford,
Percy W. Practical handbook of blacksmithing & metal-
working. II. Title.
  TT220.B43 1988   682′.4   88-8565
   ISBN 0-8306-0394-8
   ISBN 0-8306-2894-0 (pbk.)

Contents

Introduction

One of the longest established crafts known to civilized man has held its place of importance through all the changes of thousands of years, while civilizations have come, grown, and gone, and others have taken their place. The skills of the man who could work iron and steel were always needed, and the blacksmith always held an important place among his fellow men. The methods have changed little. Very early smiths mastered the principles and these still hold good today. Improvements are in detail. A smith described in the Holy Bible would be able to comprehend what was happening in a twentieth-century smith's shop, while a modern smith, provided only with the tools of 2,000 years ago, would know what to do with them and be able to achieve creditable results.

After thousands of years with little change, a good deal of change has come to blacksmithing in the last 100 years or so, due to the Industrial Revolution. When the automobile replaced the horse, a smith was no longer essential to the community.

So where does that leave us? There are still blacksmiths able to earn a living primarily from smithing, but most have to broaden their scope to embrace metalwork that was not previously considered their work. There are still apprentices to blacksmithing. There are still manufacturers of the necessary equipment, although a smith is in the fortunate position of being able to make most of his own tools. There is still a demand for wrought-iron work that shows the mark of individuality and does not obviously come from a factory where hundreds of similar pieces have been made. Above all, there is still a place for men or women determined to express themselves through craftsmanship.

Many people looking for a craft turn to wood, but not everyone wants to work wood or is capable of becoming a competent carpenter, wood turner, or carver. Much work in metal requires a considerable investment in equipment, but blacksmithing as described in this book need not be expensive. A small portable forge and an anvil of modest size (not necessarily new) are the essentials, then a few tools lead the way to making more tools. Much material can come from scrap sources. What other people throw away can be recycled by a smith into things of use or beauty or both.

Working on the anvil is a mixture of physical effort and artistic application. There is always a lot of satisfaction to be obtained from physical effort properly directed. Blacksmithing also offers this advantage: If it does not come out right the first time, it can usually go back into the fire for another attempt.

Blacksmithing can be an adjunct to another craft. A mastery of hot iron allows the making of many things that can be used with other metal or wood constructions. The smith's metalwork will be a fitting companion to the projects of other branches of craftwork.

I hope this book will show the way to a great many potential blacksmiths who will come to enjoy their work at the anvil and, in doing so, carry on a great tradition.

SECTION 1
BLACKSMITHING

1

Blacksmithing Traditions

When Stone Age man first succeeded in separating metal from ore and making something from it, blacksmithing was born. The first metals were impure copper with traces of other metals; these have become known to us as bronze. Men of the Bronze Age made tools and weapons from this comparatively soft metal, and these were much more successful and convenient than their crude stone implements. But it was not until they discovered how to obtain iron from ore that tools and weapons of adequate strength could be made. In the Iron Age man learned to use heat to fashion iron and the foundations of smithing that were laid then have not changed in principle today.

The first evidence of smithing by hammering iron was found in Egypt and dated 1350 BC. It is a dagger, believed to have been made by a Hittite craftsman. It is fairly certain that the Hittites invented tempering and forging, then they kept their ironwork techniques secret. The Hittite empire was overthrown about 1200 BC, and a large number of migrants spread throughout what is now Europe and the Middle East, taking their ironworking skills with them first to Greece and the Balkans. This early Iron Age was from about 800 to 500 BC. Then ironworking spread further west in Europe and to Britain, during what is often called the Late Iron Age.

If was combining iron with wood that made possible the cultivation and clearing of land and the use of wheeled vehicles. Iron also made better weapons for hunting and warfare. Considering this, the smith was an important member of every community. By later Biblical times the smith was using an air-blown fire to heat his iron, and working in ways not much different from smiths today.

The smith finds a place in classical mythology—Roman and Greek, as well as Aztec and Phoenician. In Roman mythology Vulcan, son of Jupiter, is credited with being the founder of smithing. According to the stories, he made the axle for the chariot of the sun and the gates of dawn. He forged the thunderbolts his father used. In Norse mythology, Loki gave power to Thor as a smith. Quetzalcoatl of the Aztecs brought skill in ironworking and other crafts to the people. A similar story goes with Tuba-Cain of the Phoenicians.

In many mythologies, the smith is ugly or evil. Such has been the treatment in some countries of smiths in more recent times, possibly because they worked with fire in semi-darkness—things that were associated with the devil in the minds of superstitious people. Smiths were important in medieval times with the need for armor and weapons, but in some places they were almost outcasts. This did not apply everywhere; there are records of kings working with their favorite armorers. It must have made sense to take part in the production of something that had to be relied on to preserve life. Some smiths were artists in metal and proof of this is seen in surviving gates and other ornamental wrought-iron work (Fig. 1-1).

You might have noticed that the name of the craft has been given as *smith* and not *blacksmith*. The family name *Smith* indicates how many people were once concerned with the craft of smithing. Smiths in earlier times did all kinds of metalworking, as it was needed. Later developments brought specialists in working lead and other metals. In particular, the worker in lead became known as a *whitesmith*, so the worker in iron

Fig.1-1. This medieval anvil without horn or holes was probably used by an armourer.

became known as a *blacksmith*. That is the usual name today for anyone who uses heat and hammer to shape iron or steel.

To many people the name includes the craftsman responsible for the making and fitting of horseshoes. Strictly speaking, that craftsman is a *farrier*, although most smiths in the days of the great use of horse transport were also farriers. However, there was and there still is a distinction, and not every farrier or blacksmith could do the other man's job. There were other specialist smiths. A chain smith forged links in a chain. A nail smith (often a woman) did nothing but make nails. Today a blacksmith, whether professional or amateur, can expect to do all kinds of smithing and may need a knowledge of horseshoeing as well.

In the days when most countries depended on a rural economy, there was a blacksmith's shop wherever there was a cluster of dwellings. His customers were the farmers and workers who lived nearby. He probably farmed a piece of land himself. A comparable life was led by the village carpenter. Quite often they had adjoining shops and certain implements needed on the land or some piece of equipment to be used in a house would be a combined effort. Wagons and carts required both skills. In later years the wheelwright became a specialist craftsman, leaving the carpenter to other woodworking. There are many places in Europe where it is still possible to see the stone base (probably an old millstone) on which the blacksmith and the wheelwright worked together to assemble a wheel and draw the parts together with its iron tire.

There would also have always been blacksmiths working in towns, and some of them would have specialized in making gates and other wrought-iron work. There would have been armorers who made weapons as well as armor. Smiths were also employed on the great estates attached to feudal castles, and worked with other craftsmen on ecclesiastical buildings and furnishings.

Like most other craftsmen, blacksmiths were their own masters and independent, depending on payment from customers. Work might be done by barter for a share in the crop at harvest time or in return for some service rendered. These methods continued until the Industrial Revolution, not two centuries ago, when factory production began to replace the work of individual craftsmen. This affected blacksmiths in the same way as others who had enjoyed the independence of their craft. The need for individual smiths diminished, but many smiths were able to find places for their skills in industry. Many became factory workers.

The use of steam and other power introduced processes and techniques that would have been beyond the smith and his helpers, who had only their muscles for power. Gas and electric welding made possible the fabrication of parts that would have previously involved lengthy and laborious work at fire and anvil. Mass production had taken over and people had no use for the one-off products from the smith or other craftsman that cost more than the factory-made products.

Of course, horses were still being used at this time, and there was still need for rural smiths. The use of working horses did not really decline rapidly until the end of World War I. By then, the internal combustion engine in vehicles—particularly tractors—took the place of horses. Those smiths who wanted to maintain their independence had to broaden their scope. Some learned to maintain motor vehicles or they became agricultural engineers, with blacksmithing only a part of their activities.

Blacksmithing as a craft is no longer in great demand for its practical applications. Much of what a smith did for purely utilitarian purposes in the past can now be done more effectively by other means. However, there is still the need for a one-off product that would be better made by smithing, and there is still a place for the artist blacksmiths who can create wrought-iron work in a way that mass production cannot. There is no longer a need for a blacksmith in every community, but there is still a place for those who treat blacksmithing as a means of using craft skill in the same way that others may hammer a copper bowl, make furniture or pottery, carve wood, or weave a basket. Whether they do this for profit or just for the love of a craft, they will get a tremendous satisfaction out of forming iron, and carrying on one of the oldest crafts.

DESIGN

Throughout most of history the majority of blacksmiths were concerned with producing implements for use. Design work was often directed toward making the thing as suitable as possible for its intended purpose; appearance was of secondary importance.

Sword hilts and similar items were decorated with cuts and punchings. Other products often obtained any artistic effect from their layout and proportions. The art of the blacksmith is geared more to large items than small ones, and the artistic ability of individual blacksmiths can be seen in railings, gates, screens, and ecclesiastical decorations. On a smaller scale were locks and hinges, where iron was wrought to shape and decorated with cuts and stamping.

There are still in existence in Europe elaborately scrolled hinges with rather rudimentary surface decoration made with punches. Twisting strip metal into scrolls is a feature of much early wrought-iron work.

Blacksmiths concerned with decorative ironwork were influenced by the Gothic style in architecture. In the 15th century tracery intended for stone was repeated in iron, sometimes more effectively. This continued into the 16th century, when much cast iron came into use.

Up to this stage, design was the concern of the individual. There are some surviving examples of excellent work, but not of any sort of design standard. This was also true in woodworking, particularly furniture making. Craftsmen might have copied good ideas from each other, but designs were comparatively local. The printing press altered this. Chippendale and other great furniture designers and makers published pattern books and other furniture makers were able to produce chairs, tables, and many other things to these designs.

Almost the same thing happened to decorative blacksmithing. A Frenchman named Jean Tijou was called to England to work under architect Sir Christopher Wren on the ironwork for the royal palace at Hampton Court, alongside the River Thames to the west of London. He was an outstanding designer of ironwork and a very skilled blacksmith, with techniques that were mostly new to English craftsmen. He was at work on the palace ironwork in 1690 and he remained in England to publish designs in 1693. These were used by blacksmiths all over the country, and spread via immigrants to America. Much of his work was rather elaborate and flamboyant. English smiths modified his style to give a more restrained effect (Fig. 1-2). However, Tijou can be credited with having raised wrought-iron work to classical perfection. His influence can still be seen today.

Fig. 1-2. This ornate example of early smith's work is a bell pull.

2

Iron and Steel

Almost all blacksmithing is done with iron and steel. None of the other common metals can be fashioned by hammering after heating in the same way. Iron is the base metal from which steel is derived. Iron ore is the source; iron as iron and steel has to be obtained from ore by heat. Fortunately, iron is plentiful: much of this earth is composed of iron. In some places the best ore has been used, but improved methods allow iron to be obtained from inferior ore. There is no fear of iron production coming to a halt because of shortage of supplies. The world supply seems inexhaustible.

When primitive man discovered how superior iron was to the previous bronze and stone for his weapons, tools, and implements, he must have tried many ways of building up sufficient heat to extract the desired iron from the ore. The wind might have been directed through channels in the side of a hill to a pit containing the fire and ore. Where there was no suitable hill, a stone and earth tower might have been built to contain the fire and ore, with a draft hole for the prevailing wind to enter. Early fires would have been fueled by wood and later by charcoal or coal. Bellows were developed to produce the draft and remove the dependence on a fickle wind. At the end of the process, the fire was raked out and the iron brought out of the bottom of the pit. Quality could not be controlled; luck decided what could be used for tools and what might have to be discarded or used in its cast form. Iron produced in this way would have contained many impurities, and to be suitable for smithing it has to be reasonably pure. An excess of impurities causes brittleness and other faults.

Modern iron is produced from furnaces that have developed primitive fires into great industries. What first comes from these blast furnaces is called pig iron. This pig iron contains a great many impurities in small quantities. It may be about 95 percent iron, with up to 4 percent carbon and the remainder including such things as silicon, sulfur, phosphorous, and manganese. The impurities have a considerable effect on the quality and characteristics of the iron.

CAST IRON

Cast iron is made from pig iron by remelting it and pouring it into molds. Its quality can be controlled by varying the contents and by cooling rapidly or slowly. It is possible to make ductile cast iron by a further process, but this is still unsuitable for smithing. Cast iron in its many forms is used extensively for machine parts, many domestic articles, and anything where weight and bulk are wanted or acceptable. The shape cannot be altered by heating and hammering. Ductile cast iron can be machined successfully, and this is the material used for parts that are turned or otherwise formed with cutting tools. Some decorative work is done in cast iron. Cast iron contains 2 percent to 4 percent carbon, plus whatever other elements are present in smaller quantities.

WROUGHT IRON

Wrought iron has been favored by smiths throughout nearly all of ironwork history. It is produced by refining and rolling after further heating the first pig iron, so as to reduce the carbon and to remove most of the impurities. The resulting iron that has been rolled to produce strips has a fibrous nature that makes it particularly suitable for shaping by hammering. It is the most tough, ductile, and malleable form of iron. It also has a greater resistance to corrosion than most other types of iron. The first light rusting forms a protective film that reduces further corrosion.

Unfortunately, wrought iron is no longer readily available. It has been replaced by mild steel, which is iron with a small amount of carbon in it. For structural work, machining, and general engineering, this is a superior material. It is not however, as satisfactory for blacksmithing. Today there is very little wrought iron produced, and anyone engaged in blacksmithing has to use mild steel. This is fine for many uses, although mild steel is not as amenable to fine work because it is more difficult to weld by the smith's method.

The amount of carbon in mild steel does not affect its hardness, and there is no way that heat treatment can have any appreciable effect in hardening or softening it. If the proportion of carbon is increased, the characteristics of the steel are altered. If the carbon content is about 2 percent, this is high carbon or tool steel. Steel with this amount of carbon can be made harder by heating and quenching, in the processes of hardening and tempering described later. Another heat treatment removes the hardness. It is this steel from which tools are made by a blacksmith. It will make springs and was used for parts of armor.

The traditional blacksmith found that wrought iron and tool steel fulfilled all his needs. The modern smith has to use mild steel instead of wrought iron for much of his work. Although there are now many special steels available, it is still advisable for a smith to only use ordinary high-carbon steel for tools. Some of the other steels—which have been alloyed with small quantities of other metals to give special qualities and are used for some industrially-produced tools—require special precise heat treatments with equipment the ordinary blacksmith would not have available.

ALLOY STEELS

Steel is often described as an alloy of iron and carbon, but this is not strictly correct. The word *alloy* applies to a mixture of two or more metals, and carbon is not a metal. Some of the special steels are collectively called *alloy steels*, indicating that other metals have been added to the steel. With modern techniques the proportions of these metals can be closely controlled. Small amounts of some other metals can make considerable differences to the steel. Nickel, chromium, copper, and tungsten are some examples.

With 18 percent, chromium and 8 percent nickel added to steel, corrosion resistance is increased and *stainless steel* produced. The addition of silicon can produce resistance to acids. *High-speed steel* is produced for cutters that retain their strength and hardness when hot. High-speed steels vary, but they can be alloyed with one or more of the following: tungsten, chromium, molybdenum, or vanadium. Cobalt added to steel improves its magnetic qualities. The range of special steels available today appears to be almost limitless. The smith wanting steel to heat and hammer into tools and then harden and temper by heat treatment should stick to a straight high-carbon steel, without any other metal alloyed to it.

Of course, iron, mild steel, and tool steel can be bought as new stock in sheet form or in strips with round, square, rectangular, hexagonal, and many other sections. For quantity production, this is the way to obtain material. But many oldtime blacksmiths had a stock of scrap material behind their forge and they would draw on this for iron or steel to make some items. It is possible to use the same iron or steel many times. A new part might be nothing like the old part it was made from. One attraction of blacksmithing is the ability to heat metal and use your skill with the hammer to form it into a new shape. It is also possible to weld pieces under the hammer to form them into a larger piece. In pioneer days, when new iron or steel was difficult to obtain, small pieces of scrap iron were joined to make a larger item. The work might have been time-consuming, but if there was no other iron available, that was the only way.

A modern blacksmith might find it worthwhile to collect suitable discarded iron and steel parts for possible future use. Cast iron is not much use to a blacksmith for making things, although a piece might be found to use as a special anvil or for some shaping purpose. Very old things made from strips, such as railings or gates, might be wrought iron and welcomed as the best material for much new shaping and welding. Even mild steel from these and other assemblies can provide the stock for new work.

Anything that has obviously been a tool has possibilities for reworking to make another tool, even if the original was worn out. A good source of high-carbon steel is any sprung vehicle. Leaf springs are good high-carbon steel suitable for making tools. Coil springs are the same steel and might not have quite as many uses, but they can be straightened and cut to make tools. Anything that has formed part of a solid structure is likely to be mild steel if it is not very old. If it is known to be very old, and particularly if it has been given much ornamental shaping to the ends, it is probably wrought iron.

The special alloy steels are mostly used in small pieces for machine tools. Larger tools—such as gardening tools, most carpenter's cutting tools and most knifelike large cutters, as well as the cutting parts of many farm implements—are likely to be straight high-carbon steel that can be used again for making tools.

Sometimes, among the scrap will be other metals that are unsuitable for smithing. When old and corroded they might appear similar to iron and steel. If they are rubbed with a file or abrasive paper, any difference should be apparent. Copper, brass, aluminum, lead, and other *non-ferrous metals* are not useful for smithing, although they might have other metalworking possibilities. *Ferrous* and *ferric* are terms derived from the Latin *ferrum*, meaning iron, and are used when it is necessary to distinguish metals and alloys that might or might not contain iron.

3

Forge and Anvil

Blacksmithing is the shaping of hot iron and steel, usually by hammering. A means of heating and something to hammer on comprise the basic required equipment.

Early smiths might have heated iron in wood fires, but they soon found that the intensity of heat could be increased with an air blast. They would have also found that wood converted to charcoal produced a better fire for their purpose. In its simplest form, the air blast was produced by air blowing through a pipe. Crude piston-type pumps were devised, usually in pairs, so a helper moving the pistons up and down in turn produced a fairly even blast. Bellows have been used for many years. Wooden pieces with leather between and simple leather flap valves over holes controlled the flow of air. Small single-acting bellows were used in pairs so a reasonably steady airflow could be maintained. Some were small enough for one helper to work with his feet. Others had to be operated by two helpers.

BELLOWS

In the Middle Ages, someone devised the double-acting bellows. It had two parts, one of which was operated by hand or foot. The other took air from it and was weighted so it forced air out while the other part was filling (Fig. 3-1A). This sort of bellows are still found today, some in blacksmiths' shops, and some in museums. There is an advantage in having a larger air capacity. A comparatively slow movement of the operating handle or lever delivers an ample flow of air to the fire. This meant that bellows in some shops were of considerable size. They did not have to be directly connected to the forge,

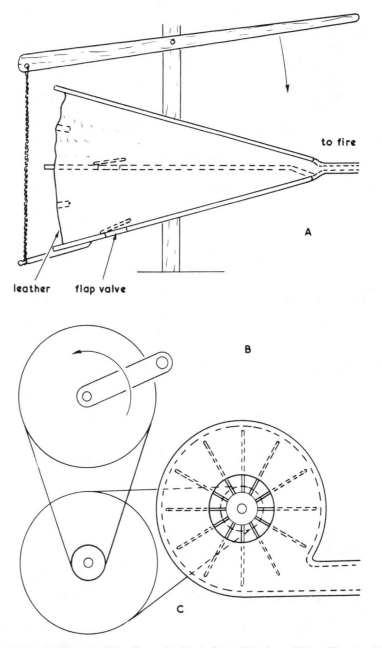

Fig. 3-1. Air blast to a forge was traditionally provided by bellows: (A) bellows; (B) fan; (C) external belting.

but could be joined by a pipe. They were usually close so that the smith or his helper could operate the bellows while tending the fire.

Portable forges were made with round, double-acting bellows under the forge pan, and a foot pedal was used to operate it. Both hands were free to tend the fire and the iron in it.

FAN BLOWERS

With advances in engineering came the development of the fan blower (Fig. 3-2). For nearly all blacksmithing purposes, this has taken over from the wood and leather bellows. The fan uses centrifugal force to take air drawn in from near the center of its casing to throw it out to a tube directed at the fire (Fig. 3-1B). The fan needs to rotate at high speed. For hand operation, the drive from the crank handle can be stepped up through internal gearing. Older types had external belting (Fig. 3-1C). The fan can also be driven electrically (Fig. 3-3). Since an electric motor is most efficient at high speeds, this suits a fan blower, often with a direct drive. However, there is a need to control the blast so the fire can be dormant when there is no steel in it to be heated or when more or less heat is required. Hand control allows this. With an electric blower, there could be a rheostat to adjust the amount of blast electrically, or there could be a damper in the air pipe. In both cases, it is best to arrange for the air blast to turn off automatically when your hand or foot is removed from the control. Otherwise the fire could go on growing dangerously.

There might still be uses for charcoal fires, but most blacksmithing is done with a coke fire. At one time, coke could be obtained cheaply as a by-product from the making of coal gas. With the general use of natural gas, this supply has ceased in most areas. Instead, the smith has to use small coal, which is converted to coke in the first burning of the fire, as described later.

When forging, it is possible to heat steel with a torch (Fig. 3-4). You can use a torch intended for welding, or a torch that uses air mixed with butane or propane gas that is primarily intended for brazing. Both types of torch produce an intense heat in a restricted space. There are occasions when this is desirable, but a greater spread of heat is usually required to get work hot over a sufficient expanse for normal smithing. A torch can be useful in the shop as an addition, but not an alternative, to the coal or coke forge.

There are gas forges in which many gas jets are used to provide a good spread of heat. They can be fixed or portable, have uses for horseshoeing, and work with rods and strips of moderate size. For general smithing, most workers prefer a coal-burning forge.

FORGES

A forge is a container for the fire, arranged at a convenient height and with an inlet for the air blast (Fig. 3-5). For indoor use, there is a hood and flue above the fire. Even for outdoor use, there is an advantage in partly enclosing the fire and providing a flue. The color of hot metal is best seen in a dim light, so the forge is normally placed away from any natural light in the smithy, while shrouding an outside forge gives shade for viewing steel drawn from the fire.

A forge can be made of sheet steel or cast iron. Many were made of stone, brick, or wood—and some still are. The wood is not as vulnerable as might be expected. The hearth is formed, inside whatever supports it, with fire bricks and fireclay or other refractory (heat-resisting) materials.

A traditional forge has a pan supported on legs with a square, open form on three sides and the back taken up to support the hood (Fig. 3-6A).

Fig. 3-2. The fan under the hearth of this portable forge is belt-driven in two stages to achieve a high speed.

Fig. 3-3. As can be seen by the flames, the electric blower maintains a steady blast in this forge.

Fig. 3-4. For heating small work a propane torch can be used over a metal tray supporting a bed of coke.

16

Fig. 3-5. This typical forge shows some of the firebrick lining and the hood and flue above.

17

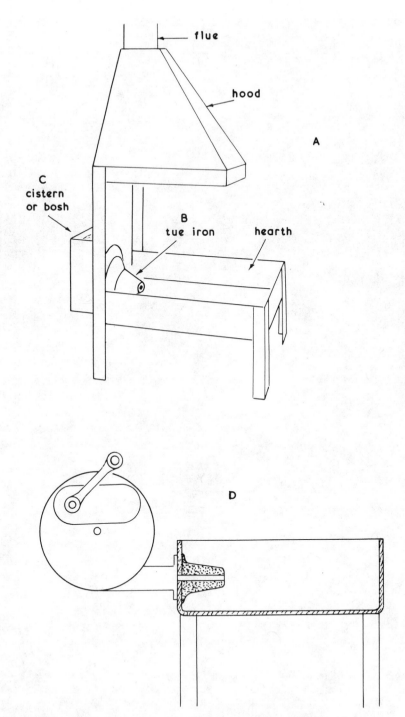

Fig. 3-6. The hearth has a hood (A) and a tue iron (B). The air blast enters through a water cistern (C). A small hearth might have a fan directly mounted on it (D).

TUE IRONS

The air pipe feeds into the fire through a *tuyere*, which is pronounced *tweer* and is of French origin. However, the English smith adapted this to *tue iron* (pronounced *twee iron*) and that seems the common term today. The two possible locations for the tue iron are at the back or in the bottom of the hearth. European forges and some used in America have the tue iron at the back. The cast-iron nozzle or tue iron projects into the fire (Fig. 3-6B) and can soon suffer from the heat, so its end begins to disintegrate. In larger forges the tue iron is made hollow and connected to a water cistern or *bosh* so water cooling prevents or delays the burning of the end of the tue iron (Fig. 3-6C). The bosh, with an open top, also serves for dipping hot steel to cool it. A smith needs a container of water within reach for cooling in any case. Some cast-iron hearths have this built into one side or the front.

A back tue iron can be connected directly to a fan blower, a convenient arrangement in a portable forge (Fig. 3-6D). In a larger forge, the blower might have to be brought to one side for convenience in turning and the blast led through a pipe. For hand turning of a fan, it is usual for the handle to be in a position for use with the left hand, leaving the right hand to deal with the fire and the steel in it.

Much good work has been done with a back tue iron, and some smiths have spent a lifetime with that type of forge. It might seem more logical to bring the air blast into the bottom of the fire, which should give a more even heat. A very simple bottom tue iron is a tube taken through the refractory material and with a pattern of holes under what will be the center of the fire (Fig. 3-7A). This does not permit easy cleaning and there is little control. It is more usual for there to be a cast-iron assembly below a central hole in the hearth. This is called a *duck's nest*. A removable perforated cover goes over the hole, then there is a door below to let out dirt and cinders that have accumulated in an extension below the air pipe (Fig. 3-7B). This assembly might also include a damper in the form of a valve that can be controlled by a long handle, to restrict the flow of air into the fire. Air from a bottom blast can be provided by a fan blower mounted similarly to one for a back tue iron, but with its outlet extended under the forge.

HEARTH SIZES

The size of a forge depends on its intended use. A large one can have a small fire, but there is a limit to the size of fire that can be made in a small one. However, space is usually important and if so, a forge no bigger than absolutely necessary will have to be chosen. The height of the hearth top above the floor should not be more than about 30 inches and might even be better a little lower. The depth inside also has to be considered. A deep fire is an advantage for welding. The hearth can be up to 1 foot deep and have its edge higher above the floor than a shallow forge. Some forges have parts cut out at one or both sides to get long bars into a deep fire.

A general-purpose smith could use a hearth up to 6 × 4 feet to accommodate anything he might have to work. Something between 30 inches and 42 inches would accommodate most work. The hood makes it higher and the addition of a blower extends the back. The steel worker who has only occasional use for a forge and the amateur who wishes to tackle blacksmithing as a hobby can manage with something light and compact. Smaller forges can be described as portable or rivet forges. Rivets for structural steelwork are

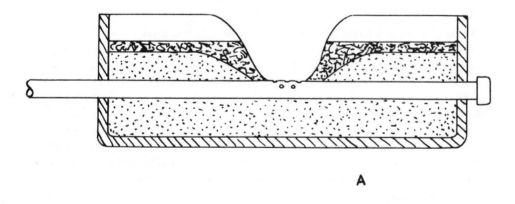

A

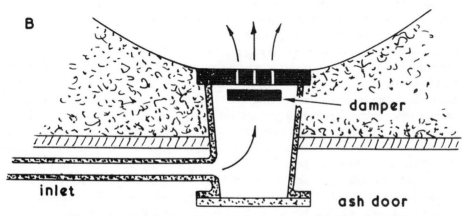

B

damper

inlet

ash door

Fig. 3-7. The air blast can be taken into the bottom of the fire through a perforated pipe (A) or a more elaborate tuyere (B).

made red hot in small forges that might have to be moved to follow the work around—so they have to be light.

Earlier portable forges had bellows mounted below the hearth. Modern versions are square or round, with four legs and a fan blower behind the hearth. These may or may not have a hood as standard equipment.

Large portable forges have fire pans or hearths 24 inches across, but they could be made down to 18 inches. A bottom blast type is preferable to a rear blast. The difference in effectiveness is more marked in the smaller forges. Some of these forges can be taken apart for ease of transport. If a portable forge is to be used outside, some sort of shrouding and flue should be devised. If it is used inside with coal, there will have to be a hood and flue. If the hood is adjustable, it can be lowered to collect smoke and increase draft when starting with coal. As the fire flames and becomes clean, it can be raised.

ANVILS

If red-hot iron or steel is to be hammered and the greatest effect is to be obtained with each blow, there has to be sufficient support under the iron so it takes the blows solidly—without bouncing or reacting. From the earliest days of the craft, an anvil made from a substantial piece of iron or steel has been used for the support (Fig. 3-8). Today there is a generally accepted form for this, with some minor variations, but anvils have had various shapes through the ages.

Some of the nearly square, flat-topped anvils were made without beaks. Some were given beaks at opposite sides (Fig. 3-9). All early anvils were iron, which suffered in use, so the original faces became misshapened and damaged. Modern anvils are formed almost entirely of steel, cast in one piece.

Traditional blacksmiths favor an anvil that rings like a bell when hit. Whether this sound signifies any special quality is debatable, but a ringing anvil is pleasant to use. Anvils are graded by their weights rather than by dimensions. The usual type for general smithing may weigh from 100 to 200 pounds. For more delicate work they might weigh as little as 50 pounds, and for heavy work they might weigh up to 800 pounds. As a guide to main sizes, the dimensions offered by one manufacturer are shown in Table 3-1.

Fig. 3-8. A modern anvil held to a piece of tree trunk with spikes.

Fig. 3-9. A medieval anvil with two horns and surprisingly thin feet.

Most modern anvils conform to the London pattern shown in Fig. 3-8. The main working surface is the face. At one end there is step down to a *table* and then the *beak* or *horn*. If a used anvil is bought, examine the state of the face and horn and check that the edges of the face form reasonably sharp and straight angles. However, a part of one edge might be deliberately rounded for special work. The table will have been used for cutting steel. It is softer than the face so as not to damage cutting tool edges, and this table might have been damaged by cuts. This is to be expected. Some damage to an old anvil can be corrected by filing or grinding, but this does not put back metal. That can only be done by welding. Building up an anvil in this way is not easily accomplished.

A proper anvil is not something that can be made by an individual. Even traditional smiths working full-time at their craft and making just about all their other tools, had to buy anvils from specialized manufacturers with the necessary heavy equipment. This means that there is really no alternative to a proper anvil. The exception is simple light work that can be done on an iron block—possibly salvaged from discarded large machinery.

At the other end of the anvil the overhang is the *heel* or *tail*. This will normally contain two or more holes going right through. One hole is square and is the *hardie*

Weight in pounds	Length in inches	Width in inches
56	15	7
84	19	7
112	23	8
168	25	10
224	28	10

Table 3-1. Anvil Sizes.

hole. A hardie is one of the tools that fits into this hole, but there are others. One or more *punch* or *pritchel* holes are there to give clearance when a punch is driven through hot steel.

The anvil is shaped down to a fairly broad square base with cutouts to leave corner feet that will stand firmly and resist tipping, even when the anvil is not fixed down. The base is usually shaped so that the corners can be held with bent spikes. However, some small anvils are pierced for bolts.

An anvil has to be mounted at a convenient height for working. The height should be such that you can stand almost upright and hold a steel rod in one hand horizontally on the face. Standing beside the anvil puts the anvil face at about the height of your knuckle—an average of 24 inches from the floor. Of course, the anvil must be firmly in position and should not move in any way while being used.

There are cast-iron and fabricated stands for anvils where the anvil base fits into a recess (Fig. 3-10A). However, these have never been popular. Most experienced blacksmiths prefer a wooden support. In an established permanent blacksmith's shop, the support is a section of hardwood tree trunk, set into the earth floor. The anvil rests on the flat top of this and is held in place with spikes made by the smith (Fig. 3-11).

For an anvil that is not set up permanently, it might be better to make what is in effect a substantial stool, giving it a slightly conical shape for steadiness and a recess in the top to hold the anvil (Figs. 3-10B and 3-12). Use thick wood so that there is plenty of bulk that will take the shock of hammering almost as well as the section of a tree trunk. The form is very similar to that of a cast-iron stand, but the iron stand is noisy and might cause rebounds of the anvil. Wooden supports do not add to the noise of hammering and they cushion the effect of heavy hammering. A leather strap can be nailed around a wooden support to provide loops into which tools can be positioned.

SWAGE BLOCKS AND MANDRELS

Specialist smiths use anvils of other sizes and patterns, and their peculiarities will be mentioned later in this book. However, there are two other anvil-like devices that most smiths use. One is a swage block and the other is a mandrel or cone.

A swage block is a basically rectangular block of iron or steel that has an assortment of hollows of different sizes and shapes around its edges and holes of many sizes and shapes through its body (Figs. 3-13A and 3-14). Patterns vary and not all hollows or holes are round. This is a bottom tool that can be moved around to get the desired shape upwards. There can be a cast-iron stand, or the swage block can be mounted on its own section of tree trunk or a made-up wooden stand. Sizes might be from 11 inches square by 5 inches thick, with a weight of about 100 pounds, up to 24 inches square by 7 inches thick, with a weight of about 700 pounds. The larger sizes need lifting tackle to turn them. A swage block is not essential for all blacksmithing, but it is convenient to have one when curves have to be made to exact sizes or many parts have to be made to match. Individual swages (see Chapter 4) that mount in the hardie hole of the anvil, will do for similar work in smaller curves.

A smith's cone or mandrel (Fig. 3-15) is a cast-iron cone with a round section and an even tape (Fig. 3-13B). It is used to make rings truly circular. Some mandrels have a long groove into which the tip of the tongs can fit when putting a ring in place. The size of a mandrel varies according to needs, but in a general blacksmith's shop it might

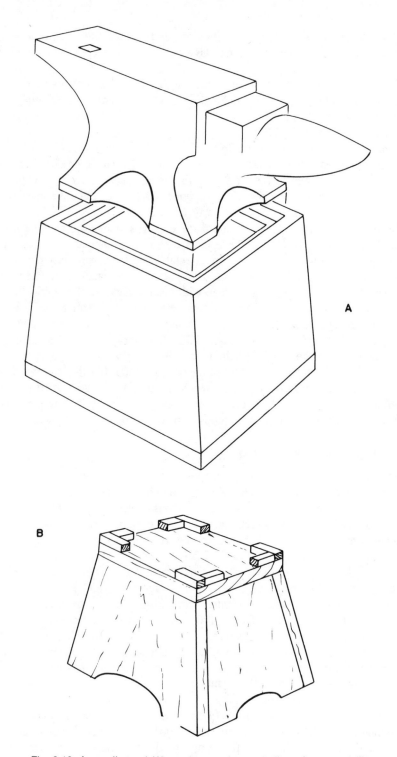

Fig. 3-10. An anvil stand (A) can be cast iron or built up from wood (B).

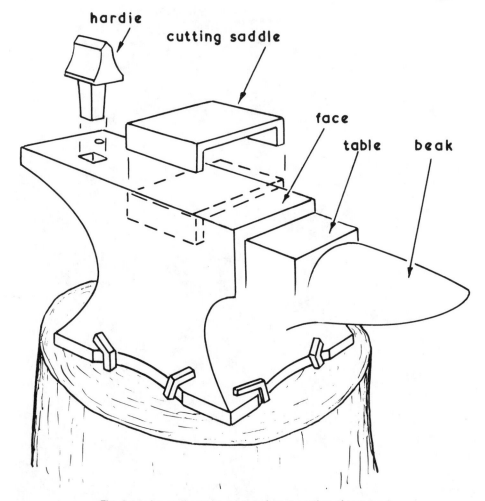

Fig. 3-11. An anvil can be mounted on a section of tree trunk.

stand up to 4 feet high and weigh over 100 pounds. For smaller rings, there could be a mandrel with a square projection to fit in the hardie hole of the anvil or be gripped by a vise (Fig. 3-13C). Some large mandrels have their tips formed by one of these pieces that can be lifted off to use elsewhere.

FIRE TOOLS

The fire is tended by tools the smith makes and remakes as they wear out. For pushing coal and coke into place, there is a poker (Fig. 3-16A) with a straight or bent end. It is given a blunt point, and the other end is shaped to form a handle and possibly an eye for hanging. A rake (Fig. 3-16B) has similar functions, but it is used for pulling fuel instead of pushing it. The simplest and most common form has a flattened end bent at right angles to the shaft. Another sort has two or three prongs bent downwards. For light work, all of these tools could be made from ⅜- or ½-inch-round rod and with an overall length

Fig. 3-12. The smith is using his anvil fitted to the top of a built-up wood support.

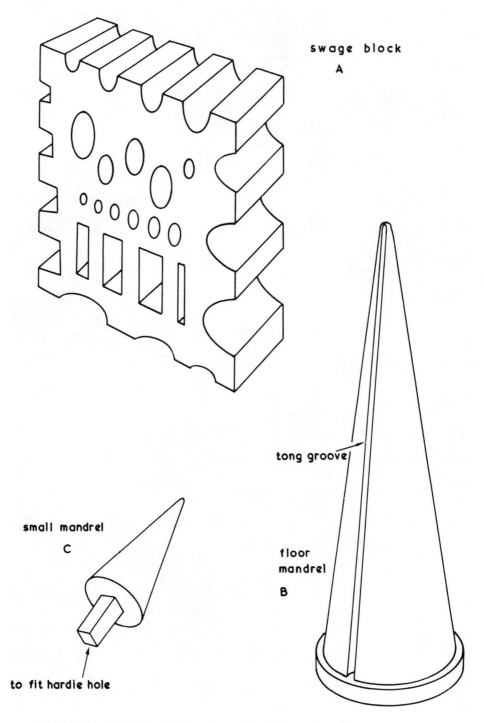

swage block
A

tong groove

small mandrel
C

floor
mandrel
B

to fit hardie hole

Fig. 3-13. Large tools, in addition to the anvil, include a swage block and mandrels.

27

Fig. 3-14. A much-used swage block in a blacksmith and farrier's shop.

Fig. 3-15. A conical floor mandrel kept outside a blacksmith's shop.

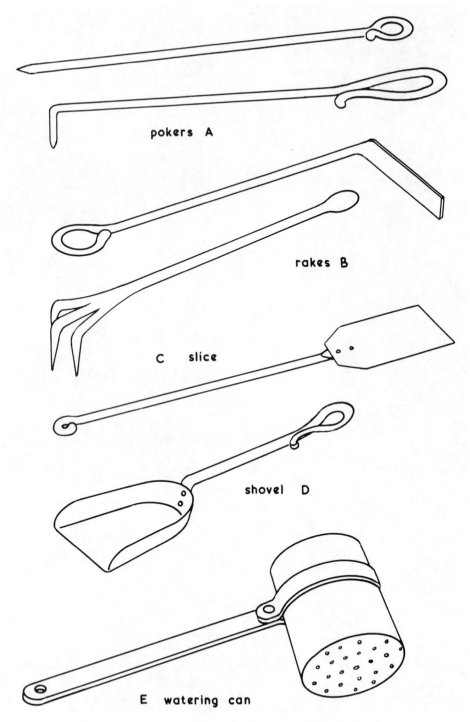

pokers A

rakes B

C slice

shovel D

E watering can

Fig. 3-16. The fire is managed with a few tools made by the smith.

Fig. 3-17. A wire brush is used to remove scale from hot steel before hammering on the anvil.

enough to keep the hand away from the heat. This depends on the size of the hearth, but 24 to 30 inches should be satisfactory.

A slice supplements the poker and rake when hot fuel has to be lifted and moved around the metal being heated. It is a simple piece of flat plate riveted to a handle (Fig. 3-16C) and about the same length as the other tools.

Reserve coke or coal can be kept in a bin or bucket near the forge, and a shovel (Fig. 3-16D) used to transfer it to the hearth. This could be a domestic type of shovel, although the smith might prefer to fashion his own of more substantial steel.

The fire has to be kept within bounds, and sometimes it is necessary to keep one part cool while another is hot. Water is sprinkled for cooling, using a watering can (Fig. 3-16E). This is just a can with an open top and a number of holes punched in its bottom. A handle can be fashioned by riveting on a bar. However, a handle that wraps around will be stronger. If a bolt is used to tighten it, the handle can be put around another can when the first has worn out.

BRUSHES

When red-hot metal is withdrawn from the fire it might be covered with scale and particles from the fire. Some of this can be removed by knocking against the anvil, but a steel wire brush (Fig. 3-17) for quickly cleaning the work before hammering is an important part of a smith's equipment. An ordinary soft bristle brush is used to clean the top of the anvil.

4

Smith's Tools

Nearly all of a blacksmith's's work is done with hand tools. Often one tool is supported on the anvil and another held over it by hand. For heavier work, power tools apply greater force, but for most things the smith has to make the only power come from his or his helper's muscles.

The tools a smith requires can be bought, but a smith can also make most of them. However, you cannot make tools without tools, and anyone starting blacksmithing will need to buy the first tools. Replacements and others of different sizes or for special purposes can be made in the shop or smithy.

Tools might take a long time to wear out and it is possible to reforge or grind old tools to make them servicable again. If used tools are available and they appear to be in poor condition, examine the possibility of putting them back into working order. Even if a tool has been worn away to the point of appearing useless, it might be possible to weld on more steel so it can be used again.

HAMMERS

By far the most commonly used tool is a hammer. There is very little that a smith does that does not call for a hammer blow, either directly onto the metal or against a tool over it. It is possible for a smith to make a hammer once some skill has been gained, but the first hammers will have to be bought.

An engineer's ball peen hammer (Fig. 4-1A) is a good general-purpose choice. This has a steel head with a flat or slightly domed face at one side and an approximately

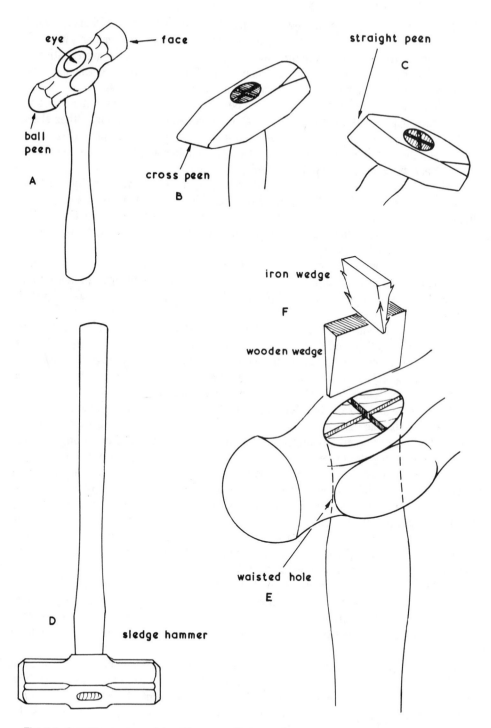

Fig. 4-1. A smith uses a variety of hammers that must be securely attached to their handles.

hemispherical face at the other side. The handle should be ash or hickory. A similar hammer with the head and shaft in one piece of steel, as are some engineer's hammers, would transfer too much shock to the hand during the frequent hammering a smith does.

The hammer should be as heavy as can be controlled. Sizes are by weight and usually up to 3 pounds. A 2-pound hammer will be easier to use.

Other lighter and heavier hammers can be added to stock. There is much less use for the face opposite the flat one, but a ball peen is useful for riveting. Other shapes with occasional uses are the cross peen (Fig. 4-1B) and the straight peen (Fig. 4-1C). These are shown in the form a smith might forge them himself, but it is possible to buy them in a general form similar to the ball peen hammer.

These hammers are used in one hand, usually by the smith working alone and controlling the work with the other hand. When heavier blows are needed, a helper also uses a hammer. This is usually the heavier, two-handed sledge hammer (Fig. 4-1D). The sledge might be double-faced, as shown, or could have ball, straight, or cross peens. The handle is usually hickory.

As with the single-handed hammers, there is an advantage in weight in a sledge hammer. But this has to be limited by what the user can control. Sledge hammer weights start at 4 pounds and may go up to 14 pounds. For amateur or occasional use, 7 pounds is a reasonable choice.

The security of the joint between the head and the handle of any hammer is obviously important. A head flying off during a swing could be very dangerous. The hole through the head is normally oval and made so that it is waisted, with a narrower section near the middle (Fig. 4-1E). Sometimes the hole is made with a single taper so that it is larger further from the handle end. However, this is less satisfactory.

The handle swells to a shoulder, bigger that the hole it is to go through. This limits the amount of handle that can enter the head. Two saw cuts are made across the handle end before it is driven in. Driving in is not done by putting the head down on the bench or anvil and hitting the other end of the handle. Instead, the different rates of inertia of wood and steel are used. Start the handle in the hole, with one hand holding the handle vertical with the head downward and not resting on anything. With the other hand, use a mallet on the end of the handle and hit until the handle is through the hole. Drive a hardwood wedge into the longer slot. There could be another hardwood wedge across it, but it is better to forge or file a steel wedge and raise teeth in it with a cold chisel (Fig. 4-1F). The wedges and handle end may project. They can be left this way, but look better if they are filed or ground level.

If the handle is dry when first fitted, it should remain tight for a long time. If it shows signs of loosening, tighten by driving the handle further in, using the inertia method just described. Instead of a mallet on the end of the handle, the hammer could be inverted and the end of the handle bounced on the anvil. Follow this by using a punch to drive the wedges tighter.

Some manufactured hammers have the handles bonded into the head by impregnating with epoxy resin. However, this is not a method that can be used in a small shop. The shoulder on the hammer limits the tightening possible in normal hammers. If a hammer has been tightened so often that there is no more shoulder left, a new handle must be fitted.

HARDIES AND SETS

There are some occasions when a smith has to cut steel with a hacksaw. A hacksaw of reasonable size and some spare blades should be included in a blacksmith's tool kit. Most cutting is done with a blow on a cutting edge, either completely through or part-way through, then the metal snapped off. If the tool is used over the metal, it is called a set (sate). If it is used underneath it is a hardie. The cutting edges and the effect might be the same, but it is the direction of cut that determines the name.

Hot metal can be cut with a more acutely angled cutting edge than cold metal. A cold set (Fig. 4-2A) might look like a hammer, but it is a handled tool for hitting with a hammer and is not intended to be swung. The head has a cutting edge at one end and a flat top to be hit. The wooden handle is usually round and held in place with a single wedge. The hot set (Fig. 4-2B) has a finer cutting edge and is usually a more slender tool.

The comparable tools used below are the hardies, which give their name to the square hole in the anvil. They are made to fit easily into the hole. As with the sets, a hot hardie (Fig. 4-2C and 4-3) is usually taller and more slender than the cold hardie (Fig. 4-2D).

Some sets are grooved around instead of made with holes through. The handle is then made from thin round rod wrapped around and with its ends welded together, as shown for the top swage (Fig. 4-4A). Either method is satisfactory. Sets and hardies are sold by weight and can be as much as 4 pounds.

Some smiths use flexible wood rods that are cut from woodland undergrowth, wrapped around in the same way as iron rod, and bound in place. This does not transfer as much shock to the hand, but renewal has to be frequent if the tools are often used.

A cold chisel (Fig. 4-2E) works like a set, but has no handle. It is common to other forms of metalworking, and a smith would use it to make lighter cuts. It can be made from round or octagonal high-carbon steel and the width of the cutting edge can be up to 1 inch.

There are many shaped cutters for special purposes. A farrier uses shaped ones when making horseshoes. A round cut-off (Fig. 4-2F) is typical.

A hardie and set can be matched for a slicing cut. The set is made with an angle at one side (Fig. 4-2G). The hardie can be straight across or hollowed (Fig. 4-2H), with its angle at one side.

SWAGES AND FULLERS

Most swages are rounding tools and are in pairs (Fig. 4-4A). They can also be made for squares and other sections. The bottom swage fits in the hardie hole. The top swage is handled and has to be located over it. Its top is shaped for hammering. Since the work and the top swage have to be held by the smith, he needs a helper for hammering. For single-handed work, the top and bottom swages can be combined with a spring handle (Fig. 4-4B). This is satisfactory for light work, but for heavier sections, the two parts and a helper are better.

The curves, or other sections, of swages have to match the intended final shape so that each pair of swages is for one size only. This means that there have to be several pairs, although it is possible to get bottom swages with several grooves to reduce the

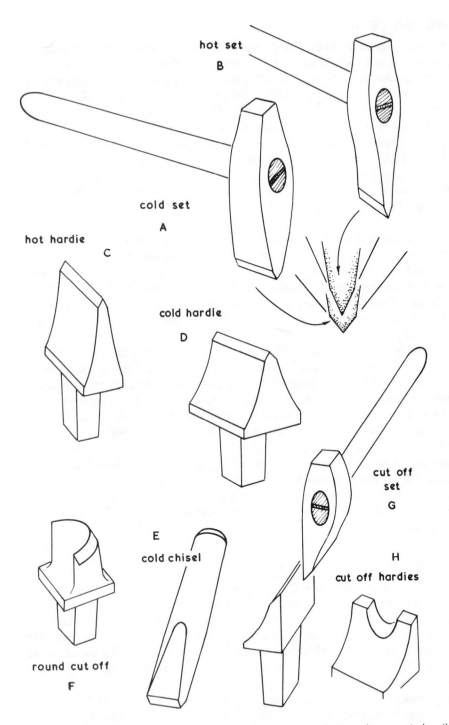

hot set
B

cold set
A

hot hardie
C

cold hardie
D

cut off
set
G

H

E

cold chisel

cut off hardies

round cut off
F

Fig. 4-2. Cutting tools for hot and cold metal can be held to cut downward or mounted on the anvil to cut upward.

Fig. 4-3. The smith has just cut the hot steel almost through by hammering over the hardie and is about to break it off over the edge of the anvil.

total number of bottom parts needed. Although swage sizes are controlled by the diameters they are intended to round, they may be sold by weight.

Fullers are also matched pairs, but their curves are the other way (Fig. 4-4C). The top fuller is hit by a hammer over the bottom fuller, which is fitted in the hardie hole. The effect is to pinch and hollow the metal held hot between them. There are fullers with different curves, but there is not such a need for a range of sizes as there is with swages.

FLATTENING AND PUNCHING

Hammering a piece of steel might get it to a general shape; a skilled smith can get a very good surface from the hammer. But to remove hammer and other tool marks and to get a truly flat surface, use a flatter (Fig. 4-4D). The important part is a square, flat surface. The tool has a top made for hitting with a hammer. Sizes vary and are graded by weight. A flatter weighing 5 or 6 pounds is usual.

An anvil stake is like a flatter reversed, so that it can fit in the hardie hole. It then has a truly flat surface upwards at a higher level than the anvil face.

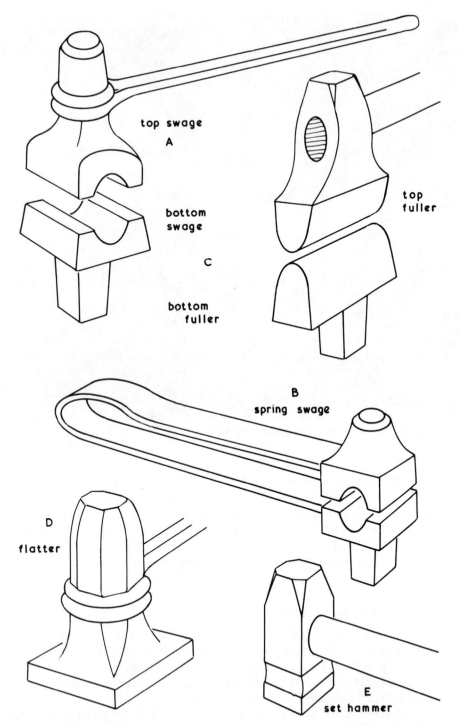

top swage
A

bottom
swage

C

bottom
fuller

top
fuller

B
spring swage

D
flatter

E
set hammer

Fig. 4-4. Some tools are used in pairs to squeeze or shape and others give flatter surfaces than can be obtained with a hammer.

A set hammer (Fig. 4-4E) is generally similar to a flatter, but the square end is smaller and deeper. Although called a hammer, it is held in position and hit with a normal hammer. It is mostly used for sharpening internal angles to shoulders.

Holes in iron or steel can be drilled in the same way as they are in most types of metal work. However, a smith, with his facility for heating metal and working on an anvil, can use a punch to fashion holes in work. Punches are in many sizes and shapes. They can be parallel or tapered. A series of punches might have to be used to enlarge a hole.

The simple punching is done over the punch or pritchel hole in the anvil. A punch for a round hole (Fig. 4-5A) has a parallel part long enough to go through the metal. Its end is ground flat. For accurate work, it helps to have a bolster underneath with a hole to match the punch. This is particularly important for square or other shaped punches (Fig. 4-5B). Punches are graded by their sizes. A hand-held punch may be used for light work (Fig. 4-6).

A punched hole usually will not finish a very accurate shape or a true size. It can be trued by driving through a drift (Fig. 4-5C). This is a round steel rod with its greatest diameter the intended size of the hole, and it tapers away in an elongated barrel shape. If it is hammered through the punched hole in hot metal, it will bring it to size and shape. Similar drifts are used for holes of other shapes. A drift can be used to alter the size of a hole or taper it, as in a hammer head.

BENDS AND SCROLLS

In decorative ironwork, much bending and twisting is done by pulling and levering instead of hammering. The smith makes tools to suit particular jobs, but there are two-pronged tools for levering strips of metal to shape. A bending fork (Fig. 4-5D) has a square neck to fit in the hardie hole or be held in a vise. Strip metal is then progressively levered to the required curve a little at a time between the pegs.

Where it is more convenient for the iron to be fixed and the pegs moved, a bending wrench can be used (Fig. 4-5E). It is called a scroll wrench if making scrolls is its main use. The handle has to be long enough to provide leverage, although a short one can be extended by slipping a tube over it.

Both tools can be made with different size gaps between the pegs. The gaps do not have to match the thickness of the metal being curved, but they should match the tightness of the curves being made. A scroll fork serves the same purpose as a bending fork, but it is made like a letter H with different spaces between the opposite ends. It is held in a vise with either end upwards.

If many scrolls have to match, as in a decorative iron gate or a length of railings, the smith makes a scroll iron. This is a pattern the iron is pulled around in order to achieve the same spiral scroll each time. It has a leg turned down to hold in a vise.

HEADS AND RIVETS

In some smith's work, the ends of rods have to be enlarged to form heads, such as are required for bolts and rivets. A heading tool (Fig. 4-5F) can be in several forms. Basically, it is a hole to match the size rod in a substantial iron or steel block. The hot iron end then projects through the hole so it can be hammered to shape.

Heads can be trued with a set having a hollow of the right shape in it. For the common round or snap-head rivets, there are pairs of sets to suit each size, both for truing the

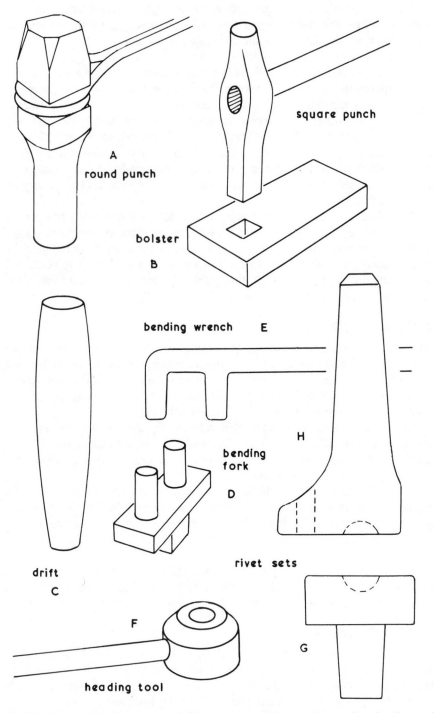

square punch

A
round punch

bolster

B

bending wrench   E

bending
fork

D

H

drift

C

rivet sets

F

G

heading tool

Fig. 4-5. Holes in hot metal can be punched. Other tools are used to bend bars or form heads on rods.

Fig. 4-6. A punch for light work can be held in the hand and used over the pritchel hole.

first head and for holding it in shape while the second head is made. The bottom rivet set (Fig. 4-5G) may fit the hardie hole, or it is held in a vise. The upper rivet set can be just a punch with a hollow of the rivet head shape in the end, or it can have a hole of the rivet size as well (Fig. 4-5H). If the rivet goes through several thicknesses of thin metal, the hole is used first over the rivet end to push the parts tightly together before hammering and setting the second head.

TONGS

Iron or steel has to be put in the fire, then held on the anvil to be worked on. In some cases the bar will be long enough so it can be held at a point where the heat has not reached enough to make gripping uncomfortable. A smith usually arranges to do as much work as possible on the end of a bar, so he can hold it for as long as possible before cutting off. However, there are many occasions when the work is too short for hand holding and some form of grip has to be used (Fig. 4-7).

Some modern wrenches (Fig. 4-8) lock on like hand vises. They can be used for gripping hot metal, but in general there are tongs for this purpose. A blacksmith's tongs are like long pliers. The length will vary according to the size of the hearth, but tongs as long as 18 inches are used. The longer the handles, the greater the leverage, and the tighter the grip for a given length of jaw.

A smith can make and alter a great many tongs. One pair of tongs can be forged to different shapes to suit the jobs at hand. There are a few standard shapes from which others are derived. In the usual construction, the pivot is a rivet and the handles are forged to taper, having a rounded section where they are gripped. When the jaws are tightened on the work, the ends of the handles should not meet. In most cases, they will be splayed outwards slightly. To lock the tongs on to the work, a sliding ring or coupler can be drawn towards the spreading ends of the handles (Fig. 4-9A).

General-purpose tongs have flat jaws. If they close completely they are closed-mouth tongs (Fig. 4-10A). They should close completely at the tips while being slightly open towards the rivet. This ensures they will hold thin material securely. If the jaws will not close completely, they are open-mouthed tongs (Fig. 4-10B). The amount of openness depends on the thickness of iron to be gripped. A smith needs open-mouthed tongs to suit ¼-inch, ½-inch, ¾-inch and other thicknesses, although each will suit sizes slightly thinner or thicker (Fig. 4-11).

To hold a shaped rod end-on, the jaws have to be hollowed, and many sizes of hollow-bit tongs are needed (Fig. 4-10C). If the hollow is rounded (Fig. 4-10D), only round rod can be held securely. Square hollows (Fig. 4-10E) will grip round or square stock. Hollow-bit tongs only suit parallel rods. If there is an enlarged end, as when a head has been forged on a rod, bolt tongs (Fig. 4-10F) are forged to suit.

If much riveting has to be done, and the comparatively small rivets have to be heated in the fire, lifted out, and put into their holes quickly so as not to lose heat, rivet tongs have to be used. They have their ends shaped to match the diameter of the rivet (Fig. 4-10G) so that it aligns as it is gripped and can be quickly positioned.

For general pick-up work, where the small items have to be taken from the fire and put in a vise or transferred to other tongs, there are pickup tongs (Fig. 4-10H) with more springy and open ends. They are not intended for holding work being hammered.

The best grip is achieved when the work is in line with the tongs. Sometimes when a piece of metal is being shaped, the end does not allow this and it has to be gripped crosswise. Holding a long piece of steel across the jaws can be rather insecure; it is better to have tongs that allow it to be alongside instead of across the line of the tongs. These are bent-bit or side tongs (Fig. 4-9, A and B). The bent or extended side part can be in various forms, depending on the section of metal to be held. Another type, also called side-bit tongs, has the ends of the jaws bent over (Fig. 4-9C).

Hollow-bit tongs will hold the iron straight. Open-or close-mouthed tongs do nothing to stop the work from slipping and twisting sideways. There are box tongs in which both

Fig. 4-7. Long tongs allow the hand to be at a comfortable distance from the fire when removing small pieces of steel.

Fig. 4-8. The lock-on wrench, at the center, is an alternative to traditional tongs for some work.

jaws have lips at the sides. The work held between them cannot twist very far from straight (Fig. 4-9D). Semi-box tongs are made like ordinary tongs, but with the boxed lips on only one jaw (Fig. 4-E). In both cases it is an advantage to have several tongs with different widths of boxing.

44

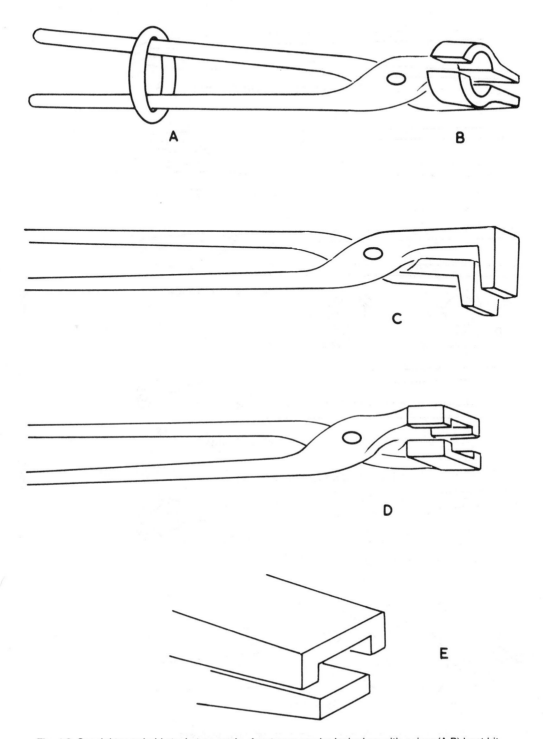

Fig. 4-9. Special tongs hold steel at an angle. Any tongs can be locked on with a ring: (A,B) bent-bit or side tongs; (C) side-bit tongs; (D) box tongs; (E) semi-box tongs.

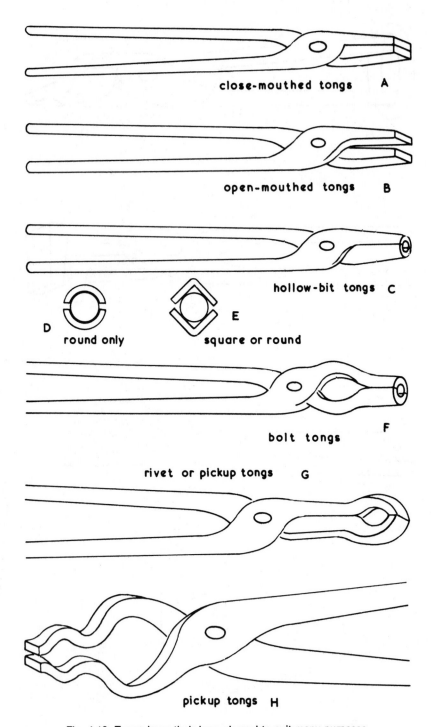

close-mouthed tongs   A

open-mouthed tongs   B

hollow-bit tongs   C

D   round only

E   square or round

bolt tongs   F

rivet or pickup tongs   G

pickup tongs   H

Fig. 4-10. Tongs have their jaws shaped to suit many purposes.

Fig. 4-11. Open-mouthed tongs are being used to hold the steel being shaped.

VISES

A blacksmith needs a vise that can stand up to a considerable amount of hammering, levering, and twisting. The modern engineer's vise is a strong tool. Much blacksmith work might have to be done with one, but it is not designed to withstand heavy hammering. An engineer's or machinist's vise is a precision tool and its jaws remain parallel at all settings. A Problem with using this type of vise for heavy hammering is that the screw thread takes much of the load and can become damaged.

The traditional blacksmith's post, box, or leg vise is made in a different way. It is almost completely of iron. It is better able to withstand hammering than steel, and it is designed so that shocks are not taken by the screw. The jaws can be steel. It bolts to the edge of a bench, but a leg extends to the floor (Fig. 4-12).

Variations in design are few. The leg forms an extension of the rear jaw. The front jaw is on an arm that is hinged quite low on the leg, and a spring helps to open the jaws as the screw is turned. The attachment to the bench is around the part carrying the rear jaw. If can be adjusted for bench height. The screw works in the normal way, but it is large and shrouded so the threaded part is protected. Both the bench and the floor where the leg pegs in should be strong—reinforced if necessary—since downward thrust goes to the floor.

A leg vise does not open parallel, and a very wide opening might not have as secure a grip as a machinist's vise. However, ability to withstand any amount of hammering outweighs this disadvantage (Fig. 4-13).

MEASURING

In blacksmithing, sizes are often checked by eye or by direct comparison, rather than by exact measurements. If a shaped part has to fit into a space, a piece of strip or sheet steel can be forged into a sort of fixed caliper for testing, if the object the part has to fit is unavailable.

Large calipers can be made by the smith, usually with an extending handle to keep the grip away from the heat. One caliper can serve two sizes (Fig. 4-14A). Joints are tight rivets.

For checking right angles, a large L-shaped piece is used (Fig. 4-14B). It could have a handle, and a large piece could have a diagonal brace. It is constructed from strip iron that is riveted or welded.

A *traveler* is a wheel on a handle (Fig. 4-14C). There is a mark or hole near the circumference. This is used for measuring, by counting the number of rotations as the wheel is rolled along or around the work. It is particularly associated with making a steel tire for a wooden wagon wheel, with the traveler run around the wheel and then along the strip of steel to make the tire, but it was used for other measuring as well. It is interesting as a curio of the past, but not much use today.

Ordinary engineer's rules are made of steel and tempered. If one is used on red-hot steel, enough heat might be transferred to draw the temper of the rule. This will make it soft and easy to bend. This can be avoided by measuring and marking along the edge of a piece of cold steel and using the rule to check dimensions of the hot steel. However, there are many occasions when the rule has to be brought to the steel being forged. Brass rules have been used by smiths. Heat has little effect on the quality of a brass

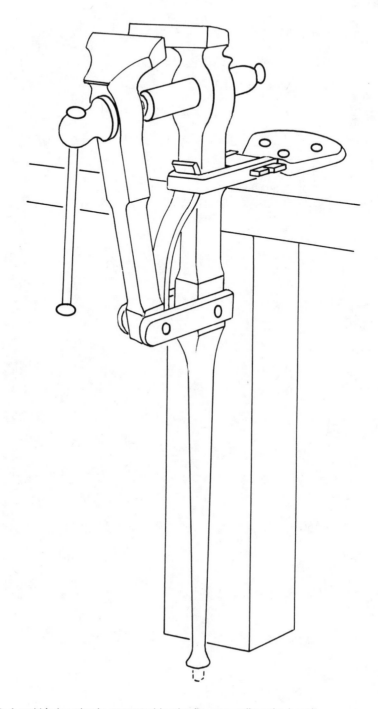

Fig. 4-12. A smith's leg vise is supported by the floor as well as the bench.

Fig. 4-13. This leg vise is bolted to a steel bench and has its legs embedded in the floor. The curved spring to open the jaws can be seen between the legs.

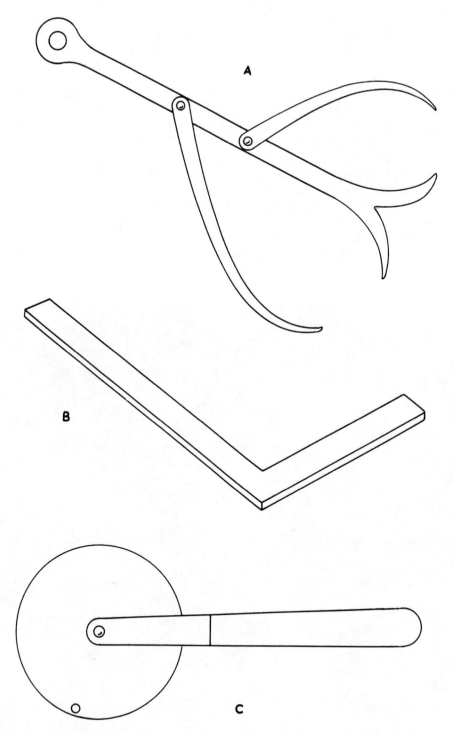

Fig. 4-14. Handled calipers (A) can be used to measure hot metal. A try square (B) is flat. A traveler (C) is run along metal to measure it.

rule, but because it is a rapid conductor of heat, a rule might soon become too hot to handle. A stainless steel rule can also be used, but its graduations are not so easily read.

CLOTHING

For anything but the lightest smithing, a smith should wear a strong apron that covers from his waist to below his knees. The best material is leather because it resists wear and knocks, and is good protection against burning. A professional apron might be made of 7 to 8 ounces of chrome-tanned leather, with a strong waist band and buckle. Joints can be glued and sewn, with rivets at stress points.

For general smithing, the apron can be in one piece, wrapping around at least halfway past each leg. For horseshoeing, the farrier usually prefers his apron divided down the front so that there are overlapping halves or chaps that hang inside as well as across the fronts of the legs (Fig. 4-15).

A good leather apron might be expensive, but it should be regarded as one of the essential tools. An occasional or amateur smith might want to use a canvas apron. This should not be a light one, such as would be suitable for general wood or metalworking

Fig. 4-15. The smith is wearing a leather apron that is reinforced over his knees and fits around his legs.

shop use; it must be a piece of quite stout canvas that will provide protection against hot metal.

Other clothing should be close-fitting. Avoid any clothing that hangs or is loose. Pictures of traditional smiths sometimes show them bare-armed and with chests bare. This might be more comfortable when working near heat, but there is a risk of burning and cutting. It is safer to work with long sleeves and a closed neck. Head covering and goggles are also a good idea. Footwear is important. There is a real risk of heavy weights being dropped on the feet. These could be hot as well as heavy, so wear stout boots. The types with reinforced toe caps are best.

OTHER TOOLS

The tools described in this chapter are those common to all kinds of smithing. A blacksmith is in a fortunate position. He is able to make most of his tools. Many smiths devise tools to suit particular work, which may be kept for the future or be adapted to suit another project.

If a smith specializes in one branch of the craft, he will have tools that will enable him to do better and faster work in that particular sphere. He may make chains or nails, or do nothing but ornamental ironwork. Specialist tools are described later in the book, where their uses show their special values. Although new or used special tools can be bought, in most cases the smith has to make his own. Being able to do this is one of the satisfying aspects of the craft.

5

Basic Techniques

The first requirement is, of course, to light a fire. How this is done and how the fire is tended is more important than might be expected. The quality and type of fire can affect the iron or steel being heated. Therefore, it may or may not be easily forged in the manner expected. Although the hearth might be large, the actual fire is usually quite small, except when working with something especially large.

At one time charcoal was used. It can still be used, but coke (breeze) is more satisfactory. If small coke is available, that is probably the best choice for a smith's fire. But it is more likely that coal will have to be used. Coke is made by heating coal, so the aim is to convert the coal to coke from around the outside. Small bituminous coal is preferred. The size of the coal should be comparable to peas. If larger coal is broken up, avoid including the dust. You can use almost any available coal. A little experience with the materials is usually all it takes.

If using charcoal, spread some around the hearth, with a hollow above a bottom tue iron or in front of a rear one. Use paper or wood shavings and a small amount of kindling wood to start a fire there. As the wood beings to burn, put charcoal over it and work the bellows or fan. Adjust the amount of blast to make the wood flame through the charcoal and ignite it. Feed on more charcoal and adjust the fire to the size you want. Maintain a blast to build up the heat when iron is put in the fire.

With coal, have a reasonable amount in the hearth, but make a hollow where the blast comes so shavings and some kindling wood can be placed there. It helps to wet some kinds of coal thoroughly with the watering can, which encourages it to stick together in a mass and more easily form coke. Unburned coal is called ''green'' coal.

Light the wood and start the blast. Push the coal towards it so that it starts to burn. With a new fire, there will be some smoke. Encourage the coal to flame by regulating the blast; this will consume much of the smoke. Rake more coal around the fire and wet the surrounding coal. Near the center of the fire coke will form. Test for coke with the poker. It should be bonding together near the middle of the fire. With the wood burned away, you should have a coke fire burning and more damped coal around the outside ready to feed. Wetting stops the fire from spreading more than is needed. For smithing with iron or steel of moderate size, the whole expanse of fire should rarely exceed 6 inches across.

While the fire is burning coal, and before much coke has formed, keep the blast going, if only at idling speed. Otherwise there is a risk of a blowback, which could damage the bellows or cause a disconcerting explosive sound in the fan. Once the fire is basically coke, it does not matter if the blast is stopped.

Once coke has formed, the fire should burn with little or no smoke. In a well-managed fire, the burning coke is surrounded by damped coal, which turns into coke as the coke inside is burned away. Coal might have to be raked in and it is probable that some smoke will be made An experienced smith keeps his fire going with a minimum of smoke. If coke is used in the first place, the smoke problem does not arise, but the fire has to be managed in a similar way.

Unfortunately, there are products of combustion that you do not want if the fire is to remain "clean," as it must for welding and some other processes. There are impurities in the coal. Some might come from the steel, while others come from the act of burning. When the fire is shut down, coke from the center should be kept for use when starting again. This allows you to start with the minimum amount of smoke; you do not want to have to start the new firing by converting coal to coke.

Besides coke, there will be some ash formed. This is the residue from burning and is not useable. With an ash pan below the tue iron of a bottom blast forge, you might be able to vibrate or open it and allow ash to drop out. Even then, and in any case with a back tue iron, you might have to scrape and shovel ash away. In addition to ash, there will be some clinker, which is hard and glassy and formed from sulfur and other impurities. In a burning fire, clinker will be seen as black dead spots in an otherwise bright fire. Clinker is heavy and will drop to the bottom of the fire, but occasionally it bonds itself into quite a large, irregular hard mass that has to be lifted out with the poker or pick-up tongs. Clinker spoils a fire for welding. It should certainly be removed when a fire is shut down, but during a long working period it will have to be looked for and removed from the burning fire. Hot clinker can bond to the surface of hot iron or steel and affect its final appearance or prevent welding.

The desirable fire for most heating is a *reducing fire*. This is a compact bed of coke surrounded by well-banked coal. The heat is then reflected inwards and consumes all the oxygen. At the other extreme is a shallow, broad, and fairly open fire with a hollow center. It has excess oxygen and can be called an *oxidizing fire*. It is difficult to heat the metal evenly in this fire, and considerable scale can form on it. It could not be welded. The best is a neutral one between these extremes.

Iron is heated in the heart of the fire, not on top of it, and is not thrust too low in it. There should be a good bed of burning coke below the iron and more raked over it. The iron should not be too close to the blast from the tue iron because the air oxidizes the metal. A steady blast of air should be maintained to keep the fire hot. Some experimenting will show how long to keep the metal in the fire to get the desired heat. Thin strips will heat faster than thick ones, and tapered pieces have to be manipulated so that the thin part does not get excessively hot and "burn" while the thicker part is still absorbing heat. It is worthwhile experimenting with pieces of scrap iron to check heating characteristics before attempting actual forging to shape on the anvil.

CUTTING

For practice in basic methods, it is convenient to use round iron or mild steel rod between ¼ and ⅜ inch in diameter. This is easier to handle in strips about 18 to 24 inches long, rather than in shorter pieces requiring tongs. Pieces could be cut to length with a hacksaw while held in a vise, but a smith prefers to cut on the anvil.

It should be possible to cut the cold metal with a cold hardie or set. If only the more acutely sharpened hot hardie or set is available, the same method can be used with the steel heated to redness. With the hardie mounted on the anvil, hold the strip over it at the place to be cut and give a good tap with a hammer (Fig. 5-1A). Turn the strip over and do the same to the other side to make two facing notches (Fig. 5-1B). Do not hit so hard that the cut goes completely through, with the risk of the hammer face meeting the hardie and damaging it. With a little practice, the notches can be taken to almost meet, then the rod broken off in the hands or pushed into the pritchel hole and levered apart.

If a set is used, work on the table (Fig. 5-1C) and not on the face of the anvil, where an inadvertent cut completely through or angling the tool might make the cutting edge meet the hardened face and become damaged. Cut from both sides and break off in the same way as using a hardie. Normally, a hardie is preferred because using a set means calling in an assistant to wield the hammer.

BENDING

Much work under the hammer is bending. This involves hitting in a way so that the blow does not pinch the steel between the hammer and the anvil. Instead the force should come to one side of the point of support, to avoid marking by compression. If the strip is put across the beak for bending, the hit should come off center (Figs. 5-2A and 5-3).

Have the rod heated to redness. Aim to get the same degree of heat for the length to be bent. How bright you get it depends on the particular mild steel, but it should be satisfactory if it glows red without being so brilliant that it is more golden. If it is bright and sparkling, you have heated it too much and the end of the rod might have been burned, leaving it semi-disintegrated and unsuitable for good work.

If you want to form an even curve, work progressively across the beak, hit off center, and alter the hitting points by moving the rod (Fig. 5-2B). As you get used to it, you can use the curve of the beak and hammer toward it (Fig. 5-2C) to get the right shape (Fig. 5-4). Avoid heavy blows tightly against the anvil. This would pinch and flatten the rod. This hammering to a curve might have to be repeated as you progress toward the shape you want. Reheat when the strip loses its redness. If you continue hammering after the steel has gone black, you will not make much progress, and you might mark the metal with the heavier hammering while you are still trying to get results.

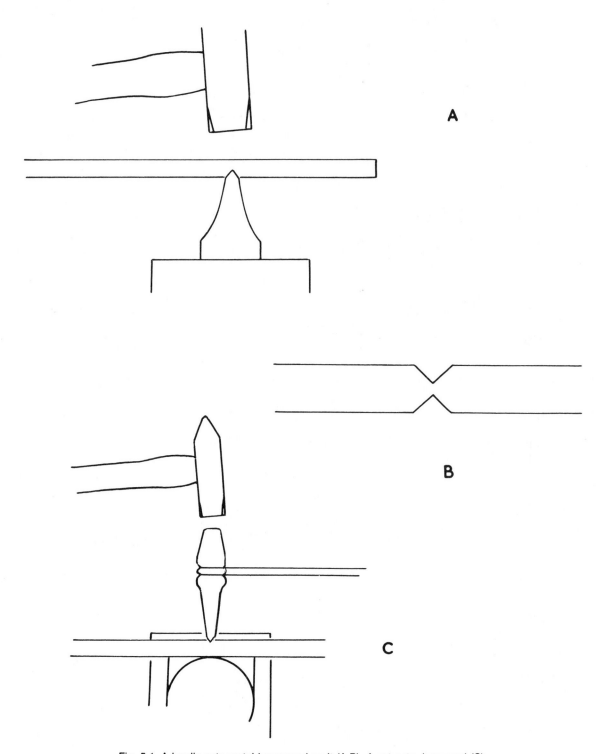

Fig. 5-1. A hardie cuts metal hammered on it (A,B). A set cuts downward (C).

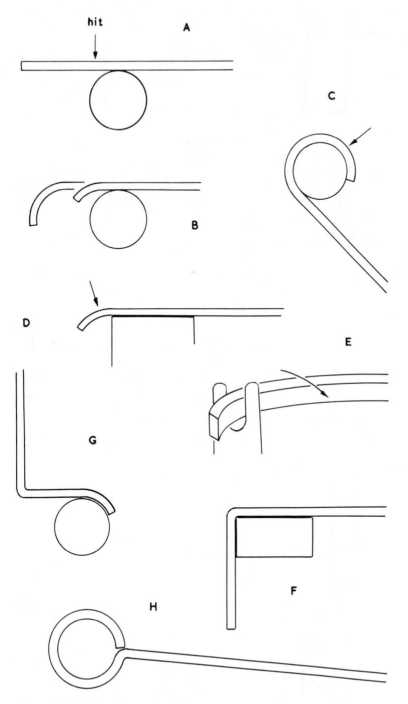

Fig. 5-2. Bending is done by hitting (A,B,C,D,F,G,H) to one side of the support or by pulling between jaws (E).

Fig. 5-3. When bending a rod over the anvil beak, hammer blows should come to one side so the steel is bent and not squeezed against the beak.

Sometimes a curve is made over the edge of the face of the anvil (Fig. 5-2D). Many smiths grind a curve on part of the edge of the face so bending can be done there without marking the inside of the curved strip with a sharp angle. As with curving over the beak, the strip is moved across to make a long curve.

Another way to make a curve is to use a scroll iron or fork, which might fit in the hardie hole or be held in the vise. Curving is done by levering the strip back a little at a time from its end (Fig. 5-2E). This is more appropriate to shaping a flat strip to produce decorative twists and curls. Simple shaping of round rod is generally better done by hammering on the anvil.

It is often necessary to put an eye on the end of a rod. It might not always be round, but a simple ring handle shows the way it is made. Decide on the size of the eye to be made and bend back the rod at a suitable distance (Fig. 5-2F). Allow about three times the intended diameter or a little more.

Choose a part of the beak that is slightly smaller than the eye is to be, and hold the rod so the red-hot end can be curved progressively over it. Work back from the end (Fig. 5-2G) so that the end can be hammered around to close as a ring (Fig. 5-2H).

Fig. 5-4. The smith is hammering towards the beak to close the end of a curve.

It is unlikely that the first attempt will produce a true circle. Another heating and some light blows to flatten on the anvil and true the curve and center it over the beak should give a reasonable shape.

DRAWING OUT

Drawing out or drawing down is the process of tapering the end of a rod (Fig. 5-5). It can be tapered in one direction, as when a square bar is tapered to a wedge section. It can also be tapered both ways to make a square spike, or the taper can form a round point. The name is also given to finishing a part of a rod—either to a parallel piece finishing at a shoulder, or to a part that is then curled into a scroll or other shape.

Drawing out a taper not only makes the steel thinner, it must also make it longer. It is impossible to compact the metal to a lesser bulk, so reducing the section in one direction must increase it in another. Drawing down the cross-section is achieved by persuading the metal to flow the other way. Work on the hot metal has to be directed towards stretching the rod.

To draw out over the beak, have the heated steel across and hit directly on top (Fig. 5-6A). The curve of the beak will force the metal towards the end as well as thin it. Do this at many positions, working back from the end (Fig. 5-6B). Turn the rod over and do it from the other side. If it is a round rod, do this from both sides at 90 degrees to the first pair of series of hits. If you want a taper and not a general reduction, you will have to work mainly near the end and not so heavily further back. At this stage the aim is to produce a taper. If the rod goes out of shape, it can be straightened on the anvil face. Reheat as necessary.

Although drawing out across the beak achieves quick tapering, slight tapering can be done on the anvil face. Hammer to spread the steel in length (Fig. 5-6C). Rotate the rod between hits to reduce both ways. Even if the rod is round, it is easier to get a good taper by working it square. If it has to go to a point, a square taper is worked (Fig. 5-6D) and the final hammering is on the angles (Fig. 5-6E). This converts the section to octagonal. More hammering on the anvil face can be directed at taking off those angles and getting the taper straight.

Most of the work in tapering should be done at a bright red heat. Be careful not to let the thinned end get too hot. Final straightening is better done at a dull red heat. During work, scale will form on the metal. It will come away during hammering and should be swept off the anvil. At a dull red heat, it does not form. Truing as a final step is better done at this heat.

An alternative to drawing down across the beak is to use the edge of the face. The bar is drawn across the edge and hammered so as to pinch against it. This produces a series of notches that force metal towards the end, stretching and thinning the shape (Fig. 5-6F). The first series of hits will curve the rod, but turn it over and do the same the other side to get that side stretched with notches. Do it again at 90 degrees to the first series and the opposite side to straighten the rod. Move to the flat of the face and straighten the tapered parts by direct hits. Twisting as you hammer can be described as *tumbling* the rod.

Fullers are used for drawing out large-sectioned bars. The effect is similar to that of the beak or the edge of the face in stretching the metal towards the end and thinning it. Heavier blows are possible for greater and faster effect.

Fig. 5-5. Drawing out a bar on the face of an anvil by rotating it through 90° while hammering.

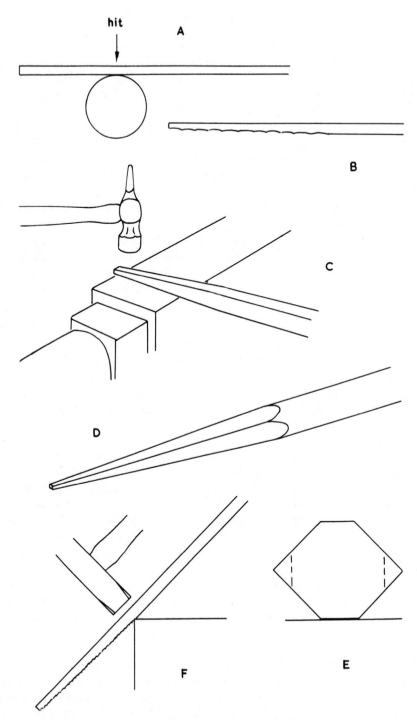

Fig. 5-6. Hitting (A) over a support compresses the metal (B,C) and is used for drawing out (D,E,F).

If the end of a bar has to be reduced in thickness without increasing in width, the top fuller can be hit into the hot steel at the end of the reduction (Fig. 5-7A). More dents are made along the part to be reduced (Fig. 5-7B), with the bar turned on edge intermediately so that there can be hammer blows on the sides to bring the bar back to width. When working alone, a bottom fuller can be used to get a similar effect. The bar will have to be returned to the anvil face occasionally for straightening. Top and bottom fullers can be used, particularly if the reduction in thickness is relatively great (Fig. 5-7C).

After overlapping dents with the fuller, the taper can be made more even by hammering on the anvil face. The tool for getting a good finish is the flatter (Fig. 5-7D). If the point of reduction has to blend with a curve, a fuller can be used diagonally (Fig. 5-7E). If a sharp angle is needed, a set hammer can be driven in (Fig. 5-7F). However, it is a good engineering principle to avoid an abrupt change of section, unless it is unavoidable. When a load is taken, it is the sharp change of section that is the weak point and that will break first.

Not all tapers are long. If all that is needed is a blunt obtuse point, as at the end of a poker, it is easier shaped on the hot steel by hammering while tumbling the rod. The rod should have one end level with the far side of the anvil and be held with its other end raised. The top and the bottom of the taper bring the point central.

UPSETTING

Making a piece of steel shorter and thicker is the reverse of drawing out. This might have to be done as the first step in forming a bolt or rivet head on a rod. It might also be needed before spreading the end of a rod. If the unprepared end of a rod is spread by hammering, the total width that can be obtained is limited by the amount of metal there is to be hammered. The result might not be enough for a particular purpose, but if the end is first thickened by upsetting, there is more metal to be spread and a greater flat area is possible.

The length to be upset should be heated evenly and brightly to a white heat. If only the extreme end is to be thickened, the heat should not extend far from it. If the heat goes further, the rod or bar might buckle. If the bar is short enough, the part away from the hot end can be dipped in water to cool the body of the bar while leaving the heat at the end. If a long bar gets heated too far, water can be poured on it. The end should be flat across and filed if necessary. Otherwise it is difficult to prevent the bar from bending. It might help if the end is beveled slightly all around, by filing, grinding, or hammering.

For example, a smith has a heavy iron block on the floor. He is upsetting with a heavy section a few feet long. With the end heated he bounces it on the iron block, using his strength as well as the weight of the rod to cause the end to shorten and spread (Fig. 5-8A). This demonstrates the principle and explains the alternative name for upsetting: *jumping up*.

If might be possible to upset a shorter piece by jumping it up on the anvil. It will probably be better to hold it with tongs or a gloved hand while hitting the cold end with a hammer (Fig. 5-8B). There will probably have to be several reheats to get a worth-while amount of upsetting. Almost certainly, there will be some bending above the part being upset, even after cooling almost up to that point. Watch what is happening and straighten on the anvil face as necessary, before bends develop too far.

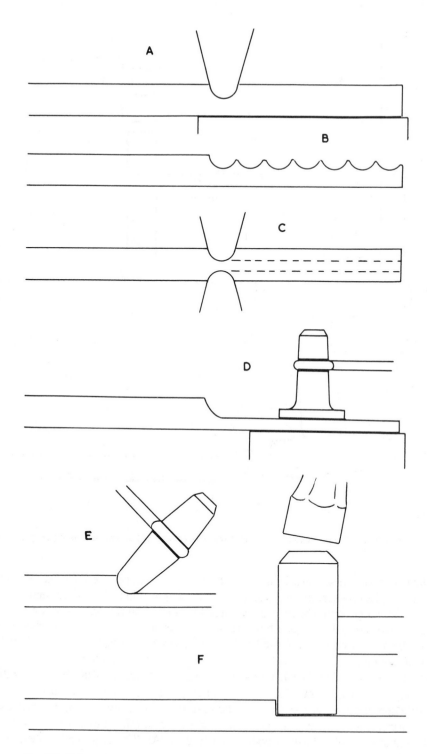

Fig. 5-7. Fullers draw out (A,B,C,) and the surface can then be flattened (D,E,F).

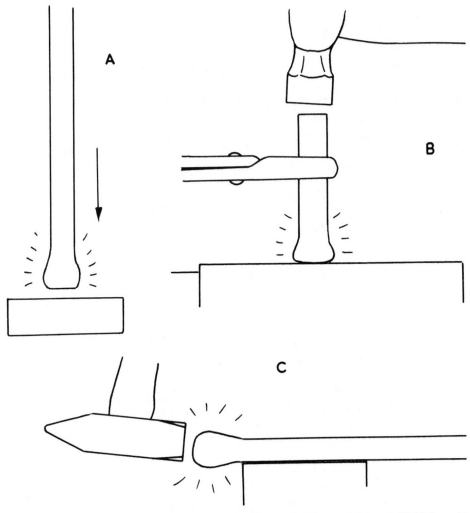

Fig. 5-8. Upsetting is the process of thickening white hot steel: (A) spread the end; (B) hit the cold end; (C) rotate the rod.

In most cases, upsetting is best started by jumping up. Once spreading and shortening has started, the process can be continued with backing-up blows from the hammer. This is particularly appropriate when a good spread is needed on the end, as when forming a head. Have the end at a good heat. Hold it so that it projects over the edge of the face of the anvil, with your holding hand braced against your thigh, ready to resist the shock of hammering. Hit the end strongly while rotating the rod between blows so as to get an even effect (Fig. 5-8C). This stance gives you a better view of how the upsetting is developing. But it is better as a follow-up step than as a first move in upsetting.

Although upsetting is necessary as the first step in forming a head, it is also used to give an increased amount of metal for spreading. An example of this is making a holdfast for driving into a wall to hold a wooden post (Fig. 5-9A). The upset end is shouldered

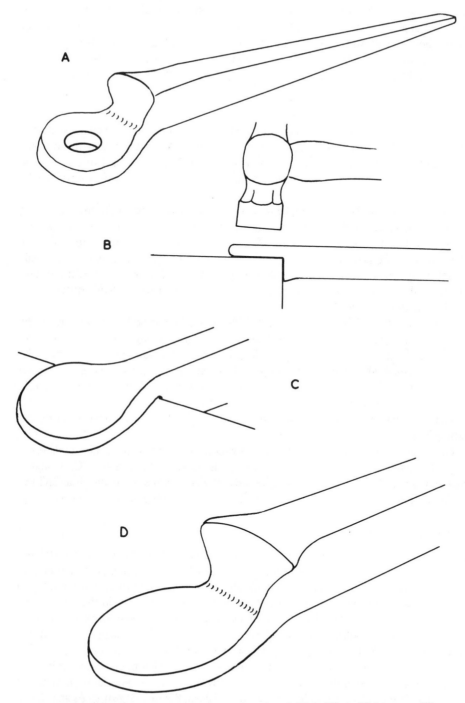

Fig. 5-9. Upsetting provides extra metal for a shaped end: (A) holdfast; (B) hammer; (C) spread the metal; (D) broaden the shoulder.

by hammering over the edge of the anvil face (Fig. 5-9B). Spread it in the same positions (Fig. 5-9C) to give a good area of sufficient thickness to take a stout screw. A set hammer squares the shoulder so that it can be hit into the wall with a hammer. If some of the upsetting continues into this part, the shoulder will be broadened to give a better area for hammering (Fig. 5-9D). Taper the other end to a point by drawing out.

TWISTING

Putting a twist in a rod is simpler than it might appear. It looks best in square sectioned bars, but could be incorporated in anything else angular. A twist in rounded rod would not be apparent, although an elliptical section has possibilities. A part of a round rod can be filed square (Fig. 5-10A) to allow a decorative twist along part of a rod handle (Fig. 5-10B).

To make a twist, heat the length that is to be twisted. Then grip one end of the intended twist in a vise and turn its other end. This can be done with an adjustable wrench or pipe grip, but it is better if you are able to twist with both hands. Use a piece of metal with a square hole near its center (Fig. 5-10C) if the work is square. This could be a screwing tap wrench, or you could use a length of flat strip metal with a square hole punched in it. If you are making a handle of round rod with a filed square, a bar could be put through the eye end.

To get an even helical twist, the part to be twisted must be heated evenly. If the heat is greater at any part, the twist will be tighter there. A long twist is more difficult to keep even than a short one, but providing the heat is the same for the length to be twisted, the result should be satisfactory. With most smithing, it is possible to reheat and correct work that is not as it should be. If a twist is unsatisfactory, there is usually nothing that can be done to put it right. This means that if a twist is to be put into a part that has smithing work to be done elsewhere on it, it might be best to tackle the twisting first.

There can be more than one twist put in a long bar by heating and holding at different points. It is also possible to put in a reversed twist next to the first one. One twist is completed and a short length that will be left untwisted comes between that and the next twist. Hold this part with a wrench while making the second twist the other way.

WELDING

A blacksmith's weld is a different thing from that made electrically or with oxy-acetylene. In a smith's weld, the parts to be joined are brought to near melting point and quickly hammered together. The principle is simple, but some skill and practice are needed to perform the task well and accurately every time. Iron is easier to weld than mild steel. If iron is available, that should be used for learning. Because most work will have to be done in mild steel, skill in welding will have to be acquired. It is easier to weld square or rectangular stock than round rods, which tend to roll on each other.

Wrought iron has a very high welding temperature, which melts away scale. It is possible to prepare the ends and hammer them together with no special treatment. All other forms of iron and steel require flux, which will clean the meeting surfaces and enable them to run together. The flux combines with the scale so that it melts and then prevents further scaling or oxidization.

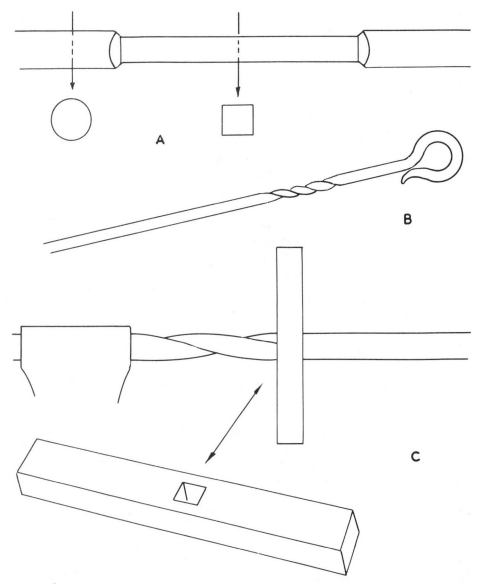

Fig. 5-10. Hot square sectioned rod (A) can be given a decorative twist (B). A hole (C) is useful for twisting.

There are welding fluxes available. Some smiths use clean, fine sand for mild steel. This might be all that is needed, but another variation used is a mixture of about four parts sand to one part borax. For welding tool steel to itself or to iron or mild steel, it might be better to get the appropriate commercially made flux.

Flux is not the complete answer to welding problems. Its plentiful use does not spell success, in fact too much is a bad thing. It could attract oxygen into the weld. There should only be enough flux to be forced out by the first hammering. Otherwise it will form a barrier to prevent the molten surfaces from uniting. A few iron filings can be included in the flux; they help to carry away the flux during the first hammering and they will burn and collect oxides away from the parts being joined.

Avoiding oxides at the meeting surfaces is important. This goes back to the heating in the fire. Make a reducing fire, with a good depth burning below where the steel is to be placed, and cover this with more fuel. Do not use too much blast, since that would cause oxidization. Keep a steady draft that will build up the center of the fire to a white heat that is so bright it is difficult to look into.

Ends to be joined have to be prepared by scarfing. They are upset and hammered to thick tapered ends (Fig. 5-11A). The surfaces that are to meet are given round shapes (Fig. 5-11B). This is so that their centers meet and force out flux and scales. If the meeting centers flow together during the first hammer blows, the weld should be satisfactory.

Heat the ends that have been prepared by scarfing. When they have reached an orange heat, pull them from the fire and sprinkle flux on them. Return the ends to the fire, and make sure they are in the center where the greatest heat will be. As the heat increases and the steel glows light yellow, turn the faces downward. Continue to heat steadily. A few sparks coming from the fire will indicate that welding heat has been reached. By then the fire and the ends of the bars will be so bright they will be difficult to look at. Do not stare into the fire too much, or you might not be able to see well enough when you turn to work on the anvil.

Have the anvil face clean and a hammer ready. Have your assistant hold one piece with its scarf upwards, and you position the other over it and hammer the parts together immediately. It is the first few blows that are critical; one problem is getting them in before the heat is lost. The cold anvil face will take heat away, and this can be reduced by bringing the parts together at a slight angle (Fig. 5-11C). The first blow brings the joint on to the anvil, but it also makes the weld. It helps to lightly tap each piece against the side of the anvil to remove any loose scales as you bring it into place.

Hammering has to be done systematically. The first few blows are at the center, then toward the ends of the scarfs to close the thin parts (Fig. 5-11D). More blows come at the edges, and the work can be turned on its side to get the width of the weld the same as the bars. It might be necessary to reheat if the weld is not fully closed all around before it cools. Use a wire brush to remove scale and dirt from the metal before returning it to the fire. Sprinkle on more flux and put the joint in the fire. Bring it to welding heat again and quickly hammer the parts that still need treatment.

There is no time to stop and examine the work while considering what to do. As soon as you take anything that is to be welded from the fire you must start hammering. When you have made the weld, continue lightly hammering all over it until it cools almost to blackness. Welding enlarges the grain in steel. Light hammering refines it to a more normal size, and makes it stronger.

HEAT TREATMENTS

All that a smith does can be described as heat treatment, but the name is specifically applied to what is done by heat to tools and other things made from high-carbon steel. Iron and mild steel are little affected by heating and cooling, but high-carbon steel can be made harder or softer by the way it is heated and cooled. There are special alloy steels for particular purposes, but many of them need controlled heat treatments that

70

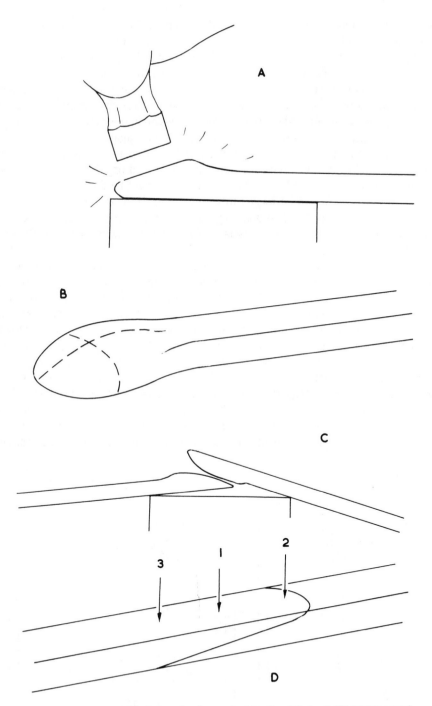

Fig. 5-11. Parts are welded after shaping and raising to white heat: (A) thick tapered end; (B) round shapes; (C) parts brought together at a slight angle; (D) the first blows (1) are at the center and more blows are made at the edges (2,3).

require equipment unavailable to an individual blacksmith. Therefore, toolmaking should be kept to high-carbon steel which is also called straight carbon steel or tool steel.

When iron or steel have been worked by the smith internal stresses are set up. This might not matter in the case of iron and mild steel, but with tool steel it might be advisable to remove them by *normalizing*. The item is heated to redness and left to cool as slowly as possible. The best way is to leave it in the fire so that it cools with the coal and coke overnight. Mild steel can be normalized in the same way, but the final effect is not so apparent. However, it is worthwhile in a much-worked piece.

The same treatment can be called *annealing*. The purpose of annealing is to make high-carbon steel as soft as possible when it has to be filed or otherwise worked with hand tools, or when it has to be machined. Annealing might be done to a tool that has been badly worn and has to be forged to a new shape. Annealing removes the effect of hardening and tempering. The annealing color is cherry red, which is about 1000 degrees Fahrenheit or 800 degrees Celsius. The longer the steel takes to cool, the softer it should be.

Hardening is done by heating to redness and cooling quickly. This will make tool steel extremely hard, but it will also be brittle. Attempting to use a tool in this state could cause it to crack or break. Some of the brittleness—and with it some of the hardness—has to be removed by *tempering*. The degree of tempering required depends on the type and purpose of the tool. In industrial tool production, the heat treatments of hardening and tempering are done with precise controls of temperatures. Fortunately there are ways that a smith can get satisfactory results with traditional methods.

For a simple pointed tool, the end should be finished bright by filing and using abrasive paper, or by grinding and polishing. Heat it for a short distance to a full red heat. It will not take long to reach this heat, and it is best held vertically in the fire with tongs and examined frequently. When the end is hot enough, lower the tool vertically into a container of water (Fig. 5-12A). Move it about after immersing so as to cool as quickly as possible.

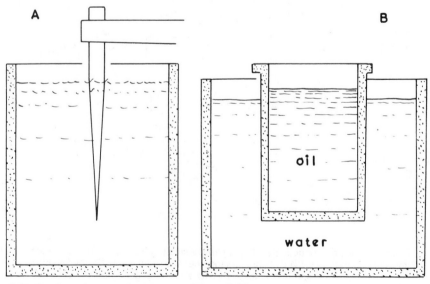

Fig. 5-12. Steel can be quenched in water (A) or oil (B).

The brightened end will discolor, but the preliminary polishing will help in later stages and will get a good finish on the completed tool.

For tools that are broader than pointed ones, it is important to cool them all over rapidly and as close to the same time as possible. Otherwise there is a risk of cracking or distorting. Thin items such as knife blades are more prone to this trouble. For something that has to be given an all-over hardness, turn it about in the fire to heat evenly and try to get the same degree of heat everywhere. Quench the tool as soon as the correct heat has been reached. Steel might suffer if heating is prolonged excessively.

Quenching by dipping the hot steel in the bosh or water tank that is used for all other cooling is generally satisfactory. However, there are other quenching baths that have advantages. Cold water can give maximum hardness, but it could induce surface cracks. Tepid water (60°F) might be better. Hardness might not be quite as great, but the risk of cracking is reduced.

Brine makes a good cooling bath that conducts heat away quickly. This should be a saturated solution of common salt—as much as the water will dissolve. Sal ammoniac can be used, but ordinary salt is more readily available.

Oil is also used for quenching. Obviously it must not be an oil that will burst into a flame when red-hot steel is put into it, but many oils have possibilities. Quenching oils can be bought, but olive oil is a clean one suitable for small tools. Crankcase oil can be used, but is more messy. Water and brine can be placed in almost any container, but with oil it is advisable to keep it within bounds by suspending the container of oil in another of water (Fig. 5-12B). This way spilled oil is trapped by the water, which will also quench any flame.

Another way of using oil as a quenching bath is to float it on a container of water. This can be mineral oil, vegetable oil, or even grease. As the hot tool is lowered through the oil, it gathers a layer of this surface film and takes it through into the water. This is claimed to produce a tougher steel with freedom from cracks. Whatever quenching bath is used, it should be deep enough for the tool to be fully immersed and moved about in enough liquid to carry away the heat. For small hand tools use at least 2 gallons of liquid.

Tempering is the process of heating again to a lower temperature and quenching again. Although it is the temperature that is important, there is a very useful guide to temperature in the colored oxides that form on polished steel. The colors play no part in the treatment of steel. They are just indicators. The oxides can be cleaned off, but removing the wrong color does not put right the mistake! If a mistake is made in tempering, it is necessary to reharden the tool and temper again.

Heating for tempering and cutting pointed tools is probably better done with a propane torch than with a fire. To use a smith's fire, an iron pan filled with sand can be put on the fire and the tool rested on that. This method is better than a torch, if tempering has to be the same all over a long cutting edge, such as a knife.

If a piece of tool steel has been worked smooth before hardening, it can be rubbed bright again fairly easily with abrasive paper. An alternative popular with smiths is a flat piece of sandstone. The essential thing is that the steel should be clean and bright enough to show oxides for some way back from the end or cutting edge.

If the colors of the oxides are observed as heat is applied slowly, the first color is pale straw, which deepens to an orange and then brown, continuing to a reddish brown before deepening into purple and blue, before going on with further heat to become red hot. The temperatures these oxides represent go from about 430°F (220°C) at the straw color, to 500°F (260°C) for the deep brown, and 580° F (300°C) for blue. The tempering colors for edge cutting tools come around the middle of the range.

The higher the temperature for tempering, the softer the tool steel becomes (Table 5-1). When the desired temperature is reached, plunge the tool into any of the cooling baths suggested for hardening. The oxide color will still be visible after cooling.

The steps in hardening and tempering are best observed by dealing with a simple pointed tool such as a scriber. This is drawn out to a point. When doing this, or making anything from high-carbon steel, do not be tempted to cool the tool in water while forging because this will harden it and make it brittle. Having forged the point to your satisfaction, anneal it by leaving it to cool for several hours in a dying fire or in the coal at the edge of the fire if that is still in use.

The body of the tool can be left black. A few inches back from the point, file it smooth and round. Then brighten it by pulling abrasive paper around it (Fig. 5-13A). Harden the point in the fire or by using a propane torch. Heat to redness followed by quenching. Use the abrasive paper or a piece of sandstone to brighten the point again. Be careful not to treat it roughly, because the brittle steel could snap off.

Use the torch to heat about 2 inches back from the point. In quite a short time, the oxide colors will begin to appear and spread out from the place you are heating. They will continue to spread, showing how the heat travels towards the point even after the torch flame has been removed. Watch their travel. If they stop, apply the flame again.

Table 5-1. Heat Treatment.

Oxide color	Temperature F	C	Tools
	400	205	
	410	210	
Yellow	420	216	Engravers, scrapers, razors, burnishers
Pale straw	430	220	
	440	227	Stone drills, reamers
Straw or orange	450	232	Saws for metalcutting
	460	238	
Deep straw	470	243	Scribers, knives, punches
Brown	480	250	
	490	255	Dies
	500	260	Knives, plane irons, taps
	510	263	Chisels, twist drills
Bronze	520	270	Surgical instruments
Light purple	530	275	Hammers
	540	281	Axes, center punches
Purple	550	285	Cold chisels, stone-working tools
	560	293	
Blue	570	300	Screwdrivers
	580	306	
Dark blue	590	310	Wood saws, Springs
	600	317	Large saws
	610	322	springs
	620	327	
Greenish blue	630	332	

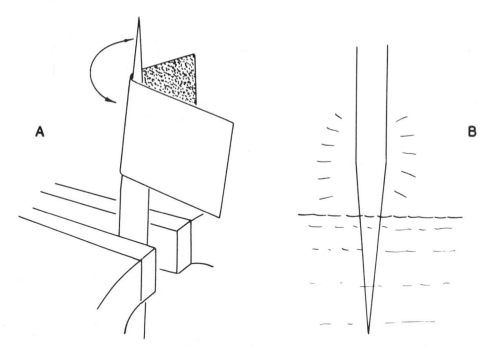

Fig. 5-13. Polish a point (A) for tempering and partially quench (B) for hardening and tempering with one heat.

The greater the spread of the colored oxides, the better it will be for the tool. The straw color will reach the end and deepen there into orange, which will get darker and begin to change to brown. At that stage, quickly quench the tool. The oxides will still be there. All of the darker orange part will be correct for a scriber. This is likely to extend for about ½ inch, and all of that will be available for sharpening before the tool needs rehardening and tempering. If more heat had been used, the colors would have moved faster and closer. Only a shorter part near the point would have been at the correct temper for a scriber.

There is another way of hardening and tempering an end-cutting tool, that only requires one heating. The tool starts with a bright surface and its tip is heated to redness for hardening. When it is quenched, only the point is lowered into the liquid; there is still a hot part above the surface (Fig. 5-13B). The point that has been under the surface is then dried and quickly rubbed bright with a piece of sandstone. There is still plenty of heat in the body of the tool and this travels towards the point. As before, watch the oxide colors and quench the tool completely when the correct color reaches the point.

For a steel tool that needs an overall equal tempering, use an iron tray filled with sand and placed over the fire. It might be necessary to pick up the tool frequently with tongs to see the colors. The colors do not move from one part to another. You have to act quickly because the sequence of colors appears all over, and you have to catch and quench at the color you want. Cold tongs can be prevented from affecting the temper at the point of grip if they are allowed to heat at the same time and place as the tool being worked on.

An alternative to the tray of sand is a fairly thick iron plate that is larger than the tool to be tempered. This is heated almost to redness on the fire, then pulled to the side of the fire and the tool to be tempered placed on it. Heat will transfer from the iron to the tool laid on it, and the colors can be observed in the same way as with sand. However, this method suits a thin steel piece such as a knife blade, but a more bulky item heats better if it is partly buried in the hot sand.

Colored oxides are not exclusive to tool steel. They will appear on polished iron or mild steel that is heated. They do not indicate any change in its characteristics, as they do with tool steel. Do not be misled into thinking that you have a piece of tool steel just because you get the oxide colors. Do not try this tempering method with stainless steel or other special alloy steels. Their characteristics are different and not all can be hardened and tempered, even by special methods that are available only in the industry.

Because much smithing is done with steel that has been salvaged, it is not always easy to know if what you have is mild steel or high-carbon steel. Heat will not harden mild steel. To check, go through the motions of hardening, by heating to redness and quenching. Then try to file the steel. If the file slides over the surface without cutting, it is tool steel. If it can be filed, you have mild steel. The hardened tool steel will blunt the file, so an alternative is to grind the end of the file across so that it makes a cutter, and then try to scrape the steel. If it will not produce a scratch on the heat-treated steel, you are dealing with tool steel (high-carbon steel). It should easily make a mark on iron or mild steel after that has been heated and quenched.

CASE-HARDENING

The difference between mild steel and tool or high-carbon steel is the amount of carbon alloyed with the iron. This difference affects the characteristics of the steel. Untreated high-carbon steel is harder than mild steel, and it can be hardened and tempered to adjust its relative hardness to further degrees. If more carbon can be added to mild steel, it should be possible to convert it to high-carbon steel. Unfortunately there is no way this can be done throughout the steel by the blacksmith. However, there is a way of giving mild steel a thin outer layer of high-carbon steel.

The process is called case-hardening or carburizing. The conversion of the outer layer can only be about $\frac{1}{32}$ inch, and at the best is unlikely to reach $\frac{1}{8}$ inch. The effect of case-hardening is to provide a wear-resistant surface that can be hardened and tempered. The whole thing will benefit from the toughness of the mild steel core with the hardness of the skin. This property is worth having if the skin is subject to considerable wear. For instance, a much-used screw on a machine might suffer from the frequent use of a wrench on its head, but if the head is case-hardened the risk of damage from the wrench is reduced.

Case-hardening is done by heating the mild steel in contact with something of high carbon content. The amount of heat and the length it is applied affects the degree of penetration. Some carbonizing agents are charred bone, wood, charcoal, charred leather, and parings of hoofs and horns. There are also some commercial case-hardening preparations. Carbonates of barium, calcium, and sodium can be added to the mixture in small quantities. They help carbon to penetrate.

Because the articles to be case-hardened and the carburizing materials have to be heated together for a long time, they have to be put in a container that can be heated without damage or disintegration. A steel box with a lid could be used, or a piece of iron pipe might have its ends sealed with fireclay. Allow spaces so the pieces being treated can be separated, and be sure each has an ample supply of carburizing material around it.

The carburizing agents should be in an even granulated form, not a mixture of solids and dust. Charcoal from hardwood can be the main agent. A mixture consisting of about 50 percent charcoal and the rest of equal quantities of the three carbonates should be satisfactory. Charred bone is even more effective. Do not use uncharred bone, which can build up pressure as it burns. A larger proportion of charred bone can be used than charcoal.

Sealing is best done with fireclay cement intended for fire brick. It is possible to put the steel and the carburizing material in a cloth and encase this thickly with fireclay. However, a steel container presents less risk of failure during a long heating.

Heating should be taken at least to the stage where a steel container glows cherry red. Maintaining this temperature for six hours might only achieve a penetration of $\frac{1}{32}$ inch. Raising the temperature shortens the time, but even at a bright orange heat there would have to be about three hours for the same result. Obviously, if there is a fire for central heating or some other purpose that is burning continuously, this would be better than keeping the forge fire going for a long time.

Another way to case-harden is to use a commercially available powder. One type has to be sprinkled on the red-hot steel or the hot steel rolled in it. Reheating then causes carbon penetration. The process has to be repeated several times. The result is a very thin layer of high-carbon steel, but it might be sufficient as wear protection.

When mild steel has been case-hardened by any method, it should be treated in the same way as high-carbon steel. After case-hardening, it should be allowed to anneal by cooling very slowly. If it is to be hardened it can be quenched in water or oil. The hardened surface might chip or crack during heavy use, so it is common practice to reduce some of the hardness and brittleness of tempering. Of course, any heat treatment only affects the skin, while the core is not affected any differently than when the whole thing was completely mild steel.

6

Advanced Processes

For a great many things that can be made by a smith, you will use combinations of the basic techniques described in Chapter 5. It is useful practice for anyone new to blacksmithing to examine something that has been made at the forge by someone else, and try to break it down into the sequence of operations that made up the whole. Try to visualize the steps and how they relate to the final shape. You will usually find that each step is quite basic and comparatively simple, despite the apparent complication of the final article.

The saying "strike while the iron is hot" obviously comes from the smithy, and is very pertinent to the blacksmith's work. It is no use taking the iron from the fire and wondering what to do with it or to have to search for the tools needed. Iron does not hold its working heat for long. You must know in advance what you intend to do and have everything ready to do it. In that way, you can get the maximum amount of progress out of each heating of the metal. The difference between an expert blacksmith and a beginner is often shown in the way the experienced smith completes his work with far fewer returns to heating in the fire. He will also get more for his actions. He knows from experience what the effect of an action will be on the iron and he works in a way that gets the best results. He might also be stronger. It is not essential to have powerful arm muscles, but if you have them, you can wield a hammer with greater force and get more effect for each stroke. Of course, strength in the correct muscles comes with practice and special exercises are not really necessary.

A newcomer to blacksmithing should learn to appreciate the ways of steel and how to get the effect he wants by making simple things that involve the basic techniques. Then he can tackle work that combines the basics as well as the more advanced processes described in this chapter. An important skill is the ability to make a weld with certainty, particularly some of the variations described later. Much work can be done without including welding, but the range of possible designs increases if you are able to weld as required.

Much blacksmithing is pure utility, but there are decorative and artistic possibilities also. Even with the utility items, there is beauty in good design. If an object is made so that it is fit for its purpose, it can be a very satisfying thing to the user as well as to the maker. If you examine ironwork of the past, you can usually find some little decorative touch that was not essential to the functioning of the article. There might be twists and curls that do not make the item work any better, but they make it look more attractive.

Examples of decorative ironwork can be seen in old churches, where grills and partitions show considerable skill, both practically and artistically. Gates and railings are other examples worth examining for the detailed artistic work that was lovingly done. Even a blacksmith with little artistic knowledge can produce attractive decorative work if he uses examples found in drawings and photographs. A smith who is also an artist might use his own ideas. Iron and steel are not the easiest materials to work with, but they do offer a challenge. Many smiths in the past took on the challenge and worked the materials into beautiful forms. There is no reason why modern smiths should not produce work equally beautiful. Some guidance on decorative work is given later in the book, but before tackling that sort of smithing, a great many relatively simple steps must be mastered.

HEADING

Upsetting has been described previously. In some work, the thickening of the end or a preliminary to spreading the end—as described in Chapter 5—are all that are needed. More often, upsetting is a preliminary to forming a head on the rod. This might be a knob to prevent the rod from sliding through another part, a head for riveting, or a bolt head. In a small size, it could be the head for a nail. The methods of working are generally similar, whatever the size.

A heading tool is needed. One example was shown in Fig. 4-5F. This is particularly suitable for nails because the raised top gives space to work around the head. A simpler tool is a piece of steel with a tapered hole to suit the rod. One piece of steel could have a number of holes of different sizes to suit more than one size of rod.

If the heading tool is made, its thickness should be enough to resist buckling under heavy hammering. Providing this is taken care of, it need not be much thicker than about half the diameter of the rod it is to hold. Too great a thickness increases the difficulty of punching it and making it accurately. For smaller sizes, it is satisfactory to drill the hole if power drilling facilities are available. Make the hole slightly smaller than the finished size to allow for tapering.

It is customary to punch the hole. Use a flat-ended punch of a smaller diameter than the rod over the pritchel hole in the anvil (Fig. 6-1A). Have the steel cherry red. It might help to put the steel on the anvil face and drive the punch a short distance from each

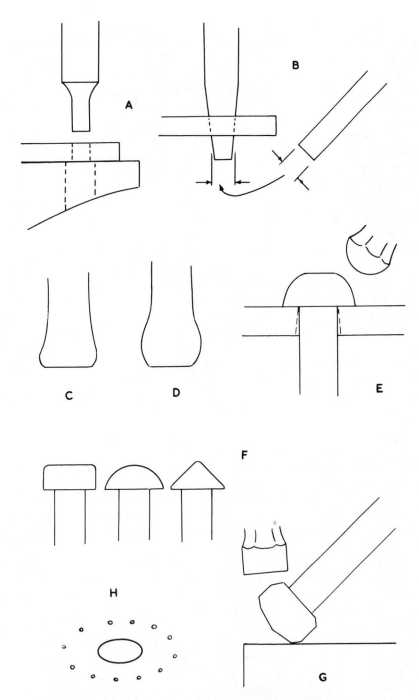

Fig. 6-1. A header tool can be punched and used to support an upset end for forming a head: (A) punch the hole; (B) match the size of the hole; (C) a tapered swelling; (D) enlarge the part; (E) hammer the end and top; (F) form the head as you prefer; (G) invert the rod; (H) center punch dots as a reference for shaping.

side before putting it over the pritchel hole to drive through. If the steel distorts, it can be hammered reasonably flat. Finishing is done after the next stage.

Use a tapered punch with its small end less than the size of the rod and the larger part of the taper greater than the size of the rod. It could have a handle, although a tapered steel punch held in a gloved hand is easier to control for small sizes. Reheat the steel and drive in the tapered punch until the smaller size of the hole matches the rod (Fig. 6-1B). Test with the rod to see if it will slide through easily. After heating, its diameter will increase slightly. Flatten the steel.

The amount of upsetting has to be arranged so that there is sufficient thickened steel to form the head. You cannot make a head of a certain size if the volume of metal is not sufficient. At the same time, try to keep the thickening as near the end as possible. It will have to taper, but keep the bulk confined to where you want it by cooling with water the part that has to remain parallel. The first upsetting will produce a tapered swelling (Fig. 6-1C). After probably three heatings and jumping up and backing up with a hammer, the enlarged part will be almost bulbous (Fig. 6-1D).

To make the head, place the heading tool or plate over the pritchel hole—if that is large enough—or over the hardie hole, with the smaller side of the hold uppermost. If your intention is to make a knob end to the rod, have your hammer ready on the anvil. Heat the end to cherry red and quickly drop the rod into the tapered hold. Make sure enough projects to make the knob. If too much projects, the rod can probably be driven down so the tapered hole cuts and compresses the rod. Hammer around the end as well as on its top (Fig. 6-1E). Hitting downward will spread the steel, but the hits around the edge will force the metal downward and form the head into shape. The head formed might not need to be a particular shape, but it could be cheese, snap, or conical (Fig. 6-1F) for a neat appearance. If it is to be a rounded knob, the top has to be formed. The rod is then removed from the plate and inverted in the anvil so that the hammer can be used around the lower edge of the head (Fig. 6-1G).

If a circular heading tool is used, the truth of the head in relation to the rod can be seen. With a broad flat plate, any eccentricity might not be noticed. A circle of center punch dots (Fig. 6-1H) will provide references for watching the shape the head is taking. Hammer blows can be directed accordingly to get a concentric result.

RIVET HEADS

If you want a half-round head of good shape to serve as a rivet, top and bottom rivet sets (Fig. 4-5G and H) or cupping tools are needed to make two heads. Examples that the smith will almost certainly soon be using are the rivets in tongs, which he can make for himself. The rivets may only be ¼ inch in diameter. Forming their heads is a straightforward process.

You need a ball or half a ball in steel of the size you want the head to be. Rivet heads are usually twice the diameter of their shanks, so a ¼-inch rivet may have a head about ½ inch across. The end of a ½-inch steel rod can be ground to shape or a ball bearing can be used (Fig. 6-2A). Support the ball on the anvil or grip the ground rod in a vise.

Upset the end of a piece of steel rod that has a greater diameter than the rivet head will have. This will be the upper set, and should be long enough for convenient holding.

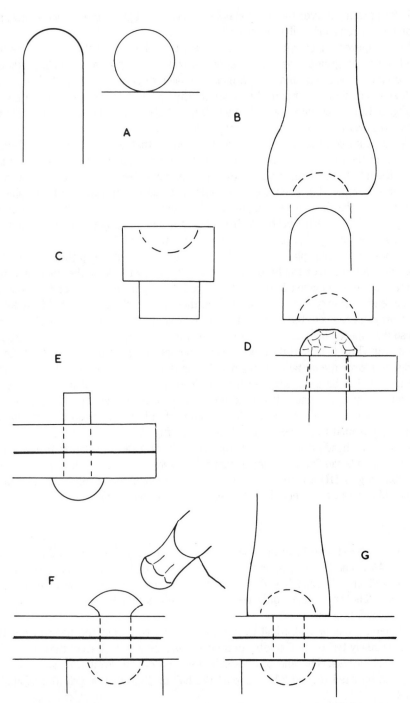

Fig. 6-2. A rivet set holds and shapes a rivet head: (A) use a steel rod or a ball bearing; (B) drive the end onto the rod or ball; (C) give the bottom rivet set a shoulder; (D) drive on the cupping tool; (E) make the second head; (F) hammer to start spreading; (G) drive the end down.

When the end has been upset so that its diameter is about twice that of the rivet head, see if the end is reasonably flat. If it is not, file or grind it flat. Heat the end again and drive it on to the rounded rod or the ball (Fig. 6-2B). There might have to be more than one heat to allow you to drive it on far enough. If a manufactured rivet head is examined, it will usually be slightly less than a complete hemisphere. There is no need to make the hollow that far, although you must allow for a little leveling of the bottom to make it ready for use.

The bottom rivet set could be a similar piece to hold in the vise, but it would be better if given a slight shoulder (Fig. 6-2C). It could be shouldered more so that it would fit in the hardie hole. In both cases, the shouldering is an application of the technique described in Chapter 5 using fuller, flatter, and set hammer.

Following the method for forming a knob on a rod, position the upset end of the rivet through the heading plate and do the first shaping by hammering. Be careful to stop the head from spreading too much. It is better to leave a little excess height so that when the cupping tool is driven on, it pushes down and does the last spreading (Fig. 6-2D). You have to estimate the exact amount of metal required for a head. If there is too little you might finish with a flat top to the round head or a part that does not take a good curve. If there is too much metal, you will get a full round head, but there will be a rim at the bottom. If the first attempt with the cupping tool is unsatisfactory, you can go back to hammering and try again.

When you assemble the tongs or something else with the rivet, start with it too long. There will not be an upset end to work on, so estimate how much you should stand up to make the second head (Fig. 6-2E). You cannot reheat the end once you have started shaping, so know exactly what you will do and have everything ready. Support the lower head in its set, and hammer around the projecting end quickly to start spreading (Fig. 6-2F). Then put the cupping tool over while there is still plenty of heat in the end, and drive it down (Fig. 6-2G). Make sure the hammering gets the edges of the head close to the surface. Driving directly downward might cause the rivet to bend in the hole slightly, instead of becoming shaped above the surface.

REDUCED RIVETS

The method of heading just described starts with a rod and makes the head larger. For some things, there is the alternative of starting with rod of the head diameter and reducing the part for the neck of the rivet. This would not be satisfactory for a long rod, but where the rivet or other part is quite short, this method is sometimes preferable. For satisfactory work, there must be a pair of swages of the size the rivet is to be.

For a ¼-inch rivet with a ½-inch head, start with a ½-inch rod that is long enough to hold. Reduce the end for slightly more than the final intended length by hammering while the rod is rotated. Check constantly that the work is remaining central. Use a set hammer to sharpen the shoulder (Fig. 6-3A) and turn the rod between blows. In this way, bring the reduced part almost to size. Check with calipers. Put the steel between the pair of swages and true the shape (Fig. 6-3B). If the shoulder under the head is untrue, pass the reduced end into the heading plate while it is red hot and hammer downward with light blows.

Use the hardie to cut around and above what will be the head (Fig. 6-3C), until there is only a small amount left to snap off. This could be done in the heading plate (Fig. 6-3D).

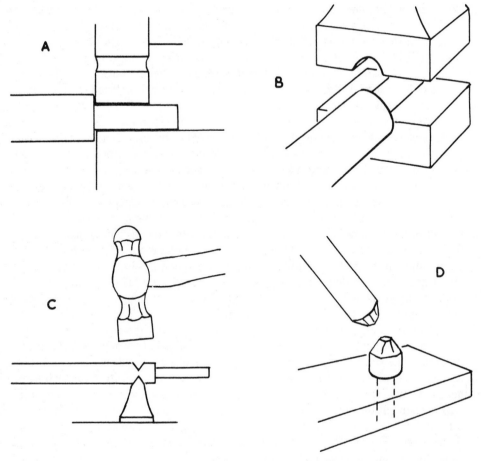

Fig. 6-3. Instead of upsetting, a rod can be reduced to make a bolt or rivet. (A) sharpen the shoulder; (B) true the shape; (C) cut the head; (D) use the heading plate.

From that point on, forming the head is the same as in the earlier example.

There should be no difficulty in tapping a rivet or other rod out of the heading tool. The tool or plate should not be allowed to get too hot because that would soften it and might cause the hole to be damaged. Dip the plate in water whenever necessary. If this is done with a finished rivet in place, it will usually fall out.

Trivet

A trivet was originally used in front of an open fire so a kettle could be slid off, but kept warm. Although there might not be much need for this today, a trivet is decorative and can be used as a plant or pot stand. It makes an interesting light bending, drawing down, and riveting project. Sufficient heat for forging can be obtained from a propane torch. The example in Fig. 6-4 has a brass top and mild steel framing. Its size is intended to suit an average kettle and a grate 5 inches above the hearth, but sizes can be adjusted without affecting construction.

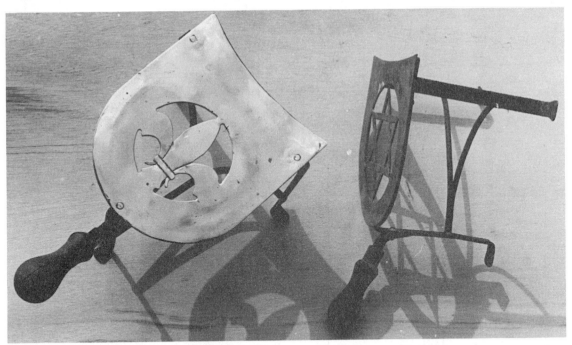

Fig. 6-4. Trivets provide practice in bending and riveting.

It is the top shape that controls most other sizes (Fig. 6-5A). Brass that is 18 gauge is suitable. The fretted Boy Scout badge can be cut with a piercing saw. Choose any other design you wish, but allow some open spaces to dissipate heat. Make the top completely, except for rivet holes.

Forge a strip of ⅛-by-½-inch mild steel to go under the top ⅛ inch in from the edge (Fig. 6-6A and 6-5B). Make three legs from a similar strip (Fig. 6-6B and C and 6-5C). Spread as well as bend the feet.

Make the tang for the handle (Fig. 6-5D) from ¼-inch round rod. Flatten one end to take a rivet. Point the other end and bend it at about 30° (Fig. 6-6D). The tang may be brazed as well as riveted to the back leg.

Drill the parts for ⅛-inch rivets through the top, the U-shaped piece and the legs, but do not rivet these parts yet.

The underframing is made from ¼-inch round rod. Curve the parts (Fig. 6-6E) so they will meet the side legs squarely. At the back leg, file the parts to meet and braze them together (Fig. 6-6F). At each leg file down to make ⅛-inch riveting ends through the leg holes. While doing this it is advisable to make a trial assembly with loose rivets in the top holes, so the underframing can be adjusted to hold the legs upright.

When the shape is satisfactory, rivet at the three top positions—preferably with brass rivets in countersunk holes—and rivet the ends of the underframing. Drive on a wood handle. The top should be polished and the other parts could be painted.

Hand Hoe

There are several garden tools that can be made using basic smithing techniques. The

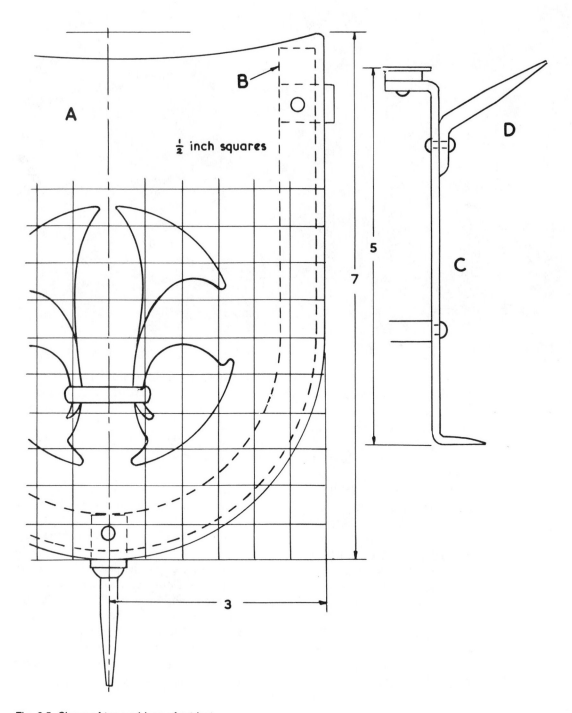

A

B

$\frac{1}{2}$ inch squares

7

5

3

C

D

Fig. 6-5. Shape of top and legs of a trivet.

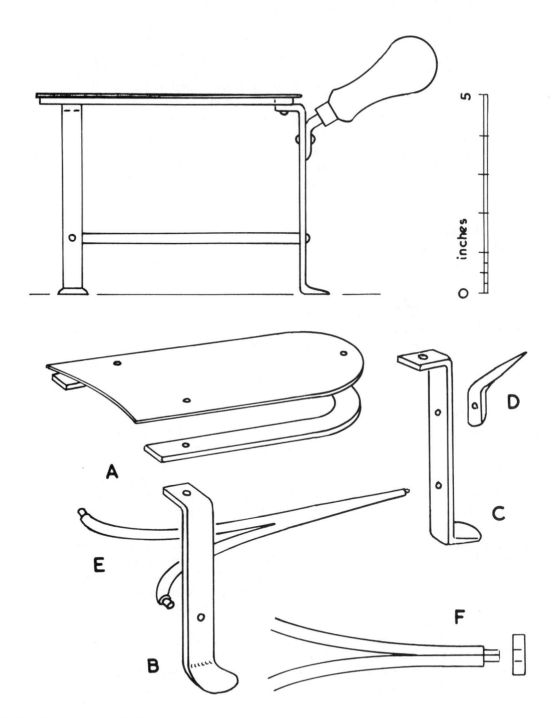

Fig. 6-6. The sizes and parts of a trivet.

example in Fig. 6-7 is a small hoe, but it could be made larger, and other tools could be made in a similar way. The blade is 3 × 5 inches and up to ⅛ inch thick. The shaft is ⅜-inch round rod, and the metal part of the tool is about 14 inches overall.

Start with rod for the shaft longer than needed. At the blade end it can merely be flattened, but you can make a stouter palm to take rivets (Fig. 6-7A) if it is upset first. If it is upset more, you can make it wider so the rivets are parallel to the edge (Fig. 6-7B). Do not reduce the thickness to less than half that of the rod.

Bend the end to a suitable curve that will hold the blade at about 15° to vertical; the exact angle however, is not critical (Fig. 6-7C).

Cut the rod to length and forge a tang about 3 inches long, either round or square (Fig. 6-7D). To help it grip the wood handle, use a cold chisel to cut teeth (Fig. 6-7E).

If the blade is mild steel, make it about ⅛ inch thick. If you use tool steel, it need only be about ¹⁄₁₆ inch thick. There is no need to harden and temper it. In both cases file or grind the cutting edge thin.

Mark and drill for rivets—³⁄₁₆-inch diameter will be suitable. Form round heads at both sides.

Use a file or similar handle. Drill it undersize and drive in the tang. The teeth should grip adequately, but for extra security drill through the ferrule and rod for a thin rivet. You could attach along handle in a similar way.

There is an alternative method of attaching the shaft to the blade by brazing (see Chapter 17). Do not thin the end of the rod, but cut it centrally for about 1 inch. Open these ends and put them over a piece of metal the same thickness as the blade (Fig. 6-7F). Squeeze them together in a vise. Drill this and the blade for one or two ⅛-inch rivets. Lightly rivet (Fig. 6-7G) and run spelter into the joint.

BOLT HEADS

Making a head from an upset end is suitable for many purposes. If the head has to be very large in relation to the diameter of the rod, upsetting sufficiently without distorting the rod below the head can be very difficult or impossible. Making a bolt head is a case where standard size to fit a wrench requires quite a lot of metal on the end of a rod. The distance across the corners of a square or hexagonal head is about twice the diameter of the rod. With the thickness needed to make a parallel head of sufficient depth, much more metal has to be built up than for a rivet head.

The alternative way of making a bolt head is to wrap and weld a strip of metal around the end of the rod. This is circular, and enough steel must be used so that you can hammer the material into a square or hexagon that can be made to match a wrench. Before the days of standardized screws and heads, a smith made bolt heads and then made wrenches to match. It is better now to make heads to the accepted standards for the particular diameter.

Cut strip steel—of the correct width for the depth of the bolt head and of enough thickness to allow for the build-up needed—to a length that will wrap around the rod but not quite meet. The best way to do this is to forge the ring around the rod (Fig. 6-8A) until it is almost a circle. Then saw and file the end. The facing ends should be fairly flat, but the gap between them has to be estimated to allow for them being stretched and drawn together under the hammer (Fig. 6-8B)

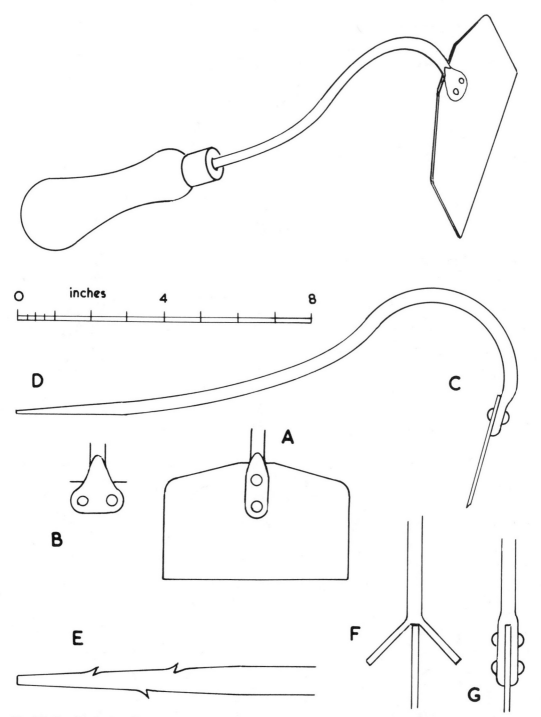

inches   4   8

D

C

A

B

E

F

G

Fig. 6-7. Details of a hand hoe.

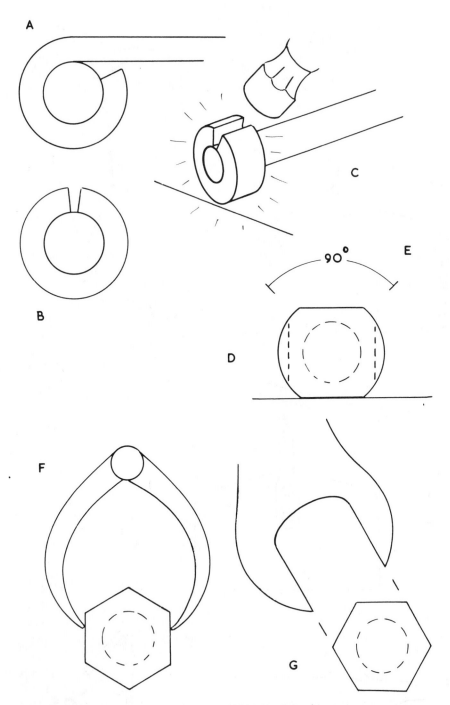

Fig. 6-8. A bolt head can be made by welding a strip around a rod: (A) forge the ring around the rod; (B) estimate the gap; (C) hammer around the strip and over the ends; (D) the opposite side is flattened; (E) convert to square in stages; (F) set calipers; (G) obtain the correct size.

Wrap the strip around the end of the rod, with a little welding flux between. Bring the head to welding heat quickly and hammer around the strip and over the ends (Fig. 6-8C). The idea is to stretch the strip and weld the ends of the ring together, which will weld the tightened ring around the rod.

The head, at this stage, should be reasonably round and the shoulder under it should be flat. If necessary, put it in a heading plate or a hole of the right size is a scrap piece of steel and hammer the head down to get it flat.

The head shape has to be obtained freehand. When the hammer is used, the side opposite that hit is also flattened against the anvil (Fig. 6-8D). A square head is made by turning the rod through 90° at intervals to that the circular head is converted to square in stages (Fig. 6-8E). Do not try to get the flats on opposite sides in one direction right down to size before working in the other direction.

For a hexagon, there are three directions to hit, the rod has to be turned 60° at a time. It might help to draw a hexagon of the size required and set calipers to the distance across the flats (Fig. 6-8F), so that checks will show when the correct size in obtained in all three directions (Fig. 6-8G). Getting a regular hexagon might involve several reheats and hammering sessions. Follow hammering with hits over a flatter to get the surfaces true. Then check in all directions with a wrench.

MAKING NAILS

At one time, all nails were made by smiths. Specialist smiths did nothing else and had tools to speed production and allow maximum convenience. But even then output was quite slow and nails comparatively valuable. Old woodwork was burned so the nails could be salvaged (Fig. 6-9).

There probably will be no need now to make individual nails, except for use in reproduction work—when the appearance of a typically handmade head would lend authenticity.

Nearly all handmade nails were tapered and square. A farrier might still use tapered nails to match the tapered pritchel holes in a horseshoe. For nailmaking, a heading tool with a square hole might have to be made. This is similar to that for round rod, except that the hole should be made with a square punch, followed by a tapered square punch or drift (Fig. 6-10A). Because most nails are comparatively small, the heading tool should be extended at one side to act as a handle when positioning over the pritchel hole.

Taper the end of a rod to the size nail you want, with a little extra for the head. The rod need not be square, but the taper should be drawn out square (Fig. 6-10B). The size has to suit the heading tool. The tapered part should go through the distance the nail shaft will be, but should stop with enough above to form the head. Try the nail in the heading tool and mark where it should be cut off. Nick the steel at opposite sides with the hardie at this point (Fig. 6-10C).

Heat the rod in the fire and put the nail in the heading tool, so that the unwanted rod can be broken off (Fig. 6-10D). Immediately use the remaining part to hammer into the head shape (Fig. 6-10E). A round heading tool with a raised center allows easier hammering, particularly if the head is to be patterned. It should be possible to break off and make a head in one heating. If a small nail has to be reheated, it should be held carefully or it might be lost in the fire.

Fig. 6-9. This old door is made and the handle attached with smith-made nails, which would have been salvaged by burning the wood away if the door was to be scrapped.

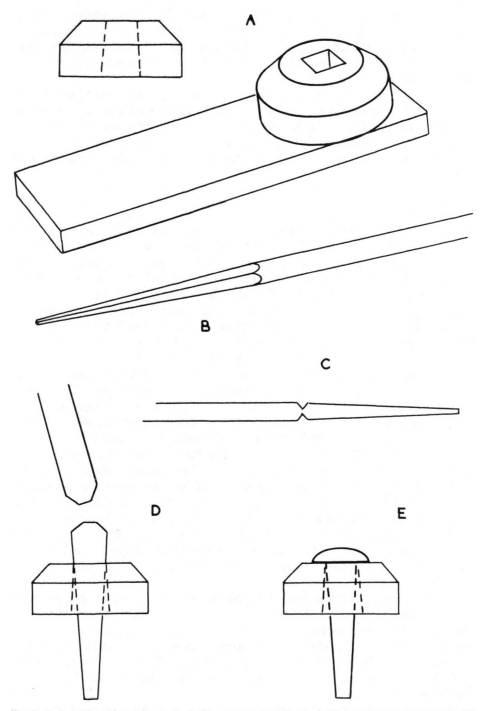

Fig. 6-10. A nail head is made on a rod with a square heading tool: (A) a square tapered punch; (B) draw out a square taper; (C) nick the steel at opposite sides; (D) place the rod in the heading tool; (E) hammer into the head shape.

There are several traditional form of handmade nails and some examples are shown (Figs. 6-11 and 6-12). There is not much scope for decoration of the visible parts of the heads of small nails, but larger nails can be given various patterns. Doors of castles, churches, and other old buildings in Europe are often decorated with large nails with ornamental heads.

Clout nails are those with larger heads than usual. The name comes from the hits or clouts that the smith gave nail heads to decorate them. A common arrangement is three or four clouts around a broad head (Fig. 6-13A), possibly with another flat at the center (Fig. 6-13B) to take the driving blows. A variation was a pattern of rounded dents made with a ball peen hammer (Fig. 6-13C). Any of these nails can be described as rose heads.

WELDS

The method of joining two bars by welding, described in Chapter 5, covers the basic method of making a blacksmith's weld. Other welding situations require similar treatments—adapted to the particular circumstances. It is always necessary to get just the right heat in a clean fire, the surfaces have to be prepared the right shape, there has to be freedom from scale, and flux has to be used. A beginner should master a weld between two bars so that he appreciates what is involved and can get a satisfactory result. However, welding two separate pieces requires a helper. A weld between two parts of the same piece of iron or steel allows holding with one hand and hitting with the other. It is also easier to keep the joining surfaces in the correct relation to each other.

An example is a welded eye. For something like a poker handle, where there is no appreciable load on the eye, it is sufficient to merely bend the rod around without making any firm joint between the end and the main part of the rod. However, if the eye is to come under strain, the end should be welded—for example, when making a lifting hook for the end of a chain. When properly welded, both sides of the eye should be of equal strength. Although it is possible to weld the end of a circular eye, it is easier and better for resisting a load if the sides of the eye meet at an acute angle (Fig. 6-14A).

Prepare the end by upsetting it and giving it a scarfed shape with a rounded surface, as would be needed for an end-to-end weld (Fig. 6-14B). The round section of the main part of the shaft where the weld will be made is already of a suitable shape.

Allow enough length to go round the loop and bend the rod back over the edge of the face of the anvil (Fig. 6-14C). Form the eye so that the part to be welded comes in the right place (Fig. 6-14D) and the loop has taken the correct shape—although there can be final correction after welding.

Bring the steel to welding heat and position the joint on the edge of the face of the anvil, with the end upwards. Hit first at the center of the weld, then at the thin edge, and finally at the thicker part of the joint. Turn the rod about so more blows can come around the edges and shape the welded parts into a whole. There should be a neat taper from the eye into the rod. This hammering will probably distort the eye, so a further heat might be needed to allow the curve to be trued over the beak and flattened the other way on the face.

An example of the welded eye is a two-pronged poker. This can be of use at the forge or at the domestic hearth. The handled end could be another welded loop or it

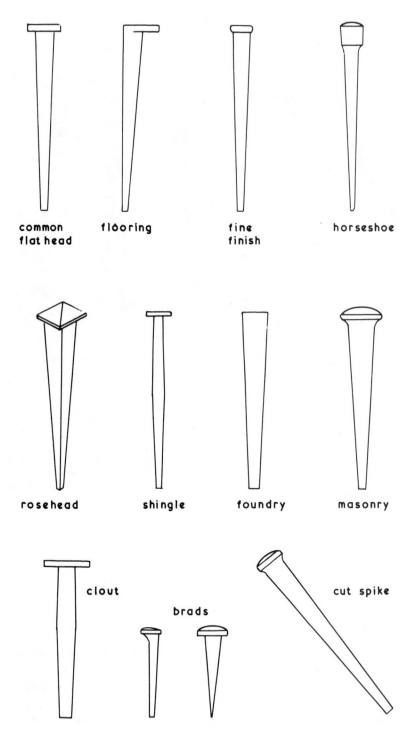

common flat head　　flooring　　fine finish　　horseshoe

rosehead　　shingle　　foundry　　masonry

clout

brads

cut spike

Fig. 6-11. Handmade nails differ mainly in the shapes of their heads.

Fig. 6-12. A selection of smith-made nails, tapered and with different types of heads.

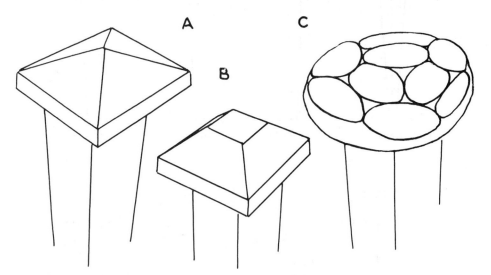

Fig. 6-13. Nail heads can be patterned to provide decoration: (A) broad head; (B) flat center; (C) rounded with dents.

might be made into a more decorative shape (Fig. 6-15). The two prongs could be shaped and pointed so that one can be used for pushing and the other for pulling (Fig. 6-16A).

Make a welded loop of sufficient size to allow for cutting through (Fig. 6-16B) and for the longer part to be straightened. Bend the long part back out of the way and draw out the point on the short piece. Next, curve it to a hook over the beak (Fig. 6-16C).

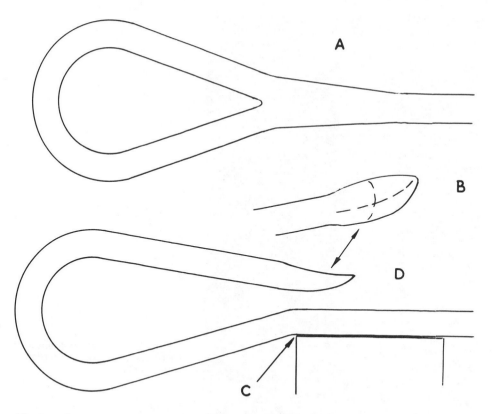

Fig. 6-14. An eye can be welded on the end of a bar: (A) sides of the eye meet at an acute angle; (B) scarfed shape; (C) bend the rod back over the edge of an anvil; (D) form the eye.

Draw out the long piece and shape that. Although a straight end might be functional, a curve will look better. This curve could be carried back in a double sweep into the main shaft. Although long tapers look graceful, if the poker is to get much use and if the ends become red hot, it is better to avoid needle points. The ends will be more durable and just as functional if given long tapers to thick ends, which are then made into obtuse points.

Similar welds can be used to make forks. A welded eye can be cut at its head, and the two sides straightened and pointed. Alternatively, one piece with its prepared end can be held against the other and welded. In both cases the prongs have to be shaped and pointed. Such a small fork can be used for toasting bread in front of the fire or dealing with meat at a barbecue (Fig. 6-16D). A larger one could be used to throw bales of hay.

Faggot Weld

Another weld in one piece of rod is a faggot weld. It is used as an alternative to upsetting in order to thicken an end. A faggot weld would be better than upsetting in places that have to be thickened for a greater length than could be conveniently upset. Although this method puts the thickening to one side, it can be forged to bring it central after the weld has been made.

Fig. 6-15. A two-pronged poker or toasting fork with a twisted and double spiral handle.

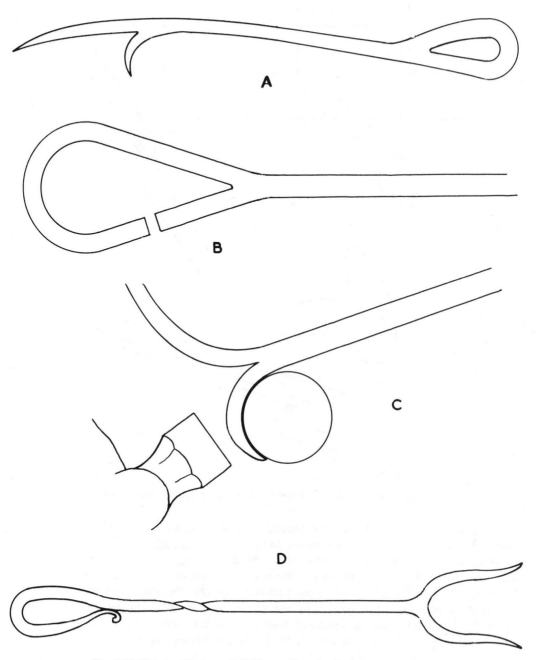

Fig. 6-16. Cut a welded eye (A,B,C) to make a hooked poker or fork (D).

If the rod to be faggot-welded is round, there is no need for much preparation of the end: it is simply folded back and welded (Fig. 6-17A). If the cross-section is flat, the surfaces that will meet in the fold should be given a curved cross-section (Fig. 6-17B) by grinding, filing, or hammering.

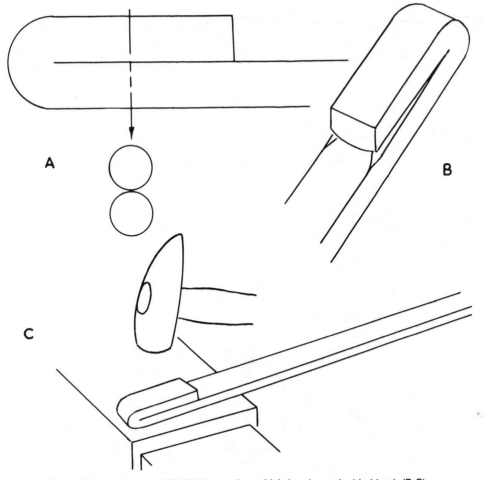

Fig. 6-17. A faggot weld (A) thickens a bar which has been doubled back (B,C).

It might be possible to fold back the end and weld all in one heating, but it is easier in two steps. Bend and fold back the amount to be dealt with. Sprinkle flux in the joint and along the edges as the piece is returned to the fire to bring to welding heat. Tap off any dirt and quickly position the end, with the fold upwards on the face of the anvil. Then hammer along it (Fig. 6-17C). Turn it on edge and true the sides. Concentrate on making a good weld at this stage. Any shaping can be done with a further heating (Fig. 6-18). For a very large thickening in relation to the bar section, it is possible to fold the end over again and make another weld with the further overlap.

Angular Welds

If bars have to be joined other than end-to-end, their preparation is mainly an adaption of scarfs to that method. For a right-angled corner, the ends are forged so that the scarfs project on to the other piece (Fig. 6-19A). Get the meeting surfaces slightly domed, so that the first hit at the center drives out scale, impurities, and flux. This means quickly

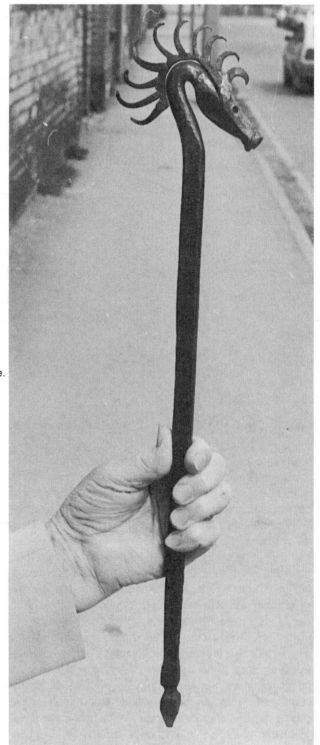

Fig. 6-18. After welding, further shaping can be done.

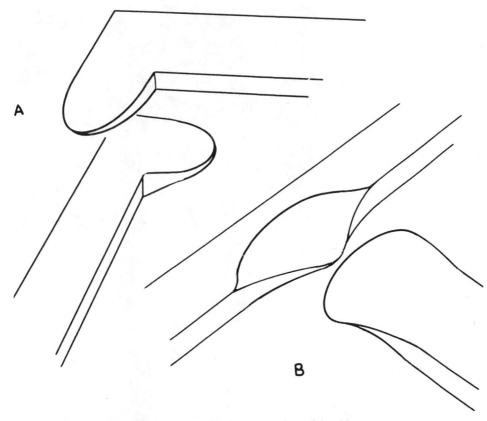

Fig. 6-19. Corners (A) and T-joints (B) in flat frames need special welds.

positioning the parts and hitting over the corner, to be quickly followed by hits at the thin edges on top. The work is then turned over for hits on the thin edges at the other side. The right angle will have to be observed by eye as the parts are brought together, but slight correction is possible after a further heating.

Another variation comes with a T-joint. The piece that is to have its end against the other can be upset and the scarf formed in the usual way. The body of the other part cannot be upset, but it can be thinned to match the other piece (Fig. 6-19B). Make sure that when the parts come together their centers meet, so the first welding hit is effective. Start welding with the end piece on top, but quickly turn over after a few blows to hammer the other side.

Many older tools can be found with bodies made of iron and only the cutting edges made of high-carbon steel. This was done for economy; iron was plentiful and steel was not. It was also done to take advantage of the toughness of iron, which is better able to stand up to heavy use. Iron was also easier to work. Because iron is now almost unobtainable and because it does not possess the characteristics of older iron anyway, cutting edges are no longer welded to it. Tools are now more often than not made completely of high-carbon steel. The body is made tough by tempering the edge to cut, while the rest of the tool is made softer.

If tool steel is to be welded to mild steel, it is not arranged as a direct lap, as can be done between two meeting piece of mild steel. Instead, the tool steel is held between two parts of the mild steel in readiness for welding. Traditional axes and hatchets had their heads made by wrapping iron to form the main part and putting the steel for the cutting edge between the ends of the wrap (Fig. 6-20A). For an end-cutting tool, the steel went into a split end of the iron (Fig. 6-20B).

To weld steel into the end of a mild steel rod, prepare the mild steel piece by bringing it to a bright red heat. Grip it end upwards in the vise and split it with a chisel (Fig. 6-20C) as far as the joint is to be. Hammer the outsides to a taper (Fig. 6-20D). Prepare the piece of tool steel by grinding or forging to a taper so that it can go into the split, which has to be closed on it (Fig. 6-20E). Use a flux that suits high-carbon steel. Mild steel needs a higher welding heat than the tool steel. Position the work in the fire so that the tool steel is out of the center of the fire, at least until welding heat is approached. Then it can be pulled back through the fire as you withdraw the work. Shake off the scale and dirt and hammer the parts together. Overheating the tool steel might burn it and spoil it for its intended purpose. Remember not to quench the work in water, at least not until you do so to harden and temper the tool. Forge or grind the tool shape so the outline blends the two steels together.

CHAIN MAKING

Chains have been made by blacksmiths for a very long time. They were needed in agriculture for traces and to use with implements. They were also needed at sea for anchoring. Castle drawbridges and many other articles of war and defense were operated by chains. Chains for various purposes vary in size and weight. For practice, it is easier to work with links of moderate size, possibly made from ⅜-inch rod, 6 to 8 inches in circumference.

For some simple decorative purposes, chain links merely can be bent so that the ends meet instead of being welded. However, for all load-carrying chains the ends should be welded. The actual welds are those described in Chapter 5; the complications arise when links need to be joined.

Links can be round or other shapes, but they are usually oval and about twice as long as they are wide. In some large links the weld might be in the center of a side. It is more common to arrange it at an end, particularly in moderate sizes, because this keeps the previous link as far as possible out of the way and gives the maximum amount of space for welding hammering.

If a length of chain is to be made, it is more efficient to make all or most of the links up to the joining stages at the same time. Do each step of preparation to each link before moving to next step on any of them. It might also help to speed production if a long piece of chain is made in several sections so that work can be done on one part while another part is in the fire. Then link these parts together in the final stages.

Links should be of uniform size, although for some purposes there might be a larger link or one with a special shape at the end. Cut the rods for the links to the same lengths. Bend each at its center for one end. Bending could be done over the beak, but because this tapers and could cause variations, it is better to use a rod held in the vise (Fig. 6-21A).

Prepare the two ends by hammering them to the usual scarf shapes (Fig. 6-21B) while they are straight. Do not taper excessively thin or the link might finish thinner

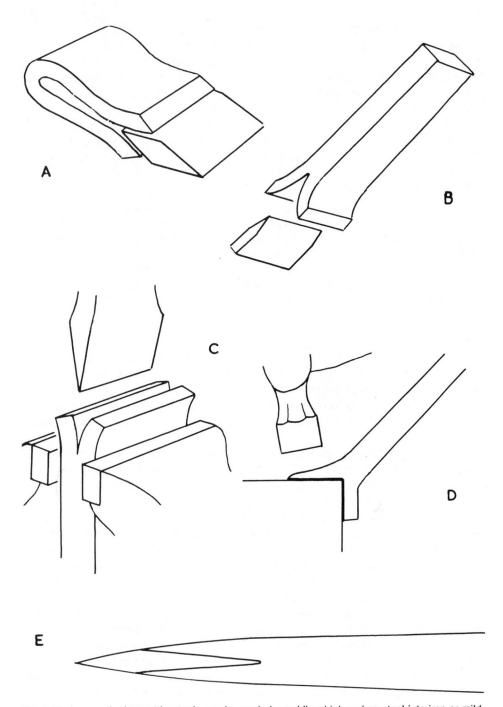

Fig. 6-20. Axes and other cutting tools can be made by welding high-carbon steel into iron or mild steel: (A) the cutting edge is between the ends of the wrap; (B) split end of the iron; (C) split with a chisel; (D) hammer, (E) grind or forge to a taper.

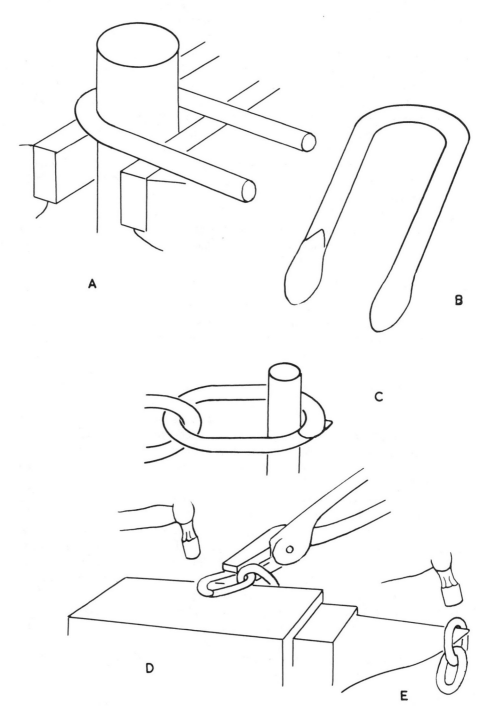

Fig. 6-21. Chain links have their ends prepared and welded: (A) hold the rod in a vise; (B) hammer to shape; (C) hook; (D) hammer on top of the face; (E) match the opposite end.

at the weld. If so, you might have difficulty in completing the weld because the edges lose heat rapidly. Complete the shaping of the link around the rod in the vise. If this is not the first link, hook the previous one in while there is still space (Fig. 6-21C).

Holding is best done with tongs locked on at the end of a link furthest from the weld, and arranged so that a previous link is kept away from the heat and cannot slip around when the chain is brought to the anvil. The work is comparatively light and will quickly heat, but the same considerations have to be met as when welding larger material. Beware of oxidizing when putting the link too near the air blast. Have the part to be heated enclosed in the hot part of the fire, but avoid overheating earlier links. Heat to a cherry red, withdraw, and sprinkle with flux. Then put back into the fire to reach welding heat. Hammering is the same as with any other scarfed weld, but there is some restriction of movement due to the enclosed shape. Use a light hammer with a narrow peen. Get the first blows in quickly at the center of the weld, on top of the face (Fig. 6-21D). Then manipulate the link on the point of the beak so blows can be made around the sides of the weld. At the same heat, it should be possible to hammer the welded end into a shape to match the opposite end (Fig. 6-21E).

CHAIN HOOK

There are two ways of making a chain hook. The eye can either be welded or made from an upset end. A hook is normally of stouter section than the chain to which it is attached because it has to take the same load without the benefit of a closed loop. If made of the same section rod as the links, there is a risk that it might begin to straighten under a strain that would not affect the links. If all loads likely to be taken are much less than this, the hook could be made of rod nearer the size of the links and given a welded eye.

The simplest hook is made of round rod that maintains the same section throughout its length, except for the point. This can have a welded eye around a chain link (Fig. 6-22A). In this or any other hook, make the shape so that the load comes in the curve directly below the eye and there is a good length of the open-ended point extending upwards and outwards (Fig. 6-22B).

If an eye is made from an upset end, upset to a good thickness, which will probably require several heats (Fig. 6-22C), until there is enough metal built up for a thicker part to be hammered (Fig. 6-22D). Such a hook is best made with the thickest part of the hook where the load hangs. It can be drawn out to a rounded point and might be reduced slightly towards the eye, while the rod is straight (Fig. 6-22E). Curl out its point and forge the loop to shape around the anvil beak. Keep the load-bearing part under the end that will be the eye. Either punch or drill the hole to go on the link (Fig. 6-22F). Have the hole tapered outward to each side so that it does not put sharp edges against the link. This can be done with a tapered punch from each side, but if it is a drilled hole, use a countersink bit on each side. The hole could be arranged to come across the hook or in line with it; however, it is more common to have the link through the hole in line with the metal of the hook.

SPLITTING

Besides cutting off bars, sets and hardies can be used to split rods and bars. This was often done with wrought iron. Mild steel does not split as readily, but is a technique that has many uses.

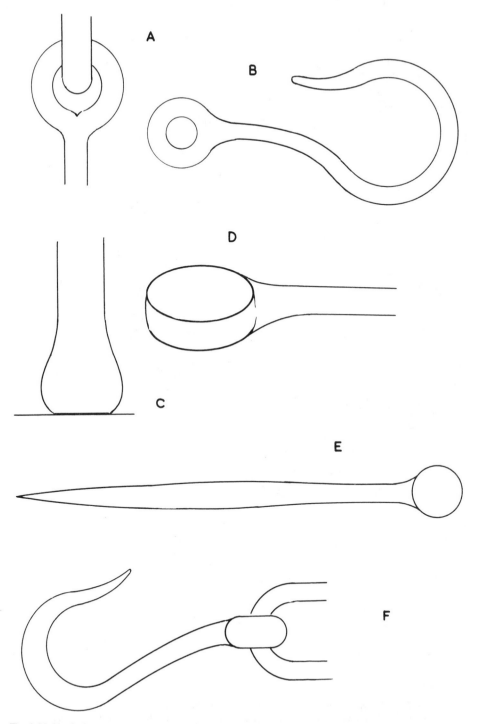

Fig. 6-22. Hooks have welded eyes (A) and are shaped for a direct pull (B): (C) upset to a good thickness; (D) hammer the thicker part; (E) draw out to a point; (F) punch or drill a hole to link.

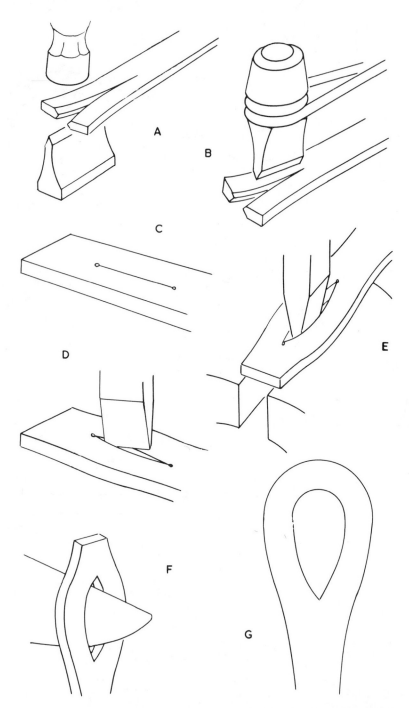

Fig. 6-23. Bar can be split (A) and the cut part (B) forged to shape: (C) the split is marked by small punched holes; (D) tilt the set into each hole; (E) drive to force the gap wider; (F) shape over the anvil beak; (G) forge to a curve.

A split can be made in the end of a flat bar by hammering it hot on a hardie, turning over so as to cut in from both sides, and working back from the end (Fig. 6-23A). The danger there is cutting completely through so that the hardie edge meets the hammer and is damaged. The risk is avoided if the cut is made from above with a hot set (Fig. 6-23B). Again, this should be done from both sides and should work back from the end. If cuts are made on the face and the set goes through, it could be blunted and damage the hardened anvil face. Cutting can be done on the table, but there would be more room to manipulate the work if the cutting is done over an iron block on the face. This could be a cutting saddle (Fig. 3-12), which is a piece of flat iron (½ inch thick would be suitable) bent so that it fits easily over the face and is prevented from moving.

Splitting from the end could make the two prongs of a fork, instead of welding two rods together. After the parts have been split, they are forged separately to remove the marks of cutting and produce round tapered prongs. A two-pronged poker could have its parts made by splitting, instead of being produced from a welded eye.

Another use of splitting is in forming a long eye in the body of a bar. In this case, the limits of the split are marked by two small punched holes (Fig. 6-23C). Use a hot set along a line between the holes. Tilt the set into each hole first (Fig. 6-23D) and then use it flat on the steel. Do this at both sides until the split goes right through. There might have to be several reheats of a large piece. Cool the set between heats.

When the set has broken through, the steel can be put over the partly open vise so that the set or a steel wedge can be driven further to force the gap wider (Fig. 6-23E). What is done after that depends on the purpose of the split, but it often has to be finished in an elliptical shape, which can be done over the anvil beak (Fig. 6-23F). The punched holes should stop the split from going further than intended. Their appearance in the finished hole might be acceptable, but it is possible to forge the whole end to a curve (Fig. 6-23G) so that the original form is not apparent.

7

Handles

Much interesting blacksmithing is involved in making handles on the end of square or round rods. For most purposes, the rods do not have to be very large section. The work can be done with light equipment, mostly single-handed and without great physical effort. Handles for the ends of domestic hearth tools, garden tools, and other implements can be tackled by a beginner.

Most handles are made on the ends of round rods, usually ⅜ or ½ inch in diameter. Some might be thicker or thinner, but they have to be related to the capacity of the hand. If the handle is on thin rod it might have to be made sufficiently bulky to provide a secure grip. If the rod is already thick, the handle might finish a little thicker or might be merely a knob or other stop on the end. The handle will also have to be related to the use of the implement. If it is for picking up with a grasp, it must be long enough and shaped to be a reasonable fit in the palm of the hand. If it is a tool that has to be thrust, the end of the handle must be shaped so the palm can push efficiently and comfortably. Many handled tools have to hang when they are out of use, so the handle might be looped or have a hole through it. Quite often, the handle will not be heavily loaded and almost any shape would suit its use. In that case, decoration might be more important than shape.

Some of the handles take on a special interest if they are made from square, octagonal, or other sectioned rod. The complete handle can be formed in the same way round rod is used, and most of the designs intended for round material will look and handle well in other sections. Another way of using angular-sectioned rod is to forge all or part of the handle to round section.

Forging handles or anything else gives the blacksmith a chance to express his artistic intentions. There is a great satisfaction to be had from working red-hot steel into a shape that pleases you. Following are a few artistic rules that might help you. Observe them and you have made a start. After that you are on your own.

Curved lines are generally more acceptable than straight ones. Some tools and other items you make will have to have straight parts. But sometimes a long sweeping curve would do just as well. The poker (Fig. 6-16) is an example of a double curve that looks better than just a straight rod. Even when the main part of the shaft has to be straight, there can be curves in the handle. It might be off-center or asymmetrical to give a more interesting shape than one that is symmetrical. Much depends on the intended use. A simple symmetrical loop handle might be more suitable for the purpose if all you are making is a tool for use in the garden. Squares look better if tilted to form diamonds (Fig. 7-1A) or if made longer one way (Fig. 7-1B).

The preference for a curve over a straight line may come in tapering. If a long taper is drawn out to make a scrolled handle, it could take a straight taper (Fig. 7-1C), but it would look better if it had a slight curve along the taper (Fig. 7-1D). Usually a hollow along the length of the taper does not look right, but it can come towards the end if that is to be rolled back or otherwise shaped tightly.

Circles are not as pleasing as ellipses or ovals. Circles are sometimes necessary, but if an ellipse would serve the purpose as well, it will usually look better (Fig. 7-1E). An oval might look even better (Fig. 7-1F) as the basic outline of a handle. Bear in mind the use of the tool. An ellipse makes a comfortable shape to hold in the palm of your hand. If there has to be a thrust, a pronounced oval with a thick knob end is better. Even when the handle is for lifting, the ellipse might look better, if given a slight oval shape, with its thicker part toward the end.

LOOP HANDLES

Some examples of variations on the basic loop handle will show how appearance can be changed while the handle remains functional. The ordinary loop is a circle centrally placed on the shaft, whether bent to butt against it or welded (Fig. 7-2A). It can be made longer than it is wide, so that it becomes an ellipse (Fig. 7-2B). This should give a more comfortable grip, but not much artistic merit. If the shape is converted to an oval (Fig. 7-2C) there is no loss of function, yet it looks better. A further step involves bringing the narrow end of the oval almost to a point, which is a help in welding, so that shape is both artistic and practical (Fig. 7-2D).

All of these shapes are symmetrical. They can be moved partly or entirely to the side, usually without loss of function. The shaft can then go along one side of the handle instead of being directed centrally at it (Fig. 7-2E). The almost conical oval need not have its sides straight or regularly curved, but can be given attractive shapes (Fig. 7-2F).

Much shaping of looped handles has to be done with a hammer over the beak of the anvil. Be careful to do most of the hitting off-center. When you hit directly toward the beak, the hammer will make a flat on the steel where it hits, and there will be another dent made on the inside by the beak. If you hit off-center, it will alter the shape more—which is what you want—and mark the steel less (Fig. 7-3A). It is very easy for a beginner to get the shape he wants by hammering often, directly toward the beak. However, he finishes with a handle that is a mass of marks or that is thinned and flattened. There

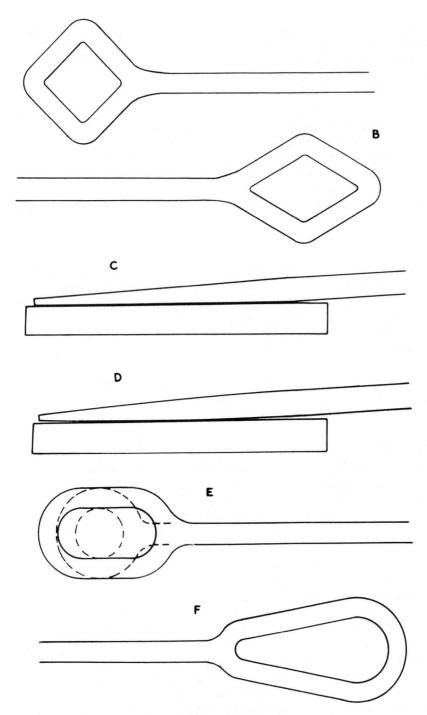

Fig. 7-1. Handles can be made into a number of shapes: (A) diamond; (B) drawn out diamond; (C) straight taper; (D) curved taper; (E) ellipse; (F) oval.

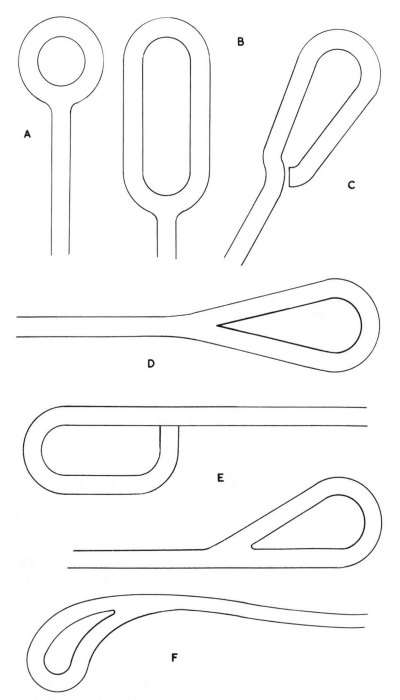

Fig. 7-2. Handles can be formed to suit special purposes or for decoration: (A) loop; (B) ellipse; (C) oval; (D) oval brought almost to a point; (E) a shaft along one side of the handle; (F) almost conical oval.

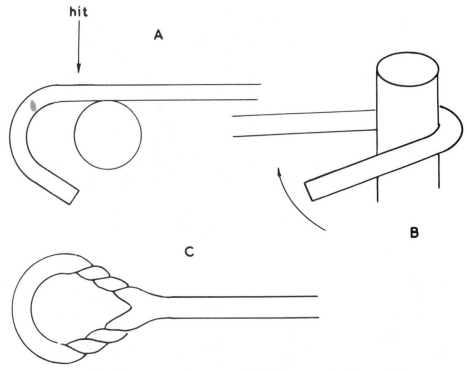

Fig. 7-3. A more advanced handle includes twists: (A) hit off center; (B) pull the end; (C) square rod can be twisted.

might have to be some blows directly pinching the metal. Keep these few and make them taps for the final steps in shaping.

The alternative to hammering is to pull the rod to shape, at least for obtaining the main curve. This can be done on the beak, but it might be easier to use a rod gripped in the vise. A rod of the right size will also help get the shape right.

The rod can be held in one hand while the end is pulled around with tongs (Fig. 7-3B). Rod heated to a good red will pull around almost effortlessly. This has the advantage of getting the rod to shape without marking it in any way with a hammer. The section around the curve should be as clean as along the rod. This is particularly important if the rod is square or angular and the appearance would be spoiled if sharpness was knocked off the section. Square rod can be twisted before bending, either partly or completely around the handle (Fig. 7-3C). This should be pulled to shape; hammering would damage the projecting angles of the twist.

SCROLLED HANDLES

The variations on handles include ends welded into the shaft or butting against it. For most lightly used implements, such as those for tending a domestic fire, there is no need for a weld. The untreated plain end does not have a very good finish; it would be better to do something to improve its appearance. One way is to taper the rod and provide a small scroll or pigtail on the end (Fig. 7-4A). This has to be done before shaping the handle.

Draw out the end for the amount needed to make the pigtail—far enough to come almost to the crown of the loop. In most handles it looks better to keep the full thickness of the rod up one side of the handle and across the top. Taper to about one-quarter the thickness of the rod (Fig. 7-4B). Tapering to a point could result in the end being burned during further work. Also, a point does not usually look as good as an end with some thickness.

Heat the end for a short distance. The thin metal will heat quickly, so be careful not to overheat. Bring it to a yellow heat and hold it over the edge of the anvil face so you can hit it (Fig. 7-4C). Hit mostly at the end and it will curl inwards.

As the curl develops (Fig. 7-4D), continue to hit on what is now the end so that more metal curls (Fig. 7-4E). You will have to reheat as you make progress because the thinned part will soon lose heat. The curl might have to be trued by light hits against the edge of the anvil (Fig. 7-4F), but do not hit heavily in this direction. Best progress is made in shaping by using a light hammer and light blows on yellow-hot metal. The end should finish as a fairly tight helix, but not so close that it no longer shows light through.

Forge the loop handle to shape by hammering or pulling around and close it so the scroll is outward and against the shaft. The scroll end is effective whatever basic shape is chosen for the loop (Fig. 7-4G).

Examine decorative ironwork and you will see that some of the twists and twirls in gates and other examples will finish with pigtails, as just described, but others might have a broadened, flattened end. This can also be used on a poker or similar handle. It does not matter if the rod is square or round. Taper the end, but instead of going almost to a point, flatten and spread one way while thinning the other way. For a handle, it is advisable to keep the flat part narrow unless the twist will come outside the grip. This will roll narrow (Fig. 7-5A). A widened end will give a different effect (Fig. 7-5B). Variations in the outline of the flattened part give different rolled patterns. These ends can be rolled in the same way, as described for the pointed rod. Another way is to use round-nosed pliers to start the curl with yellow-hot steel.

KNOTTED HANDLES

The end does not have to finish alongside the shaft. In the example in Fig. 7-6A, it is twisted around. Draw out a long taper for the twisted part, then form an eye in the usual way. Make it round or any other shape, and leave the tapered part across the shaft. With another heat, pull the tapered end around the shaft with pliers or tongs. Then hammer lightly to get it close and its turns evenly spaced.

An ordinary overhand knot could be tied in the end (Fig. 7-6B). The tip could be a scroll, but it would be better to upset it before shaping and making a knob there. By carefully manipulating the parts of the knot, a balanced handle can be formed. To get it to center more naturally, a figure 8 knot is more symmetrical. Turn an eye in the rod (Fig. 7-6C) with enough end left to complete the knot. Then pull the end through the eye after going around the shaft to the other side (Fig. 7-6D). The rod could finish with an upset knob or be tapered and made into a small eye (Fig. 7-6E).

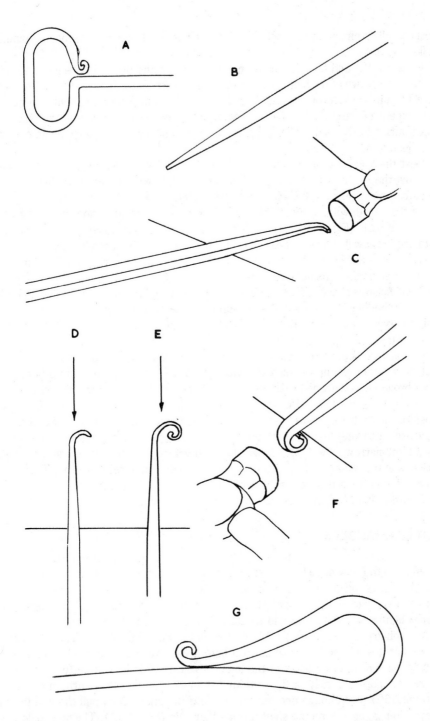

Fig. 7-4. A drawn out end can be turned into a scroll to decorate a handle: (A) small scroll; (B) taper; (C) heat and hit the edge; (D,E,F) continue to curl; (G) forge the loop handle.

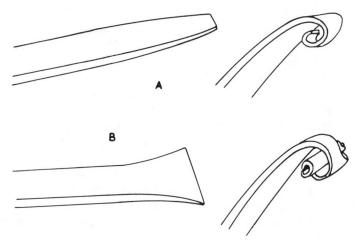

Fig. 7-5. By flattening (A) and altering the outline (B) different scrolls can be made.

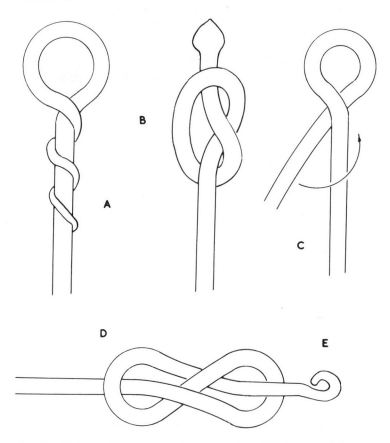

Fig. 7-6. Twists and knots make different handles: (A) twist around; (B) a tied overhand knot; (C) an eye in the knot; (D) pull the end through; (E) upset knob with small eye.

UPSET HANDLE

If thickening the handle would produce a handle large enough to grip, the rod can be upset for a sufficient length and this part shaped to provide a grip. Alternatively, thicker material can be used and the shaft swaged down from it. A piece of ½-inch or ⁷⁄₁₆-inch rod could be upset enough to make a handle with the greatest diameter about ¾ inch.

Make the handle before forging any other part of the rod. Heat the end and upset it first by spreading the extreme part (Fig. 7-7A). When this has spread, heat further back so more of the rod gets bigger (Fig. 7-7B). Do this in stages until the length of the handle is built up. From this point on, heat to red and forge the handle to the shape required. It could be round, but it looks attractive and gives a firmer grip if there are flats on it. Most are simply arranged by forming an octagonal section.

Forge to the general outline first, usually with an oval side view that has a knob at the end (Fig. 7-7C). The knob can be separated by using narrow fullers to lightly tap in the groove while the work is rotated between blows. Upsetting will have provided the taper towards the shaft. When the shape is satisfactory in a round section, use the hammer lightly with the poker over the face of the anvil. First hammer flats in a square pattern, then hammer the corners to make an octagon (Fig. 7-7D).

CAGE HANDLE

A handle that looks like a spiral cage has the advantage of remaining cool as well as being an attractive decoration (Fig. 7-8A). Because making it involves welding, the work would

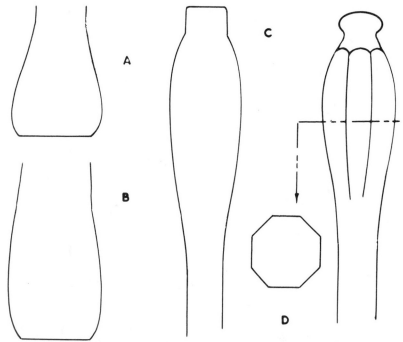

Fig. 7-7. An upset end can be forged into an octagonal handle: (A) heat and spread the extreme part; (B) heat and enlarge; (C) forge to the general outline; (D) make an octagon.

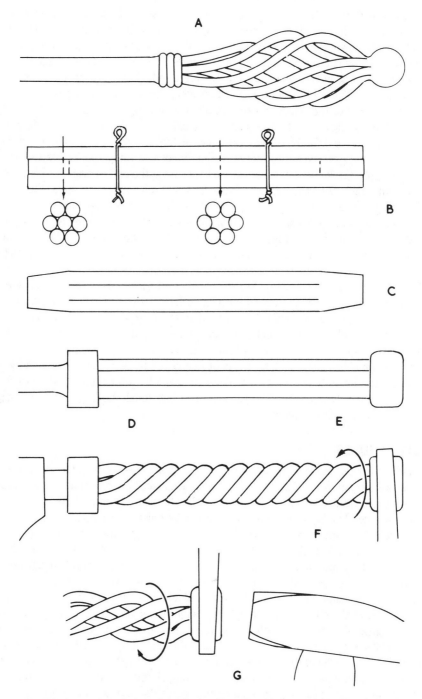

Fig. 7-8. A cage handle is built up from rods and welded to a shaft: (A) spiral cage; (B) rods wired together; (C) ends are hammered slightly smaller; (D) fit roll collars over the ends of the handle; (E) form the top collar into a knob; (F) twist the handle; (G) place in a vise and unwind slightly while tapping with a hammer.

be easier in iron than in steel. The handle and shaft are separate parts welded together.

The handle itself is made of six pieces of identical rods. Diameters of ³⁄₁₆ inch would be suitable. They could be 5 inches long. Pieces about 1 inch long are put between their ends so that they can be tied together with iron wire in a regular hexagonal section (Fig. 7-8B). Weld each end in turn while holding the other end with hollow-bit tongs. Remove the binding wire. The ends will be slightly smaller, due to hammering (Fig. 7-8C).

Upset one end of the handle enough to allow a welding scarf to be made. Do the same with the rod that is to be the shaft and weld the handle to it. Roll collars from ³⁄₄- × -³⁄₁₆-inch strip and fit them over the ends of the handle (Fig. 7-8D). Weld them on. That completes the welding. Further steps involve forging the handle to shape.

The end collar looks best if formed into a knob. Heat the end to bright red and shape this by hammering around the edges of the collar while rolling it on the anvil (Fig. 7-8E).

The twist is made mainly in the upper half of the length of the rods. Heat evenly from the end knob to within about 1 inch of the lower collar. When ready, quickly grip the shaft in the vise and use tongs or a pipe wrench on the knob to twist the handle (Fig. 7-8F). Give enough twists to make a close screw-like shape, with the rods tightly touching.

Heat again for the same length. Quickly put the shaft back in the vise. Use the wrench the other way on the knob to unwind partially, while at the same time tapping with a hammer on the knob. (Fig. 7-8G). This will open the cage and spread the parts. It is unlikely that they will form a perfect shape first time, but after a further heating, pliers can be used to get all the rods into a balanced form.

The bottom collar could be left as it is or decorated by filing grooves around it. An interesting variation is to introduce a ball into the cage by forcing two rods apart to let it in, then bringing them back to the pattern. The ball should be larger than any gaps, but loose enough to move about.

ADDED HANDLES

The handle does not have to be one with the shaft and need not be steel. If it is for a tool that will get hot, a wooden handle would provide insulation from heat. Brass, copper, and plastics can be used to provide color and brightness to contrast the steel.

For a wooden handle, the end of the shaft can be finished as a spike or tang, usually square, even if the rod is round. Teeth could be raised by cutting into the spike with a cold chisel (Fig. 7-9A) to give the maximum grip. The best handle is made of hardwood and fitted with a ferrule to resist splitting. The hole is then drilled slightly undersize and made with two or three drills, to reduce in steps (Fig. 7-9B).

Some plastics can be softened with heat, and a handle made of this material can be shrunk on. Leave the shaft round except for a slight taper near its end. Drill the plastic only slightly undersize. Soften it with boiling water or in an oven, depending on the amount of heat required for the particular plastic. Warm the end of the shaft to about the same temperature. Tap the handle on with a wooden or rubber mallet. Leave to set and shrink.

Another wooden handle can be made by putting cheeks each side of the steel. The end of the shaft is flattened and given a curved outline so that it can be drilled for two or more rivets (Fig. 7-10A). Usually the handle is the end, but it is possible to add a decorative twirl that might also serve for hanging the tool (Fig. 7-10B).

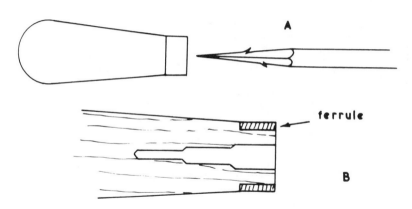

Fig. 7-9. Cutting barbs (A) on a tang help it grip a wooden handle (B).

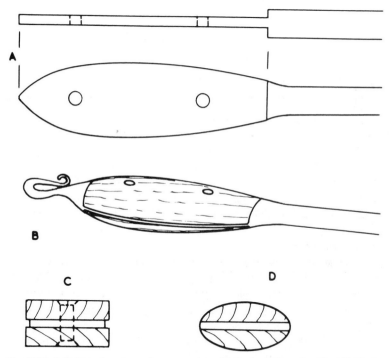

Fig. 7-10. A flattened part can have wooden cheeks to make a handle: (A) shaft end; (B) decorative twirl; (C) rod can be used to fill hollows; (D) file to get a rounded handle.

Make two hardwood slabs to fit on the flat parts, but keep them slightly too wide at this stage. Put one under the steel and drill through, then turn over and drill the other slab. The rivets could be brass or copper with countersunk heads. They need not be prepared rivets; they can be rod hammered on alternate sides until they fill the hollows in the wood (Fig. 7-10C). When the wooden sides are secure, file the wood and the edges of the flattened steel to give an elliptical cross-section and a neatly rounded handle (Fig. 7-10D). Remove file marks with abrasive paper and finish the wood with varnish.

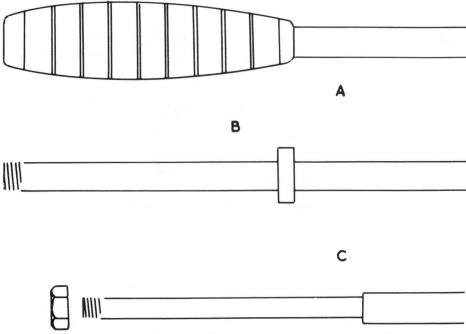

Fig. 7-11. Pieces of plastic and metal can be threaded on a rod to make a handle: (A) brass and colored plastic; (B) a collar on the shaft; (C) swage to form a shoulder.

Another form of handle has discs of many sorts of material threaded on the shaft. Brass washers can be used to alternate with colored plastics (Fig. 7-11A).

A collar can be welded around the shaft to mark the limit of the handle (Fig. 7-11B). Another way of limiting the discs is to swage down the shaft slightly to provide a shoulder (Fig. 7-11C). At the other end, cut a thread to take a nut that will be shaped to match the other parts of the handle.

Build up the length of the handle with metal and plastic. Tighten the nut at the end, lightly riveting the end of the shaft to prevent the nut from loosening. What can be done to the handle depends on the facilities available. If the job can be mounted in a lathe, it can be turned to an elliptical or other outline. Otherwise, similar shapes can be obtained by filing. The section need not be round, but can be filed in an octagonal or oval shape. Follow by sanding to remove file marks, then polish the handle all over.

A similar idea works with a wood or plastic rod handle that is drilled through the middle. It could be turned before or after fitting, or it might be carved to make a head. In the case, the nut should be sunk below the surface of the wood.

Handles of other metals can be turned or cast and then attached to their shafts, usually by screwing. A brass or bronze handle on a steel shaft looks attractive. There should be enough screwed length to make a firm joint and to keep the handle and shaft in line. On a ⅜-inch shaft, the threaded part should be at least ¾ inch. In the other part, make the hole deeper than that to give clearance for the screwing tap and to allow all of the thread on the rod to disappear when the handle is fitted. This also ensures a tight joint (Fig. 7-12). If the handle is turned, the hole can be drilled in the lathe to make

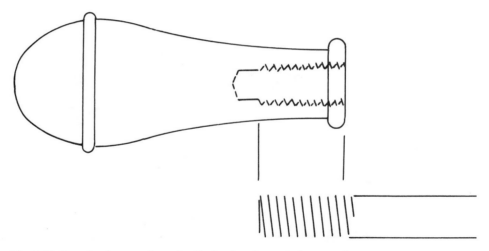

Fig. 7-12. Screwing is a good way to attach a handle made from another metal.

sure it is in line. If it is a cast patterned handle, have the flat end center-punched where the hole is to come. Make sure the flat end is level when the handle is held in a vise under a drill press.

CROSS HANDLES

If a handle is required to provide leverage to twist the shaft with much force, it has to be across the line from the shaft. A simple traditional way of arranging this is to forge the end of the shaft into a long flattened point (Fig. 7-13A), which can be driven into a hole in a wooden cross handle. The point could go completely through, so a small washer would allow it to be riveted (Fig. 7-13B). The twisting action puts a splitting action on the shaft in the wood. With suitable hardwood of sufficient size, the handle should survive this.

A better arrangement encloses the wood in the iron so that there is no tendency to split. This necessitates making an eye at the end of the shaft so that the wood can be pushed through. If there is much load anticipated, the eye should be welded.

It is difficult to weld a full circle; it is better to make an oval eye first and bring it to round after welding. Flatten enough of the end to make the eye (Fig. 7-13C). Prepare its extremity for welding. Bend the eye and position the end on the shaft. Prepare it with flux and weld it (Fig. 7-13D). Having made a good joint, forge the eye round on the anvil beak or a mandrel so that a round piece of wood can pass through (Fig. 7-13E).

An iron rod or tube could be put through the eye instead of the wooden rod. A more permanent T-shaped handle might be made by welding a rod across the end of the shaft (Fig. 7-13F).

Another way of providing a twisting action is to upset the end of the shaft and forge it to a tapered square. Punch a square hole at the center of a flat bar so that it will fit over the end of the shaft. Reduce the ends of the bar and swage them round to provide grips (Fig. 7-13G). The handle can be taken off for convenience in storage or transport, or the end of the shaft can be riveted over to hold the two parts together. If the tool

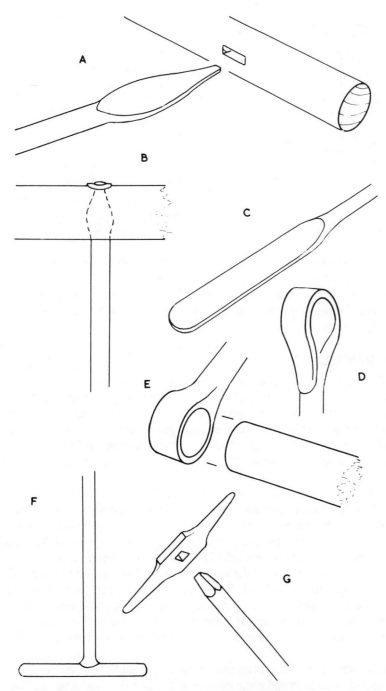

Fig. 7-13. If a tool has to be turned, the attachment to the handle must resist torque: (A) a long flattened point; (B) rivet with a small washer; (C) the eye; (D) weld; (E) forge the eye; (F) weld a T-shaped handle; (G) reduce and swage the ends of the bar.

is for lifting, as when the shaft forms a hook, the cross handle should be riveted or welded on.

RING HANDLES

Another type of handle is a swinging ring that can be used as a drawer pull, or a heavier version could be a door knocker. An oval version can be used as a lifting handle on the end of a chest. There are many ways of decorating the handle and its backplate; only a few are suggested here. Similar items can become hitching rings, mooring points, or lashing anchorages.

For a basic handle or ring bolt—without decoration—a length of rod can be made into a circle and given a pivot. One way of making a true circle is to first have a rod of the internal size ready. Then heat a long piece of rod for the ring, and grip its end and the pattern rod in a vise. The hot steel can be pulled around to more than a complete circle (Fig. 7-14A). Remove the steel from the vise and cut through at the overlap. Do no more at this stage if the ring is to go through a hole in a solid bar.

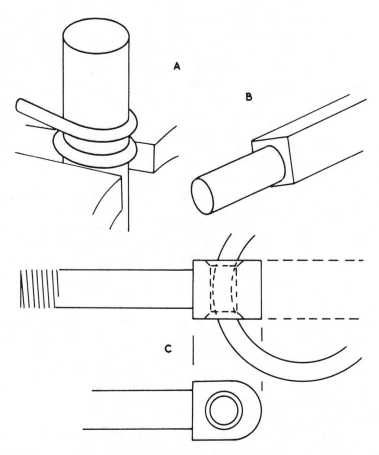

Fig. 7-14. A ring handle fits a hole in a bolt head: (A) pull the hot steel around; (B) reduce the end and swage to round with a sharp shoulder; (C) drill a hole and countersink.

For the bolt, use a piece of square bar about three times as thick as the rod used for the ring. If it is a bolt that is to go through wood and be held with a nut at the other side, reduce enough of the end and swage this to round with a sharp shoulder (Fig. 7-14B).

Drill a hole that the ring will pass through easily and countersink both sides (Fig. 7-14C). Cut off the surplus bar and file the end that remains rounded. Pass the ring through the hole and prepare its ends for welding in the same way as chain links. Make the weld and true the joint by hammering if possible, but if necessary, file the weld to the same section as the rest of the ring so that it will move through the hole without catching.

Cut a thread for a sufficient distance on the end of the bolt and provide it with a nut and large washer. There can be another washer under the bolt head to prevent it from pulling into wood, or a decorative piece as described below.

If the assembly is to mount on the surface instead of going completely through, there has to be a backplate to take the screws. It could be a plain circle, square, or diamond of flat plate, with edges and corners rounded or beveled (Fig. 7-15A). The surface could be hammered all over with a ball peen hammer (Fig. 7-15B), or only the edges hammered (Fig. 7-15C).

Make a tenon on the end of the square rod, long enough to go through the backplate and far enough for riveting (Fig. 7-15D). Keep the tenon as large as conveniently possible, while leaving enough of the square part for a shoulder. If the wood the handle is attached to can be hollowed, make the stronger rivet head on the surface (Fig. 7-15E). If it has to be kept flush, the rivet must be countersunk (Fig. 7-15F). For an oval handle, there can be two supports on a longer backplate (Fig. 7-15G).

For a drawer, door, box handle, or a door knocker, the ring and the backplate should be decorated. The ring looks better if it is tapered so that the hanging part is thicker than the part entering the support. If the handle is to be used for lifting or dragging a heavy weight, the handle should have its ends welded. For most purposes, it is sufficient for the ring ends to go into the support without meeting.

Even with a tapered and decorated ring, it is easier to pull the hot steel around a rod of the correct diameter than to hammer it to shape over the beak of the anvil. There is also less risk of damage. Leave some surplus length—maybe a few inches at each end—so one end can be gripped in the vise and the other end pulled around with tongs.

If the ring is made from round rod, draw out both ends (Fig. 7-16A). This need not be much—⅜-inch rod could taper to about ¼ inch. There could be some filed decoration each side of the center (Fig. 7-16B). Heat the rod and pull it to shape in the vise so the ends overlap.

There could be a bolt or riveted support (Fig. 7-16C), or it might be sufficient to form a clip from sheet metal (Fig. 7-16D). For tapered ⅜-inch rod, it should be about ¹⁄₁₆-inch thick.

Cut the overlapping ends of the rings, and file pins on the ends that go into the hole of a bolt or that are small enough to allow the sheet metal clip to be wrapped between the shoulders (Fig. 7-16E). To get the pins into place, heat the central thick part of the ring to redness and squeeze the sides gently in a vise.

If a clip is used, it will probably not need heating. It can be bent cold around a rod of the same diameter as the pins, then the projecting ends squeezed together in the vise (Fig. 7-16F). The ends must be long enough to spread behind the backplate.

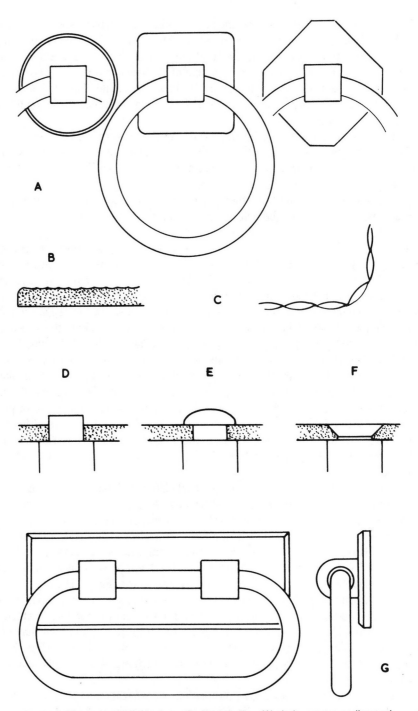

Fig. 7-15. Shaped backplates decorate ring handles: (A) circle, square or diamond flat plate; (B) hammered surface; (C) hammered edges; (D) a tenon; (E) rivet on the surface; (F) a countersunk rivet; (G) two supports for an oval backplate.

If the ring is to be used as a door knocker, it is better to have a knob at the center (Fig. 7-16G). This is a piece of steel with a hole through it. If the hole is very slightly undersize when both parts are cold, the knob can be shrunk on. Prepare the knob and heat it to redness. Put it over the pritchel hole of the anvil or a partly open vise, and drive the straight piece for the ring into it. Then shape the handle. The knob might have to be filed, or it can be shaped by hammering after fitting. Hammer marks on it can be regarded as decoration.

Square bar can be used to make rings with twisted centers, with either one twist (Fig. 7-17A) or a reversed twist (Fig. 7-17B). You could make a knob with a square punched hole arranged between the twists, or just a striker (Fig. 7-17C) welded or held with a pin on the underside.

The twist should be done first, then the ends drawn down so that they are round at the parts where they enter the bolt or clip. File pins in the same way as the previous rings.

The backplate can be any shape, but it will look best if it is symmetrical around the hanging ring (Fig. 7-18). It could be a circle with hammered treatment on the surface or edges, or the edges could be filed (Fig. 7-17D). Whatever the shape, the attachment comes near the top and there have to be holes for screws. If the attachment is a bolt going right through the wood, there need only be one wood screw located at the bottom where it will be hidden by the hanging handle. If it is a door knocker, the screw could go through a raised block to serve as a striker plate (Fig. 7-17E). If the wood screws have to hold the handle in place, there should be at least three holes for screws.

A bolt or rivet will go through a round drilled hole, but the clip will need a punched slot. A tool might have to be forged for this. Because the slot is small and the metal thin, the punch can be quite light. Assemble the parts and support the curve of the clip on something softer than the anvil face. A lead block is best, but a piece of hardwood will do. These support without much risk of marking or distorting the clip. Use a cold chisel to open the ends of the clip (Fig. 7-17F), then flatten the open ends by direct hammering.

An interesting decorative feature for the backplate is a domed center (Fig. 7-19A). There has to be a flat rim for the bolt and wood screws, but the center is raised to a moderate curve. If the plate is 1/16 inch or less, doming can be done cold. Use the ball peen hammer to make a slight hollow in a block of lead or in the end grain of a piece of hardwood. Hold the backplate over this, with its front downward, and use the hammer on it (Fig. 7-19B). Work from the center, pulling the metal around between blows that are given in increasing circles. Tilt the work as necessary (Fig. 7-19C).

If the backplate is thicker, the work has to be done in a similar way, but the steel must be made red hot. This makes lead or wood unsuitable for support. Instead, use a hole in a swage block or one drilled in a piece of scrap iron. It does not have to be very large, but should be bigger than the diameter of the ball peen (Fig. 7-19D). Countersinking the hole helps to soften the edge, but there will be some marking of the hot metal.

Hammering the front can remove the marks, but whether thin cold or thicker hot steel has been used, the front can be decorated by planishing. The hollowed part has to be supported on a stake, which is a rod with rounded top of less curvature than that of the backplate (Fig. 7-19E). Stakes of this sort are made for sheet metalwork, but

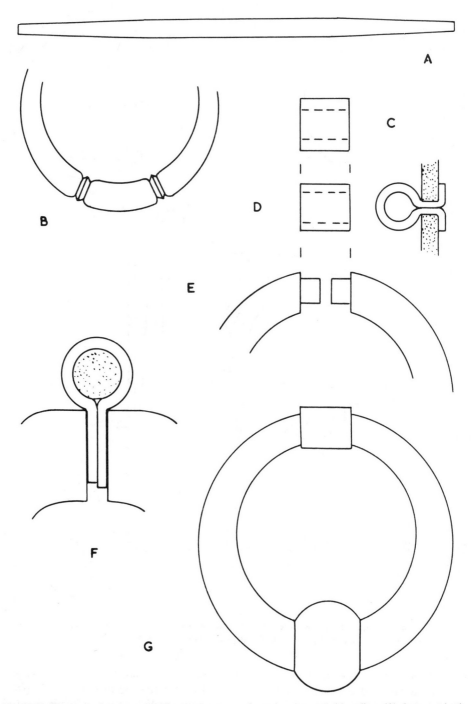

Fig. 7-16. Rings can be decorated in many ways and can be supported by clips: (A) draw out both ends; (B) filed decoration; (C) riveted support; (D) a clip from sheet metal; (E) cut overlapping ends and file pins; (F) squeeze in a vise; (G) finished door knocker.

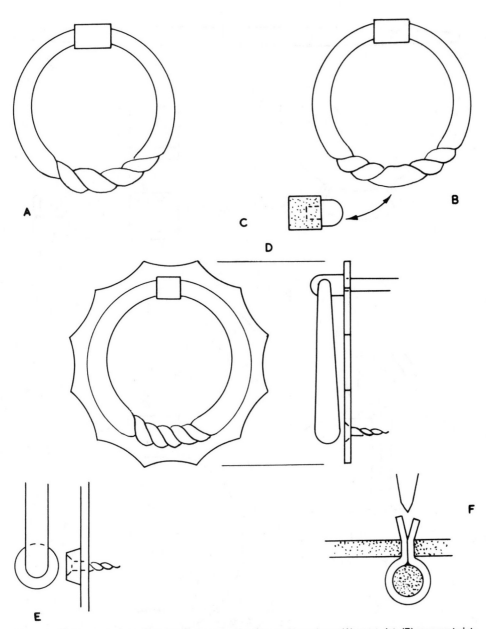

Fig. 7-17. Twists are appropriate decorations for handles and knockers: (A) one twist; (B) reverse twist; (C) a striker; (D) filed edges; (E) striker plate; (F) open the clip with a chisel.

there is no need for one of these; the end of a rod ground to an approximate curve will be good enough. Use a ball peen hammer directly over the top of the stake to pinch the metal at each blow. Move the plate around until the whole front surface is covered with overlapping dents from the hammer (Fig. 7-19F). When the flat rim is reached, the work can continue on the anvil face or any other flat surface.

Fig. 7-18. A twisted ring door handle swings over a hammered backplate.

131

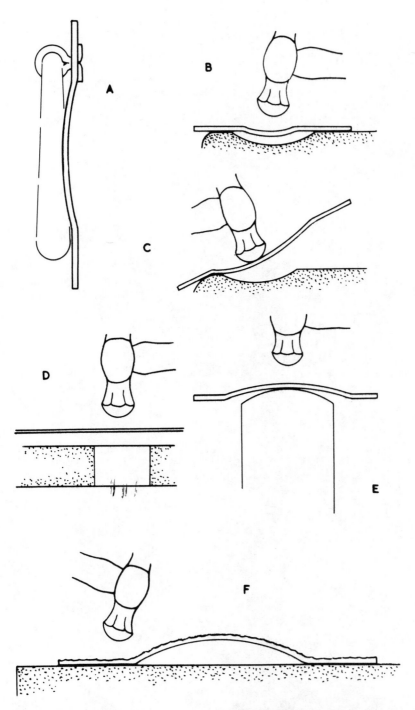

Fig. 7-19. A domed backplate can match a ring handle. (A) domed center; (B,C) hammer over the backplate; (D) use a swage block; (E,F) hammer to shape.

8

Easy Tools To Make

A good introduction to toolmaking is forming things such as punches, chisels, and spikes with steel bar. Successful end products are fairly easy to achieve, and they are useful tools that will serve their purpose at least as well as any bought from a tool store. In the process of learning to forge high-carbon steel, a beginner blacksmith can add to his stock of tools for working in both wood and metal.

There are minor variations between tool steels and you might have to experiment to get a tool hardened and tempered to your liking. Table 5-1 gives a guide to oxide colors that can be expected to give the correct temper for a particular purpose. There would only be slight variations in any case. The way you heat the steel is probably more important. It should not remain in the fire any longer than necessary. When it has reached the correct heat, withdraw it and work on it. If the steel is left to "soak" in the fire, the surface becomes decarbonized and forms a soft skin. This can be quite thin, but it means that after heat treatment the outer surface might not be as hard and tough as the steel below the surface.

There is an old blacksmith's couplet that emphasizes the point:

> He that will a good edge win
> Must forge thick and grind thin.

To allow for some softening of the skin, a tool should be forged so that what will be the cutting edge is thicker than necessary, and so that some of it can be ground away to get the size required. In doing this, any decarbonized surface will be removed. What is left will have its full proportion of carbon and will be as hard as required. When working on a tool that will be finished to a point or a thin edge, do not hammer too far. Leave the edge thick, so it has to be finished to size by grinding. About ⅛ inch should be enough.

One cause of decarbonizing is exposure to air while heating. Do not put the steel to heat on or near the top of the fire. Let there be fire above and below the steel. Thrust the steel into the heart of fire. Beware of putting it too near the tuyere where the blast might direct air on to the steel. Hardening and tempering are best kept apart from forging. Even if the final work on the steel leaves it with enough heat for hardening, it is unwise to go straight into hardening. There is a risk that the internal stresses set up in forging might cause cracking or distortion when suddenly cooled. It is better to normalize the steel by heating to a cherry red and allowing it to cool slowly with the fire or in ashes or sand.

The tool is then as placid as it is likely to be and as soft as it can be. This is the stage where it is better to file, drill, or do any other non-forge work, as well as grinding or polishing. If the operative part is ground, there is no need to take it to a cutting edge yet. The taper towards the end should be bright so that the tempering colors will be easy to distinguish later. For an attractive finish, rub with abrasive paper and buff with a rotating mop after grinding. The brightness will disappear with hardening, but it is easy to restore if it was there in the first place. Trying to brighten unpolished steel after hardening is an almost impossible task. Hardening and tempering have previously been described, and for end-cutting tools the process is straightforward.

Steel of almost any section can be made into a tool. For a tool that is to be held in your hand like a pencil or hit with a hammer, steel can be round, square, rectangular, hexagonal, or octagonal. Square or rectangular bar, with small bevels on the corners, is comfortable and a good shape to resist twisting (Fig. 8-1).

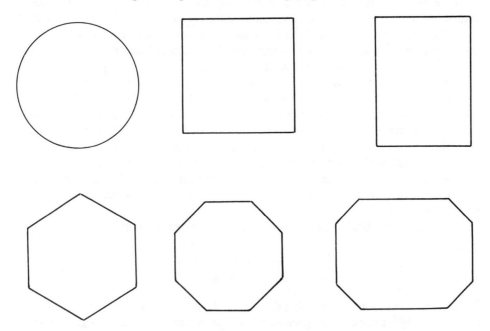

Fig. 8-1. Tools can be made from high-carbon steel of several sections.

If the steel to be used has already been made into something and you are forming a tool from it, first normalize the steel. This removes any existing temper and any internal stresses that might have built up during its previous use. This also applies if an old tool has been worn away and there is still enough steel in it to forge a new end. It might be satisfactory to go straight into forging, but to assure quality in the new work, normalize first.

Do the work on a new tool on the end of a bar that is long enough to hold, and do all the work possible before cutting off. Otherwise, make sure you have tongs that will hold the steel firmly and can be locked on. When you are working on thin tapered sections, if you have not planned ahead it is very easy to lose the heat while trying to get the steel gripped and in position for hammering.

PUNCHES

Center and nail punches can be made in sizes starting with rod no more that ¼ inch thick and up to any size that can be gripped. The amount of taper has to be a compromise between what is necessary for strength, and what looks more graceful and allows more length for grinding back later. A slender taper might be appropriate for light work and is pleasant to use, but it could bend or break under heavy blows. A taper that is three to four times as long as the thickness of the bar is usually right (Fig. 8-2A).

Draw out the end to about one-third the thickness of the bar (Fig. 8-2B). There is no need to try to make the point of the center punch by hammering. If possible, grind the taper at this stage. With the extra length to control the ends, it should be possible to rotate the taper across the tool rest of the grinder (Fig. 8-2C).

Cut off the length required. Many punches are too short. Unless it is a very small diameter rod, the length should be 6 inches or more. Cutting can be with a set or hardie, or it might be more convenient to saw through. Bevel the top of the punch all around (Fig. 8-2D) to delay spreading under hammer blows. Eventually the end will spread and the taper should be ground again. For a small diameter punch, grinding will be all that is needed to shape the top. For thicker rod that is ⅝-inch or more, the end can be heated and a bevel hammered all around while the rod is rolled on the anvil face (Fig. 8-2E). There should then be little need for grinding, except to even the shape.

The top that will be hit should be left soft. Any tool that has to be hit should be soft. Hammer heads are hardened and tempered. If the hammer comes against something else that is hardened and tempered, there is a risk of one or both being damaged. Also, tiny splinters of steel could break off and hurt your eyes.

The working end should be hardened and tempered. Heat the body of the tool for tempering to get a slow spread of oxide colors and wide bands of each color. When the correct color is reached at the end, there will be a reasonable length of similar color behind it to allow for sharpening before retempering will be needed.

Nail punches usually have round ends that are ground flat (Fig. 8-2F). For some nails, it is better to forge and grind the end square or rectangular (Fig. 8-2G). Several sizes can be made and similar punches can be used for driving out rivets, hinge pins, and other parts. A useful range is from just under ⅛ inch up to ½ inch across the ends, by 1/16-inch steps. Ends can be made to match the sizes of nail heads in regular use.

Center punches are usually ground with 60° points (Fig. 8-2H). That angle suits most punches, but it could be slightly more obtuse for regular use on hard materials.

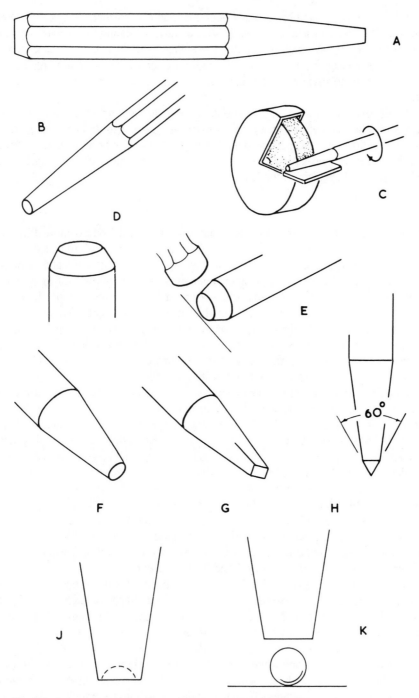

Fig. 8-2. A drawn-out rod makes a punch or it can be formed into other tools: (A,B) center punches; (C) grind the taper; (D,E) bevel; (F,G,H) nail punches; (J) hollowed end punch; (K) hot punch driven onto a steel ball bearing.

A center punch regularly used for copper, aluminum, or brass might be more acute. A similar punch used to mark hole centers in wood could be even more acute. It might be necessary to have the end of a center punch for hard materials fairly wide to provide strength, but it is difficult to see the location of the actual point. For general use, the top of the cone should not be more than ⅛ inch across.

Some nail punches have a hollow end (Fig. 8-2J). This is supposed to prevent the punch from slipping off the nail. It has some advantage when punching pins or headless nails. The end of a red-hot punch could be driven on to a steel ball bearing (Fig. 8-2K). It would be easier to control if the end of a round rod was ground to half a sphere and held in the vise for the punch to be hammered on. This will have to be done during forging because there has to be some trueing of the shape around the end.

A longer punch with a slight taper is a drift for pulling holes into line (Fig. 8-3A). When assembling sheet metal parts, the drift goes through holes that should match and is either levered or hit to bring them into line. The tool is made like a nail punch, but care is needed to get a gradual taper. A useful size is made from ½-inch rod with a finished length of 10 inches to 12 inches.

Because the small end has to go into the holes, a set of drifts can be made with ends ranging from ⅛ inch to ⅜ inch. The handle might only be about ⅓ of the total length (Fig. 8-3B). Because the end does not have to withstand heavy hitting, it is better rounded for comfort in handling.

A pin punch differs from a nail punch in that it has a parallel part behind the end (Fig. 8-3C). A pin punch can be used for punching nails. However, it is mainly intended for driving out pins, such as are used through hinges, so that the parallel part can follow at least part way through the hole.

Ideally, the parallel part is finished with swages. In the smallest sizes, it might be necessary to forge by eye and get the end to a reasonable cross-section during grinding. Some very fine pin punches, such as those used by watchmakers, are made entirely by grinding. Diameters ⅛ inch and more can be forged and then ground. Do not make the parallel part any longer than necessary. A long slender parallel end could bend and buckle. Let the taper be fairly long and blend into the parallel part with a curve so that there is no sudden change.

Blacksmith's punches are similar to pin punches, only heavier. They can be forged in the same way. Smaller sizes can be hand held (Fig. 8-3D). Allow enough length of grip for your fist to go around and still leave enough projecting above so you can hit without hurting your hand or having to go so low as to be dangerously near the hot steel being punched. For strength, keep the parallel part and the taper short.

For heavier punching, either of small holes through thick steel or larger holes through any thickness, it is better for the smith's punch to have a handle. Wrapping a thin rod around is easier than making a hole for a wooden handle. There is no need for deep grooves. With square bar, the grooves can be across the corners (Fig. 8-3E). With other shapes, there can be a groove all around. This is done with a fuller, either a single over the punch resting on anvil face, or with a pair of fullers if a helper is available as a striker. Have the groove wide enough for the ¼-inch rod to make a complete round turn (Fig. 8-3F). Above this part, the punch can remain parallel and be tapered only at the top (Fig. 8-3G) or it can be drawn out slightly before making the bevel (Fig. 8-3H).

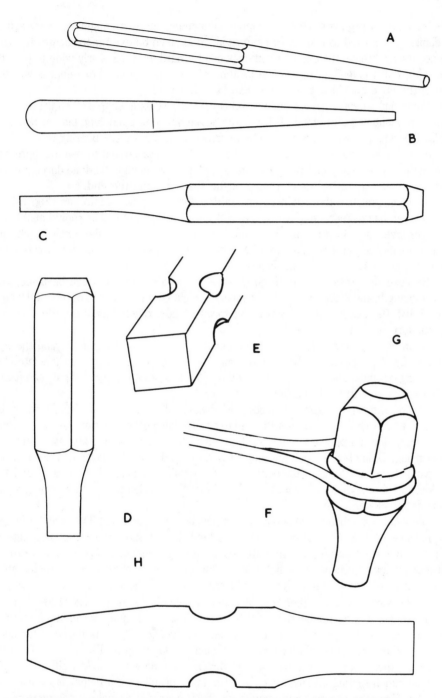

Fig. 8-3. Punches can be held in the hand or arranged to take handles: (A) longer punch with a slight taper; (B) the handle is one-third the length; (C) a pin punch; (D) a hand held punch; (E) square bar with grooves; (F) the rod should go completely around; (G) the punch is tapered at the top; (H) draw out slightly before making the bevel.

To make punches for other purposes, follow the blacksmithing procedures previously described. The smith who is interested in other crafts can make a stock of punches with blank ends ready to prepare as needed. Many special ends start by being made like nail punches.

Punches are used for leatherwork and repousse work (decorative raised sheet metalwork). The punch can be used in a haphazard pattern all over the background to make an irregular pattern of dots, lines, or other shapes. One simple and effective end can be made by filing grooves across a round or square end to leave raised points (Fig. 8-4A). Close dots made in the end with a center punch will produce a different pattern (Fig. 8-4B). Alternatively, the end of the punch can be shaped to make a pattern such as a heart (Fig. 8-4C).

The end can be made broader. Rounding it while keeping it straight across (Fig. 8-4D) allows it to be used to punch a straight border. A variation has a groove filed across it, so it produces a double straight line (Fig. 8-4E).

The end could be shaped in an arc. For a large sweep, forge the curve first and true it to shape by filing and grinding. A smaller arc can be filed on the end of a punch first forged round (Fig. 8-4F). The curved punch can be used to make corners by linking it with lines from the straight punch (Fig. 8-4G), or it can make its own decorative border (Fig. 8-4H) on leather or sheet metal. For a punch to mark complete circles, drill the end of the punch blank. Then file the outside to make an even border around the edge of the hole (Fig. 8-4J).

Design possibilities are only limited by the maker's ingenuity with a file. S or Z shapes (Fig. 8-4K) can make wavy lines or be intertwined for patterns. A broad punch can have a series of similar hollows (Fig. 8-4L) to make a scalloped border.

SPIKES

Pointed tools are needed for many purposes (Fig. 8-5).

A marline spike is an example of a plain spike (Fig. 8-6A). It is used for opening rope strands for splicing, releasing stubborn knots, or arranging the parts of decorative knotting or braiding. For general purposes, it can be made from ⅜-inch diameter rod and finished about 6 inches long. A full-length taper is usually straight, so it is a simple cone. For the three-quarters taper, the sides of the cone are given a slight curve for a more bulbous shape. That type would be thrust between rope strands up to the parallel part, minimizing the risk of the spike slipping back. For more delicate work, the straight taper is better (Fig. 8-6B).

Forge the general shape of a marline spike on the end of a rod. Then cut it off (Fig. 8-6C). As with punches, leave some thickness for grinding to a point. A marline spike should be ground and polished completely before hardening and tempering.

In one variation, the point is ground to something like a screwdriver end (Fig. 8-6D). This allows it to be forced into tightly laid rope strands and turned sideways to lift them apart. Another flattened end is broadened, so the opening forced between the strands is greater when the spike is turned (Fig. 8-6E). This is particularly useful for wire splicing where the spike has to be left in while an end wire is tucked, and there has to be a large enough space for this beside the spike. To make that type of end, draw the rod out slightly and upset the end to provide enough metal for spreading (Fig. 8-6F).

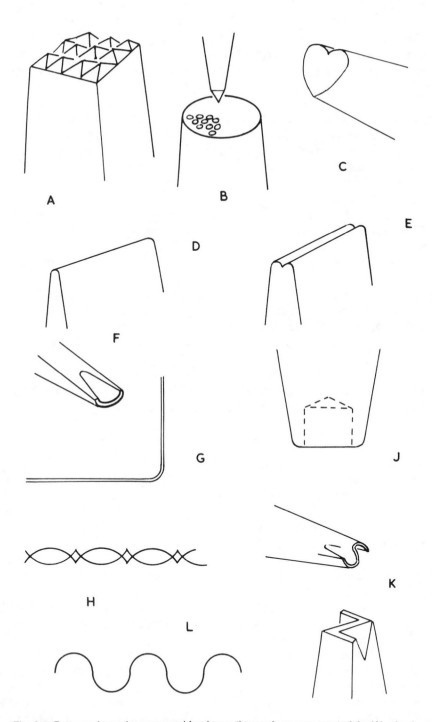

Fig. 8-4. Patterned punches are used for decorative work on many materials: (A) raised points; (B) close dots; (C) heart shaped; (D) rounded; (E) grooved; (F) a small arc; (G) corners; (H) A decorative border; (J) an even border; (K) Z shape; (L) a series of hollows.

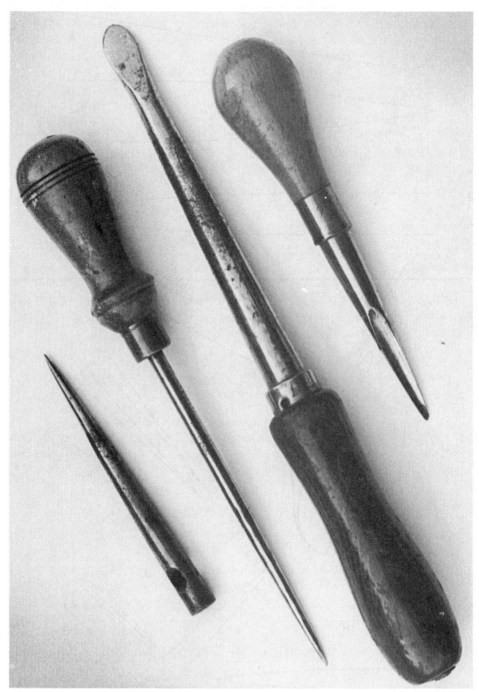

Fig. 8-5. A plain spike with a hole for a lanyard, an ice pick, a spike for splicing wire, and a grooved spike for rope splicing.

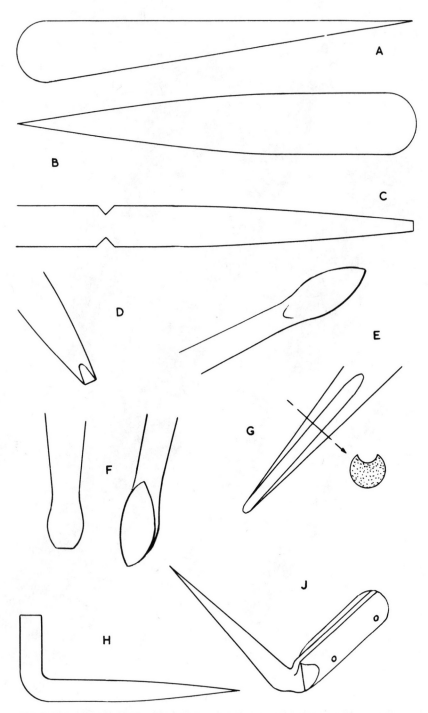

Fig. 8-6. A spike is used for rope splicing and other purposes: (A) marline spike; (B) taper can be full-length or three-fourths; (C) forge the marlin spike; (D) grind to a screwdriver end; (E) flatten and broaden the other end; (F) draw out and upset; (G) groove the spike; (H) bend the top of the spike; (J) place between wooden cheeks.

In another variation for wire splicing there is a groove along the spike (Fig. 8-6G). It is made from an ordinary pointed spike by grinding the groove on the edge of a grinding wheel. The tip then becomes more of a gouge shape than a sharp point. With the spike between wire rope strands, the end can slide along the groove in the spike which has been turned on edge.

With any sort of spike that has to be turned on edge, the end has to be gripped. Some tightly laid rope needs considerable leverage. A wooden handle, as described below, can be used. Another way of providing leverage is to bend the top of the spike as a continuation of the round rod (Fig. 8-6H), or as a flattened part that can be put between wooden cheeks to make a more comfortable grip (Fig. 8-6J).

An example of a handled spike is an ice pick, although it is used for many things besides breaking ice. The pointed part of the spike is made much like a marline spike, but the other end goes into a handle (Fig. 8-7A). That end should be given a square taper so that it grips a wooden handle and resists twisting. Further grip can be provided by raising teeth in it with a cold chisel (Fig. 8-7B).

Forge the point on the end of a rod and grind this to its finished shape. Brighten it with abrasive and polish it. Cut off, allowing sufficient length to forge the other end to a square point. It need not go to a needle point, and the taper need not be very long. When the spike is held in a vise and the handle driven on with a slightly undersize hole, the square end penetrates and grips the wood at the bottom of the hole.

An alternative to a wooden handle is a plastic handle. Many plastics will soften with heat—some in boiling water and some in an oven. Drill a slightly undersized hole in a piece of plastic rod and then soften it and push it on to the spike (Fig. 8-7C). As it cools it will shrink and grip the steel.

If the spike is fully polished before having its handle fitted, hardening and tempering can be left until this point so that the handle gives a convenient grip while heating with a torch.

Small-handled spikes are used as picks or awls. A piece of rod ¼ inch in diameter or less can be given a diamond-sectioned long taper (Fig. 8-7D) that can be used for piercing leather and canvas. Turning after pushing in allows the edge to force the hole larger. Small pointed awls, like miniature ice picks, will scratch lines on wood and mark the centers of holes. To make a small hole in wood to start a screw, file the end of a tapered piece of ³⁄₁₆-inch rod to an edge like a sharpened screwdriver (Fig. 8-7E) to make a bradawl. First push it to cut across the grain. Then twist it alternate ways while pressing it in order to sever the fibers instead of removing them, as would a drill. This will ensure a better grip on the screw threads.

If a small tool has to be pushed, there is a limit to what it can accomplish. This is particularly true if the tool has to be helped by hitting the end of the handle with a hammer or mallet. A shoulder is needed to stop the steel part from being forced further into the handle and splitting it (Fig. 8-7F).

In order for a shoulder to be forged, the steel has to be upset at the place where the shoulder is to come. Heat the end as far back as the shoulder position to a very bright heat, then grip in a vise as far back as the shoulder is to come and hammer the end to spread the hot part. More than one heating might be needed to get a sufficient spread (Fig. 8-7G).

Taper the point as far back as possible towards the shoulder by hammering. Working near the edge of the anvil face will help to get the shape (Fig. 8-7H). Then use a

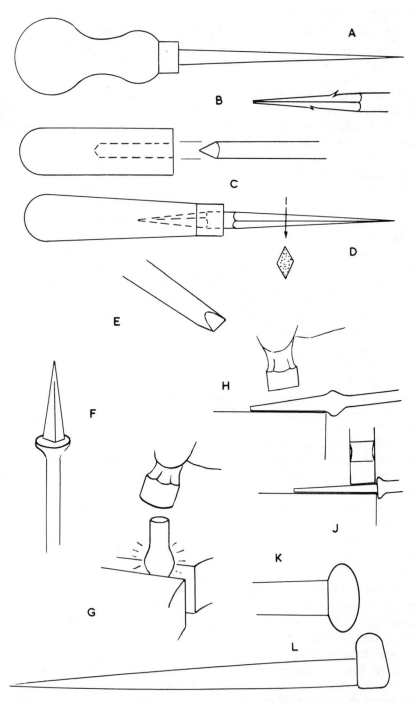

Fig. 8-7. A spike can be a pick or an awl, but if it is to be pushed it needs a shoulder: (A,B,C) one end goes into a handle; (D) diamond-sectioned long taper; (E) bradawl; (F,G) shoulder; (H) work near the anvil face; (J) use a set hammer; (K) spike with a knob; (L) spike with offset knob.

set hammer to sharpen the shoulder where it will come against the end of the handle (Fig. 8-7J).

Some spikes are better with a knob at the end (Fig. 8-7K) so that they are like large nails. The knob can be finished round so that it fits comfortably in your hand for thrusting. Larger and heavier spikes that are hammered in to force open holes or bring holes in large parts into line might be better with a knob offset to one side (Fig. 8-7L). This way the spike can be levered out or hit out after use. Make knobs as previously outlined for bolt and nail heads.

Making a scriber is a good lesson in hardening and tempering (Figs. 5-12 and 13). This long tapered spike is primarily used for scratching lines on metal, but it has other uses in craftwork (Fig. 8-8). Since its purpose is very similar to a pencil and it it convenient to carry in a pocket, the top could be made into a pocket clip (Fig. 8-9A).

If a very broad clip is needed, the end would have to be upset before flattening. It should be sufficient to flatten the end of a square bar without upsetting first. If the scriber is made from $\frac{3}{16}$-inch square bar, flattening to about $\frac{1}{16}$-inch thick should result in a spread about $\frac{1}{2}$ inch wide. Flatten on the face of the anvil so there is little of the tendency to spread in the length that there would be over the beak (Fig. 8-9B). Keep the flattened part parallel by turning it on edge and hammering there. Use a flatter to get a good surface, but let the change from square to flat blend with the curve. Do not sharpen the angle with a set hammer.

Taper the end almost to a feather edge so that it can be rolled. Start curling the end over the edge of the anvil face. If that is worn, use a stout piece of iron or steel held in the vise (Fig. 8-9C). Make about a semicircle in this way, then turn the curl upwards on the anvil and hammer it closed (Fig. 8-9D). Next, hook it over the edge of the anvil or the bar in the vise to knock it tight (Fig. 8-9E). To bend the pocket clip back, heat where the curve is to come, then pull it into shape over a piece of rod no thicker than $\frac{3}{16}$ inch projecting from the side of the vise (Fig. 8-9F). It should be possible to do this with thin-nosed pliers, without the need for hammering. There should be sufficient spring in the clip without tempering. Only the pointed end of the scriber needs to be hardened and tempered.

MARKING KNIFE

For furniture making and other precision woodworking a knife is necessary to mark lines more accurately than a pencil can. A fine awl is also needed for marking positions. These can be combined in one tool, a tool that makes an interesting blacksmithing project. This woodworking marking knife (Fig. 8-10) is made from flat tool steel, with one end pointed and the other spread to make a blade. The handle is riveted wood, but the tool could be used without it. Sizes are not critical; the knife shown (Fig. 8-11) is made from $\frac{3}{16}$-×-$\frac{5}{8}$-inch square-edged tool steel.

Start with the steel annealed. Always be careful to keep the part that is within the handle flat and unmarked. Spread the end for the blade (Fig. 8-11A) on the face of the anvil.

At the other end forge the steel cylindrical and draw down the point (Fig. 8-11B). On $\frac{3}{16}$-inch bar this will be about $\frac{1}{4}$-inch diameter, but the exact size is not important. See that both ends are straight and symmetrical.

Fig. 8-8. Three scribers: one made of round wire and the other two made by twisting square rod.

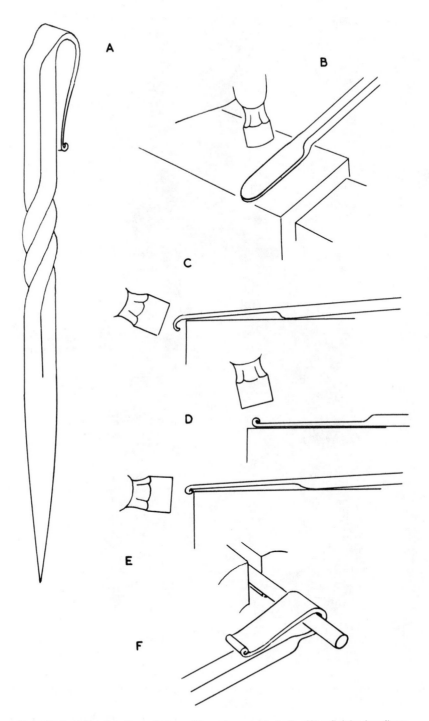

Fig. 8-9. A scriber has its end shaped to make a pocket clip: (A) a finished scriber; (B) flatten on the anvil; (C) curl the end; (D) turn the curl up and close; (E) tighten the curl; (F) bend the pocket clip.

Fig. 8-10. A woodworker's marking knife with a double-edged blade at one end and a spike at the other end.

Anneal again, if necessary. Drill for rivets (Fig. 8-11C), which will be pieces of mild steel or copper wire—$3/32$-inch is a suitable size.

Grind or file and polish both ends. The blade can be with double bevels or cut diagonally across (Fig. 8-11D). Harden and temper both ends to straw or light brown colors, then polish again. Sharpen the blade and point.

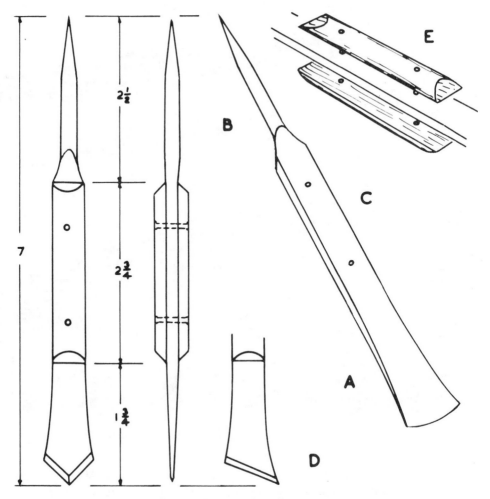

Fig. 8-11. Sizes and construction of the marking knife.

The handle can be two flat pieces of wood, but a good shape is obtained by cutting a piece of dowel rod down its center. Bevel the ends (Fig. 8-11E). Drill through the steel into one side, then turn the assembly over and drill the other way. Lightly countersink the holes in the wood. The wood could also be held to the steel with epoxy glue, although this is not essential. Cut the wire long enough to make rivet heads, then hammer lightly a little at a time from each side, while the tool is supported on the anvil. Finish the wood with varnish, if you wish.

CHISELS

Most chisels for general metalworking and smaller ones for blacksmithing are made in much the same way as a punch. Cold chisels and hot chisels differ only in the angle of the cutting edge, although hot chisels can be given a more slender taper between the body of the chisel and the cutting edge. Most often, octagonal section steel rod is used

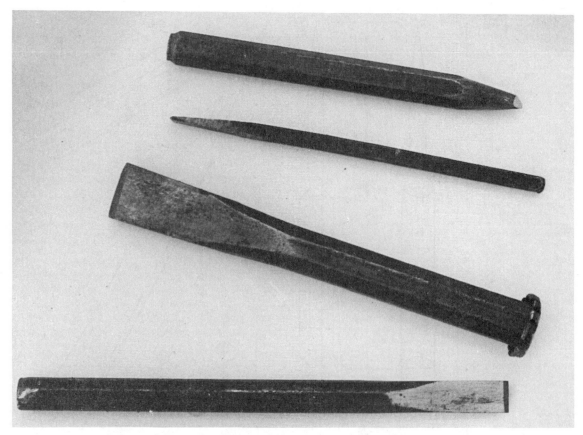

Fig. 8-12. Four cold chisels. At the top of the large are the results of considerable hammering on an end that has not been tapered.

because it provides a good grip, but other sections can be used. Most chisels are made without upsetting in order to increase the width of the cutting edge (Fig. 8-12). The thickness of bar can vary with the chisel size, from ¼ inch up to ¾ inch. Finished lengths vary. Small tools for light work can be about 4 inches long, and can be held between the fingers and thumb. Most chisels should be 6 to 8 inches long to give a good grip for your hand. For stone cutting, it is worthwhile having longer cold chisels so that they can also be used as levers.

An ordinary cold chisel is forged to a taper three to four times as long as the thickness of the bar. The end is taken to about ⅛ inch thick to leave metal there for grinding and getting through any decarbonized surfaces. If octagonal bar is used, have the tapers and the parallel sides in the same planes as the faces of the bar (Fig. 8-13A). Draw out the taper for the width of the cutting edge and turn the bar through 90° to hammer the sides parallel. Leave some metal for grinding, smoothing, and polishing. Bevel around the other end of the tool in the same way as the top of a punch. Harden and temper the cutting end before grinding the edge. For most work, the cutting angle of a cold chisel can be about 60°. A hot chisel can be more acute. Be careful of overheating the edge while grinding. If the tempering oxides appear, the edge has become too hot and the temper of the tool has been drawn. It will require hardening and tempering again.

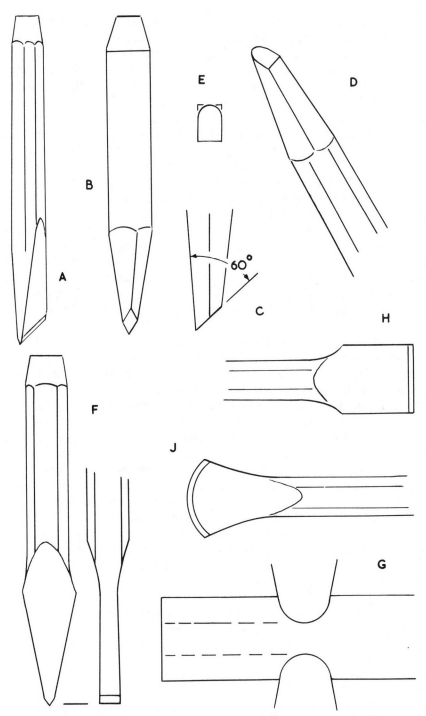

Fig. 8-13. Cold chisels can have their cutting edges shaped in many ways: (A) a standard chisel; (B) a diamond-pointed chisel; (C) a one-point cutter; (D) a round-nosed chisel; (E) round one face; (F) a crosscut chisel; (G,H,J) draw out and thin a shoulder with fullers.

A diamond-pointed chisel (Fig. 8-13B) is used to get into corners and for making V-shaped grooves. Draw out the end like a square punch, but do not make it too fine. Allow for grinding all four sides so that you leave the end about ⅛ inch square in small chisels and up to ¼ inch for those made with bar between ½ and ¾ inch. Grind the end diagonally from one corner at 60° to make a one-point cutter (Fig. 8-13C).

A half-round or round-nosed chisel (Fig. 8-13D) is first given a square taper similar to that of a diamond-pointed chisel. For greater strength it could be made wider one way to allow for one of the narrower faces being rounded (Fig. 8-13E). In the smaller sizes, the rounding can be done at the grinding stage. In larger chisels, take off the sharpness of two corners by hammering to reduce the amount of grinding needed. The width of the narrow direction is the size of the chisel, and many chisels can be made for chopping grooves of different widths. Sharpen the end at 60° to the curved face.

A crosscut chisel is expected to chop deeply, and is made to taper to a slightly thinner section behind the point so it will not bind in a groove (Fig. 8-13F). To make it, draw out to the size the point is to be and thin a shoulder with a fuller (Fig. 8-13G). Reduce from there to the end by hammering and using a flatter to get the shape, with some metal left for grinding. Do not thin excessively with the fullers or the chisel will be weak. Grinding should be slight, for the same reason. If the cutting edge is a little wider than the steel behind it, that is all the clearance needed. Grind the end from both sides to 60°.

If a chisel is needed with a wide cutting edge, first upset the end of the bar. Then draw down so the width increases and the end can be ground parallel, but wider than the bar (Fig. 8-13H). Cutting edges of special shape might be needed for sheet metalwork. A curved or half-moon end is easily adapted from a wide chisel (Fig. 8-13J).

Woodworking chisels can be made in the same way as cold chisels. The all-metal types are intended for rough work such as chopping through floor boards. The others are more suitable for exact carpentry and cabinetwork. If the cutting edge is suitably formed and sharpened, both are capable of good work.

The simplest all-steel woodworking chisel has its cutting edge no wider than the bar it is made from. It can be octagonal, round, or square bar. The end is drawn out in much the same way as a cold chisel, but the taper is kept to one side so that a flat back of the cutting edge follows down from one of the faces of the bar (Fig. 8-14A).

So that there is an allowance for grinding, forge the end slightly further out. The width should allow for grinding parallel (Fig. 8-14B). The amount of total taper could be more than for a cold chisel—about five times the thickness of the bar. Bevel around the other end that will be hammered in the usual way.

To get a good edge on a woodworking chisel, it is important that the flat side be finished as smooth as possible. Grind it flat and test with a straightedge (Fig. 8-14C). Follow by rubbing on a piece of abrasive paper that is on a flat surface, then rub flat on an oilstone. For the best edge, start on a coarse oilstone, then finish on an Arkansas or other fine whetstone.

Keep the tool absolutely flat and use a thin oil while you rub with a circular motion. On the other side of the blade, grind about 30° and almost to a feather edge. Change to the oilstone and lift the tool slightly (about 35°) to make a sharpening bevel (Fig. 8-14D). When the edge appears sharp, give the back a brief rub on the stone to remove any wire edge (a sliver of steel clinging to a sharp edge). Do subsequent sharpening on the

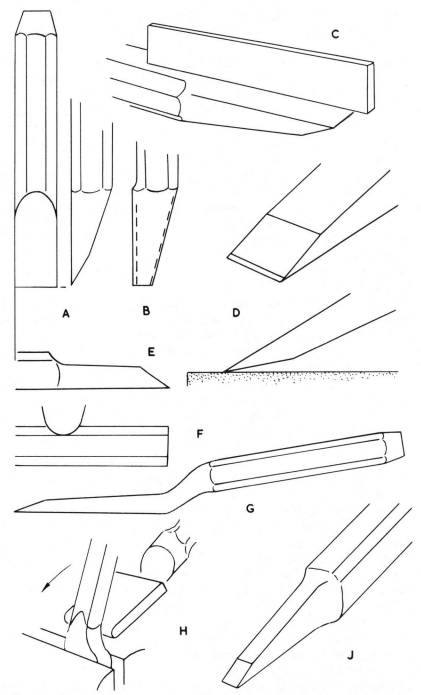

Fig. 8-14. Chisels for wood can be made in much the same way as cold chisels: (A) taper is to one side; (B) make an allowance for grinding; (C) test with a straightedge; (D) make a sharpening bevel; (E) give the bar only a slight taper; (F) hollow with a fuller before drawing out; (G) allow clearance for your fingers; (H) obtain the correct angle; (J) standard cutting edge.

oilstone until the "sharpening bevel" produced is getting long and regrinding is necessary. Beware of overheating and drawing the temper of the thin edge when grinding. Dip the tool into water frequently.

Allowing the end to taper back from the edge gives strength. However, it is more convenient to use and sharpen a chisel that keeps about the same thickness for a distance from the edge, and made so that it steps down from the bar to only a slight taper (Fig. 8-14E). Make this by hollowing with a fuller before drawing out (Fig. 8-14F).

For some work, there is an advantage in cranking the chisel so that your hand can be above a surface while the blade is along it. The amount the tool is cranked need only be enough to give clearance for fingers (Fig. 8-14G). To form the shape, draw out the end as if making a straight chisel, but draw out to a slightly greater length. Make the first bend over the edge of the anvil. Move the chisel to the vise—after another heating if necessary—and put the handle between the jaws, with enough projecting to make the second bend. Use a flat piece of steel as a punch to knock over the metal until the end is at the correct angle (Fig. 8-14H). This process is call *joggling*. With this and any other forging of tool steel, never continue to hammer after the steel has become black. All shaping must be done at a red or greater heat, otherwise damage can be done to the structure of the steel.

Chisel ends can be narrower than the bar, either by tapering to the width or by reducing to a narrow blade. If the edge is to be narrow and is expected to withstand levering to remove wood, it should be finished thicker than it is wide by forging to something like a crosscut cold chisel (Fig. 8-13F) and finishing with the usual woodworking cutting edge (Fig. 8-14J).

If the chisel edge is to be wider than the rod it is made from, upset the end with several heatings (if necessary), to give a good bulk to work with. The end can be forged in the same way as a narrower chisel, but with the required width. Some old chisels can be seen with the sides tapered (Fig. 8-15A). This obviously results in a narrower cutting edge as the tool is ground back. It is better to finish with parallel sides, with all faces ground (Fig. 8-15B). Give a slight taper in thickness and let the blade blend into the rod with a curve so that the change of section is gradual and the risk of breakage there is reduced (Fig. 8-15C).

Some woodworking chisels are very wide in relation to the handle.

Although it is possible to forge the blades quite wide after upsetting, there is a limit. If an even wider blade is needed, the process has to be reversed. The work is started with flat steel of the intended width, and it is reduced to make the handle. Use fullers to hollow as deeply as possible at first, then draw out (Fig. 8-15D). Use the fullers again and draw out more (Fig. 8-15E) until the final size is reached. Use the flatter to get the handle to a straight and even section. Hammer and flatten the corners of a square section to make a comfortable grip (Fig. 8-15F).

A very wide chisel is called *bolster*. It could be sharpened in the usual woodworking way or can be given a rather more obtuse angle for cutting bricks. A brick bolster is between 3 and 5 inches across the edge.

A mason uses a variety of tools very similar to cold chisels, but for carving stone he prefers to hit with a mallet. The usual thin end of the tool that is intended for the steel surface of a hammer would soon damage the wood of the mallet. To reduce this risk, a mason's chisel is given a rounded knob (Fig. 8-15G). The top should be upset

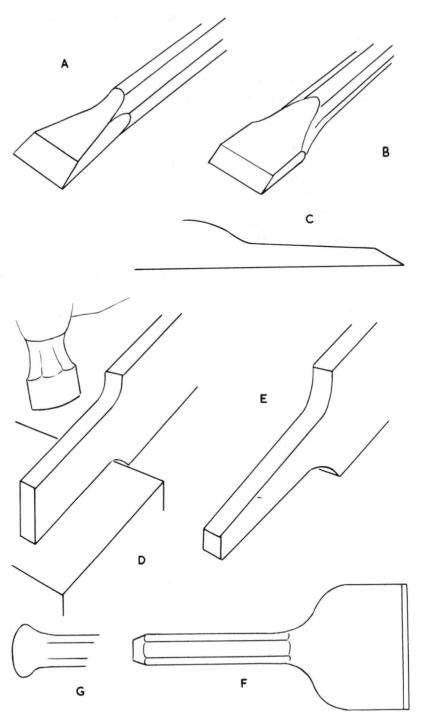

Fig. 8-15. For a wider cutting edge, rod can be widened or wide bar can be reduced: (A) chisel with tapered sides; (B) parallel sides; (C) the blade blends into the rod: (D) draw out; (E) use fullers and draw out more; (F) make a grip; (G) round the grip.

enough to hammer into a suitable shape that is finished on its surface by grinding and polishing.

A gouge is a chisel with a curve in its cross-section. Cold chisels are not usually made as gouges, but those for wood and stone can be curved. It is not very easy to get a regular curve for a great length, so it is usual to forge only the end of the tool to a curve (Fig. 8-16A). This is done with a fuller in a matching swage (Fig. 8-16B). It would be possible to hold the tool over the end of the beak and hammer it to shape, but the result would not be as even.

There is a problem of grinding a gouge. For most work, the outside of the end has the cutting bevel (Fig. 8-16C). To get a sharp edge, the inside has to be smooth. This means careful work on a grinding wheel with a rounded edge, followed by rubbing with a *slip stone* (an oilstone with a rounded edge). For some work, the gouge is ground inside and the outside has to be made smooth. This is easier to do, but a rounded grinding wheel and a slip stone are still needed.

A chisel or gouge that is to fit into a handle is given a tang. For woodturning tools and some light paring chisels, the tang is plain (Fig. 8-17A). For any tool that has to be hit, there must be a bolster or shoulder (Fig. 8-17B) to prevent the tang from going further into the handle. This type of chisel can be made from any high-carbon steel rod. It is possible to make satisfactory chisels from steel recovered from automobile springs and other sources, but it is also possible to obtain what is described as *ground flat stock*.

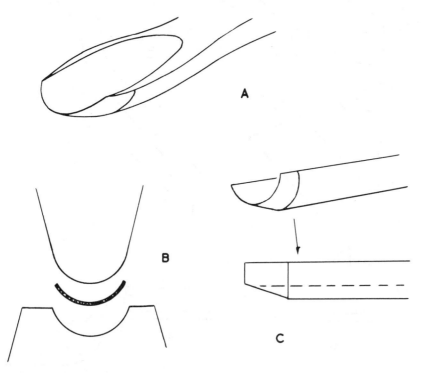

Fig. 8-16. A gouge is made by thinning and hollowing a bar: (A) forge the end; (B) use fuller in a matching swage; (C) the cutting bevel.

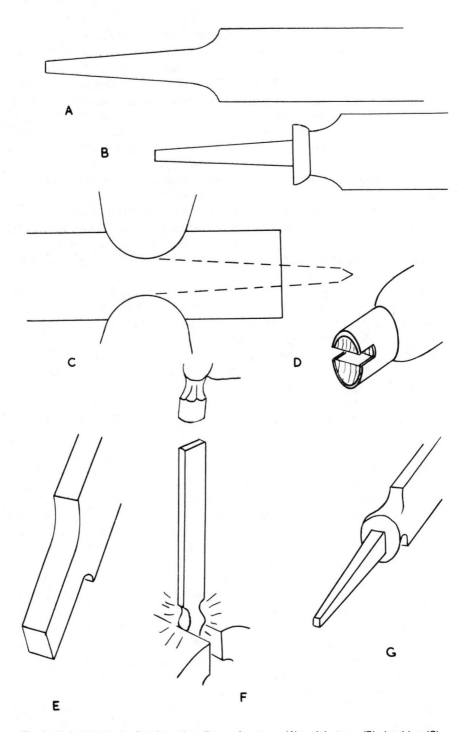

Fig. 8-17. A chisel to be fitted to a handle needs a tang: (A) a plain tang; (B) shoulder; (C) draw out the end; (D) a handle with a ferrule; (E) draw down the end for a bolster; (F) grip in a vise; (G) draw out the tang.

This is high-carbon steel that has been machined to exact sizes. Because the only forging is at the end remote from the cutting edge, such material can be made into excellent wood chisels that will be true to size and require minimum work.

To form a tang on a length of parallel steel, hollow with fullers and draw out the end (Fig. 8-17C). There is not much need to taper. With thick bar, make the tang square. If it is thin, the section might have to be rectangular. There is no need to taper to a fine point, but the extreme end can be given a short point like a nail. The handle is drilled almost as far as the tang will go, and the tip penetrates the solid wood at the end.

One way to help prevent a plain tang from being pushed further in, with a risk of the handle splitting, is to have a piece of tube as a ferrule on the handle and notch this so that the flat part of the tool goes into it (Fig. 8-17D).

If the tang is to be given a bolster, start to draw down the end, but do not make it very thin (Fig. 8-17E). Heat it locally—where the bolster is—to upsetting temperature, and grip the end of the tang in a vise so the other part of the tool can be hit (Fig. 8-17F). Upset enough to make the bolster. Hammer this to a reasonable shape on the anvil. Do not try to get a finished shape at this stage.

Draw out the tang beyond the bolster to the usual shape (Fig. 8-17G). Use the flatter or a set hammer close in to the bolster to get it to shape. There must be a flat surface to come against the end of the handle. If necessary, grind or file the bolster and the part of the tool that will be exposed after fitting to a handle.

Tools for woodturning are quite long; the blade length might be 9 inches or more. For general woodworking, the blade should be not more than 6 inches—unless it is a slender paring chisel, which could be about 8 inches. Bought woodworking gouges are hollow for most of their length. This can be done with fuller and swage, but it is simpler to only deal with the end, as described for the all-steel gouge. For heavier work on a lathe, this can give stiffness to the tool.

Handled tools for wood and stone carving can be formed in the manner just described for general-purpose chisels and gouges. For delicate work, there is a need for *spade tools*, which have blades wider than their shafts (Fig. 8-18A). A carver uses many of these tools, so they can be made in many widths and curves.

To make a carver's spade-end chisel or gouge, use a piece of round or square steel. Prepare the tang end first. If the bar is thick in relation to the finished tool, it might be sufficient to cut into it to form a shoulder against the tang (Fig. 8-18B). Otherwise it will have to be upset and a bolster made in the usual way.

With thick bar, draw out toward the cutting end, but leave the end thick (Fig. 8-18C). If there is insufficient steel to make a cutting edge as wide as required, upset the end. Otherwise flatten it to a wide fan shape (Fig. 8-18D). It could be ground as a thin flat chisel or it could be rounded to make a gouge (Fig. 8-18E). A carver does not have much use for a straight cutting edge; even flat surfaces are worked with a gouge of shallow curve. The blade could also be curved in its length (Fig. 8-18F). For some work, the shaft is better cranked slightly (Fig. 8-18G).

A carver's V or *parting tool* is made like a gouge, except that it has a V-shaped cutting edge (Fig. 8-18H). The usual angles are 60 and 90°. A problem in forging is getting the acute angle. Grind a piece of scrap steel to the angle and have this ready as a stake held in the vise. Hammer the hot steel end over this, but be careful not to hit too hard over the edge that it cuts into the steel and makes it thin. Grinding is on the outside,

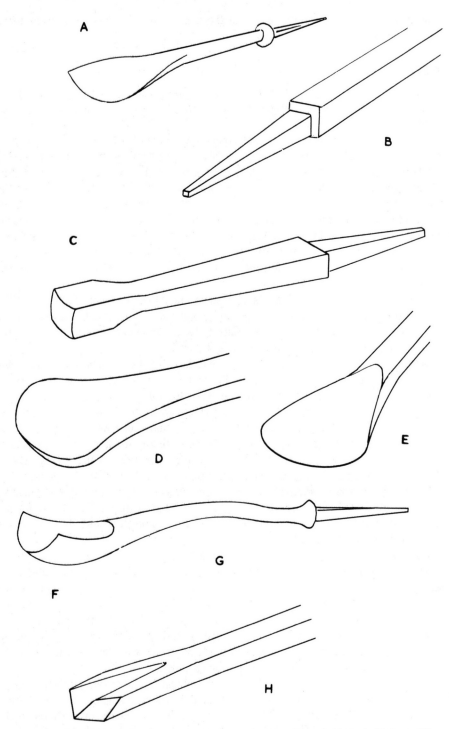

Fig. 8-18. Carving tools for wood are made in many forms: (A) a spade tool; (B) tang; (C) draw out the bar; (D) flatten; (E) grind; (F,G) curve or crank the shaft; (H) a parting tool.

but the inside has to be smooth right into the angle. This can only be done by using a knife-edge slip stone.

SCREWDRIVERS

High-carbon steel of many sizes and sections can be made into screwdrivers for the common slotted-head screws. Drivers for screws with star-shaped sockets in their heads are not so easy to make.

The simplest screwdrivers are parallel round rods. If the tip is ground to shape without increasing the size, the tool is suitable for small screws, including those in deep holes—particularly for electrical work (Fig. 8-19A). If the end is hammered to shape (Fig. 8-19B) and then ground, it can have an end wider than the shaft. There is no binding if the screwdriver has to follow down a hole. Give the end of any screwdriver a long flat taper on each side, and finish the end straight across with square corners (Fig. 8-19C). Avoid curving the tapers toward the end. Make screwdrivers to fit particular sizes of screws, and use a screw head as a gauge for the width and thickness of the blade. It is easy to make many screwdrivers of different sizes, and this is better than trying to use the wrong size driver in a screw.

Light screwdrivers can be given a simple square tang to go into a handle (Fig. 8-19D). This should be enough to resist turning with slender screwdrivers. If you think extra grip is necessary, draw out the tang, and flatten and thicken near its center (Fig. 8-19E) so this extends into the wood fibers as it is driven in.

Larger screwdrivers can be made of square or hexagonal steel. This gives something for a wrench to grip if extra leverage is needed to turn a stubborn screw. Longer screwdrivers are easier to turn than shorter ones due to the leverage gained. If there is no specific reason for a screwdriver to be short, make the blades fairly long.

There is a limit to the grip that a tapered tang can have in a wooden handle; some additional hold has to be given. One way to achieve this is to have a broader part at the tang fit into a slot in the ferrule and the handle (Fig. 8-19F). It might be sufficient to flatten the top of the driver, although upsetting might be necessary to allow enough metal there. An alternative method is to start with flat steel for the section at the handle, then swage down the shaft to round and reduce the tang to shape. The shaft does not have to be round. It can be a rectangular section, the same thickness along its length until it is tapered at the blade.

A screwdriver does not have to be given a tang to go into a handle. The end of the rod can be forged into a ring (Fig. 8-20A) or longer handle shape (Fig. 8-20B). Another handle can be made by flattening the end so that wooden cheeks can be riveted on and the handle worked to shape (Fig. 8-20C). A driver for use where there is limited access can be given maximum leverage by welding on a T-handle (Fig. 8-20D).

Sometimes a screw has to be turned in restricted space. A cranked screwdriver can be made for such a purpose. Bend the ends different ways, and sharpen one end across and one end in line with the shaft (Fig. 8-20E).

A tool that is similar to a screwdriver is an upholsterer's chisel. The end is like a broad, thin screwdriver and it is used for levering out tacks and staples. Another version has the end split and bent (Fig. 8-20F) for getting under tack heads. Make the end like a screwdriver and bend it. Then use a set to cut and spread the end. True the shape with a file.

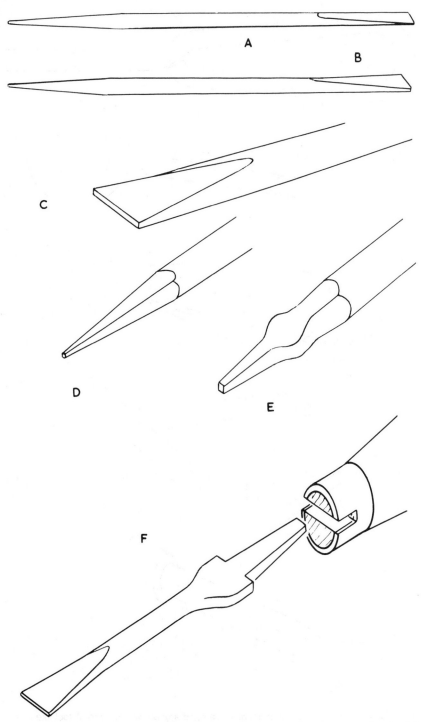

Fig. 8-19. A screwdriver needs a good resistance to twist: (A,B) parallel round rods; (C) give a long flat taper; (D) a square tang; (E) draw out for extra grip; (F) the tang fits into a slot.

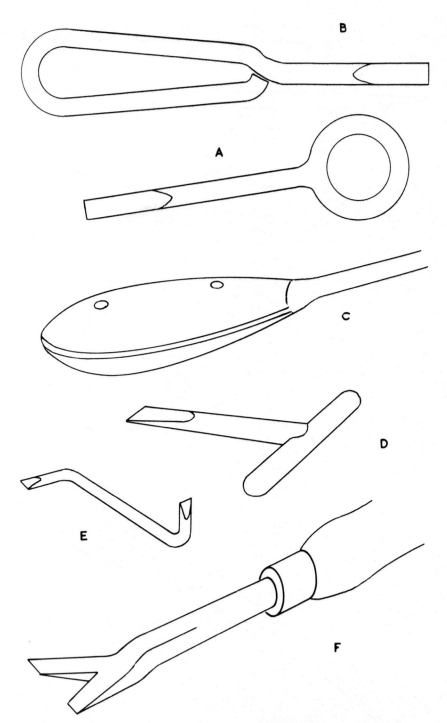

Fig. 8-20. A screwdriver handle must give the hand a good twisting grip. A tool like a split screwdriver is used by an upholsterer for lifting tacks: (A) ring; (B) handle; (C) flattened end; (D) T-handle; (E) a cranked screwdriver; (F) split screwdriver.

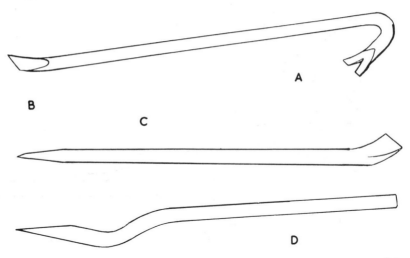

Fig. 8-21. Large tools (A) sharpened like screwdrivers (B) make wrecking bars (C,D).

CROWBAR

A crowbar or wrecking bar involves similar forging operations described for the previously mentioned tools. Sizes can vary from an overall length of 12 inches made from ½-inch octagonal or other section bar, to 24 inches made from ¾-inch bar. The material should be high-carbon steel, with the ends tempered to a dark brown color, while the rest of the bar is left in an annealed state. The bar is usually made with one end doubled back so that its split end can, for example, lever out nailed boards from a packing case (Fig. 8-21A). The other end can be given a slight curve for levering or be left straight (Fig. 8-21B). When kept straight or nearly straight, it can be driven like a cold chisel by using a hammer on the other end. If it is curved too much, hammering is ineffective.

Forge and grind both ends as if making cold chisels. Split the end that will be bent back and file the slot. Curve the ends over the anvil beak or stout rod held in the vise. When the shapes are satisfactory, harden and temper the ends. Crowbars can be made with other ends. One end can be pointed instead of having a chisel edge (Fig. 8-21C). The length can be given a dog-leg double curve instead of being left straight. One end can be cranked (Fig. 8-21D) so that the double bend allows the chisel end to be used close into an angle, while the body of the tool is levered like an upholsterer's chisel. A straight bar can be made like a long cold chisel, with a straight tapered end and the other end beveled all around for hammering.

HOLDFAST

A woodworker can use a holdfast to temporarily secure a piece of wood to the bench (Fig. 8-22A). A blacksmith uses a similar tool to hold a piece of metal on the anvil (Fig. 8-22B). In both cases the holdfast, or hold-down, can be regarded as a third hand when no assistant is available. A woodworking holdfast is sometimes thicker and larger, otherwise the two types are made the same.

In principle, the holdfast gets its grip by having a loosely fitting stem through a hole on the bench, or by having the pritchel or hardie hole of the anvil driven down so its

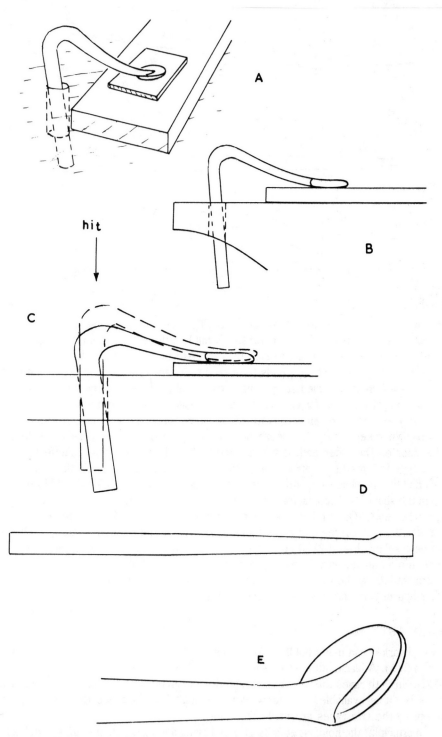

Fig. 8-22. Holdfasts (A,B,C) are used by woodworkers and metalworkers: (D) draw out the end to be shaped; (E) forge the tapered part into a curve.

angular position grips by friction (Fig. 8-22C). It is released by hitting back from underneath. The thickness that can be held is controlled by the length of the stem. The palm presses down at about the same angle regardless of the thickness being held. The angle the stem takes when hammered tight should be about the same in any position.

Choose a bar of a size that will slip easily into the hole. If it is too near the size of the hole, it is prevented from tilting sideways to get a grip. Usually it is round—even when intended for the square hardie hole—so that it can be swung around to suit the position of the work being held.

Leave the main stem parallel. Draw out the part that will be shaped and leave the end fullsize (Fig. 8-22D). If a very broad palm is wanted, upset this end to increase the amount of metal there. Wood needs a broader pressing surface than does holding steel. Forge the end to a circular or oval shape, but leave final shaping until the holdfast has been curved and tried in position.

Forge the tapered part to a curve and adjust the angle of the palm so that it will press flat when the stem is driven tight (Fig. 8-22E). Grind or file the outline of the palm to an even shape. The face can be flat or given a slight doming to allow for variations in its contact. This should be slight or it will reduce the area of contact and the hold will be weakened. For wood, there might be some advantage in filing across the palm to give teeth to bite into the surface. When holding wood, place a piece of scrap wood between the holdfast and the work so that a finished surface will not be damaged.

Hardening and tempering is probably unnecessary because the steel in its annealed state should keep its shape. If it is to be heat-treated, temper the curved arm to a spring temper.

9

Making Blacksmith's Tools

Although a smith has to start with tools bought or made by someone else, with these basic tools many others can be made. There is always a need for things like swages and fullers in various curves, and the variety of tongs in the shop might never be enough to satisfy all needs. There are also special tools to suit particular purposes that cannot be bought. The basic iron and steel used in tools does not deteriorate to any appreciable extent, so the material in one tool can be reforged and used again in others. The tools in this chapter are described as if made from new materials, but many of them could be made from the steel salvaged from something else.

TONGS

Tongs for general use are by necessity fairly large and heavy. They are about 24 inches long with jaws of perhaps 1- × -¾- inch section. There are also uses for lighter tongs. Anyone learning to make tongs will find it easier to start with small ones, about half the size of the normal ones. The method of working is the same, but it is easier to get smaller section steel. Such experience will be of use when making larger tongs.

Use mild steel. High-carbon steel might be needed for particular tongs, but for general purposes, mild steel is better. If high-carbon steel tongs become red hot and are dipped in water, they will probably become brittle and break.

For small tongs, it is possible to use rod of the size for the handles and upset the part for the jaws. For larger tongs, it is better to start with suitable sectioned steel for the jaws and reduce for the handles. Another method favored by the experienced smith is to make the jaws and short pieces toward the handles from large sectioned steel, then weld on round rod for the handles. The first method is simplest for light-duty tongs, but would be unsuitable for tongs with larger sectioned long jaws.

Light Tongs

The two parts of tongs are the same, If there are no tongs available from which to copy, make a fullsize drawing of one part. Trace it and turn the tracing over on the original to see that the parts match and there will be the intended opening. The jaws should finish closed or parallel when the handles are splayed outwards slightly. Suggested sizes for small tongs are shown in Fig. 9-1A. These are made from ⅜-inch round rod.

The hinged part needs to be wider than could be achieved by flattening only. To gain some metal there, upset each rod at the right distance from the end. Grip the rod in the vise and hammer the end (Fig. 9-1B). Upset pieces to match. For pick-up purposes, the jaws can be flattened where they meet and left rounded on their backs (Fig. 9-1C).

Use each meeting face as a guide. Hold the bar so the face is upright and flatten the upset part on the face of the anvil (Fig.9-1D). Now bend across the hinge part so the jaws and handles turn opposite ways in an S-form (Fig. 9-1E). Use your drawing as a guide and make sure the two parts match. At the other end of the handles or reins, it might be satisfactory to leave the rods as they are, but the tongs look better if they are drawn out a little. The grip is better if the ends turn out slightly (Fig. 9-1F).

Try the two parts over each other. It might be necessary to use a flatter or set hammer on the meeting surfaces. The jaws and the handles will have to be cranked slightly so that they are in the same plane when closed (Fig. 9-1G).

With a center punch, mark where the rivet is to come and drill through both pieces. This will make a better pivot than punching holes. Try the action of the tongs with a bolt temporarily through the holes. There will probably be some adjustment to make to get the jaws or handles as you want them. When you are satisfied, join the parts with a rivet. While it is still hot, open and close the tongs a few times so that the parts bend down and move over each other properly.

Heavy Tongs

For large tongs, it is still advisable to start with a drawing. However, it need not go the full length of the reins (Fig. 9-2A). If you start with ¾-inch square bar, the jaws can finish about 1 inch wide and ½ inch thick. The handles have to finish about ½-inch diameter throughout most of their length.

It should be possible to make the flattened hinge part without first upsetting. Allow sufficient end for the jaw and spread on the anvil face (Fig. 9-2B). Get the two parts the same and do further work a stage at a time on each piece. The flattened part has to be the center of a joggle, which can be done over the edge of the anvil (Fig. 9-2C).

If the jaws are to be widened, do this next. You can get maximum width without lengthening much by first using a straight-peen hammer or a fuller along the jaw (Fig. 9-2D). Follow by hammering with the flat peen, and true the surface with a flatter. To get the two jaws into line they have to be offset (Fig. 9-2E). How much they have to be offset depends on their width and the thickness left in the hinge part. Try fitting the jaws together to get the amount right.

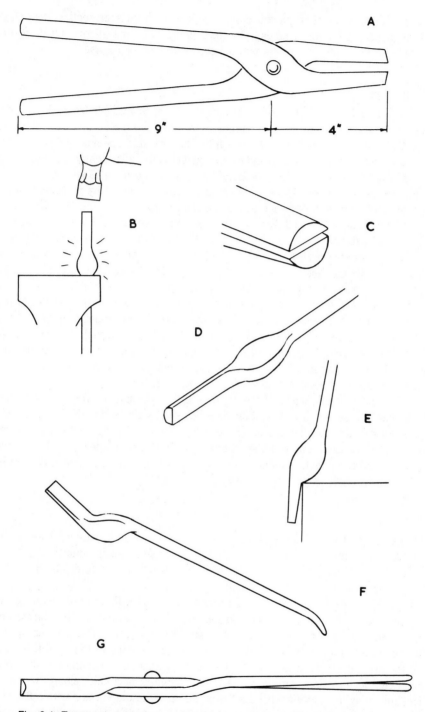

Fig. 9-1. Tongs are made from rod upset to provide enough metal at the pivot: (A) suggested size for small tongs; (B) use a vise; (C) flatten and round the jaws; (D) flatten the upset portion; (E) bend to S-form; (F) turn the end slightly; (G) crank the handles slightly.

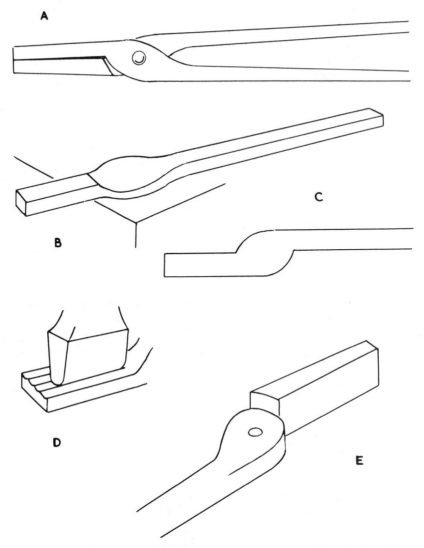

Fig. 9-2. Tong jaws (A) are shaped (B,C,D) and offset to match each other (E).

The handles have to be drawn down. Start by hammering and finishing with swages. A slight taper toward the ends looks better and lightens the part gripped. Turn the ends outward if you wish. Try the two parts together. Make sure the meeting surfaces are flat and the offset jaws will clear the other parts. The pivot holes can be punched. There is some value in using a tapered punch from each side so that the holes are bigger on the outside. When the hot rivet is driven through and the second head is started, the rivet swells to the shapes of the holes and the taper helps the rivet heads prevent the tongs from working loose.

Otherwise, drill the holes. Test with a bolt, and adjust the angles of the jaws and handles if necessary. For this size tongs, the rivet should be ⅜-inch or larger. Make sure there is a good width of metal left each side of the hole. The action of using tongs puts considerable strain on the pivot rivet and the metal around it. Rivet the parts together and work them a few times before the rivet cools.

If the handles are to be welded on after making the head of the tongs, complete the jaws with a few inches of rod projecting toward the handles. The work can be done to the stage where holes are drilled and the action tested. Only riveting is left until after welding.

Prepare scarfed ends on the handles and the head projections. Make these welds in the usual way, then assemble the tongs and test their action.

JAW SHAPES

If plain tongs are made with a reasonable amount of bulk in the jaws, it is possible to cut off the rivet and forge the jaws to any special shape needed, then rivet them together again. This could be done more than once if there is enough metal in the jaws.

Open-mouthed tongs with several different sizes of gaps are always needed, and it is better to make them to suit the common bars than to have to alter tongs. With these and close-mouthed tongs, it is always advisable to actually make them to grip at the tips (Fig. 9-3A). If they start exactly parallel, wear will cause them to open slightly, which will affect their grip.

Light tongs can be adapted for pick-up purposes. Allow more length in the jaws and curve them to a bow shape (Fig. 9-3B). They could be given a second curve if they are needed to handle rivets (Fig. 9-3C).

One way that plain jaws can be adapted without spoiling them for normal flat stock is to groove them slightly. Don't make them fully round, but leave flat surfaces on each side (Fig. 9-3D). This is done with a fuller before assembly. Keep the hollows the same depth throughout their length. If they are deeper at the tips, round stock would only be held tightly at the inner end, which would not be safe.

Other sections of jaws can be formed by forging the jaws parallel, but they are not made as thick as plain types. Form sections with fullers and swages (Fig. 9-3E). As with the other jaws, be careful to finish so the grip tightens at the tip more than it does further back.

Tongs for bolt and rivet head clearance might look like pick-up tongs, but they should be heavier. The bowed part should be rigid and not springy, as it might for picking up (Fig. 9-3F).

Boxed jaws (Fig. 9-3G) might have to be made separately and welded on. The rod could be upset sufficiently for them to be forged. Another way of getting the correct thickness and length is to make a faggot weld on the bar, then forge that to shape. Boxing one jaw is usually sufficient, then its sides lap over the other plain jaw.

Offset jaws (Fig. 9-3H) are useful for gripping the edge of a tube or cup shape. They are made like long plain jaws and then bent to match each other. Form the inner jaw first, then pivot the parts temporarily on a bolt to get the shape of the outer jaw. Arrange the jaws so that they meet or are at the intended gap before the straight parts of the jaws meet. There is no need for the straight parts from the pivot to meet; it is the offset jaws that must grip.

HAMMERS

Most hammers in use today are made of high-carbon steel. Hammers that you buy are

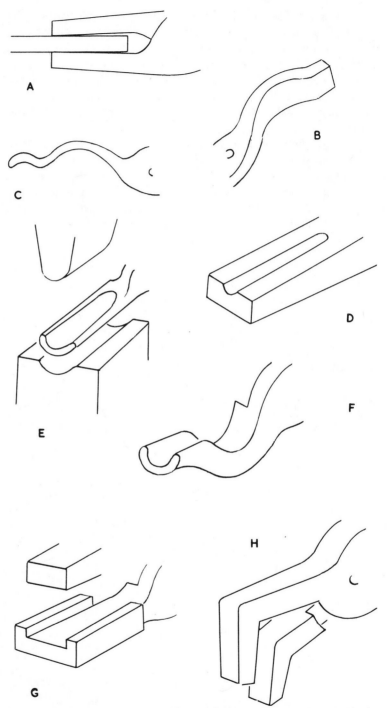

Fig. 9-3. With sufficient metal in the jaws, tongs can be specially shaped: (A) grip at the tips; (B) curve to a bow shape; (C) a second curve can be given; (D) flat surfaces; (E) form with fullers and swages; (F) the bowed portion; (G) boxed jaws; (H) offset jaws.

described as cast steel. The steel is high carbon, but the name refers to the method of manufacture. This is not the way an individual smith makes one-off hammers. At one time, many hammers made by smiths were of iron or mild steel, with high-carbon steel welded on to make a face at one or both sides. A mild steel hammer is easier to make than a tool steel one. Obviously, it would suffer in use without the harder steel face. But for practice, a hammer head can be made from mild steel and it would have limited uses. Some durability could be gained by case-hardening the faces, then hardening and tempering them.

If welding high-carbon steel to a mild steel hammer head, make the head completely and allow for the steel to be welded on. This should be about ½-inch thick and could be the end of a flat bar. Cut off the excess after welding. Slightly dome the end of the hammer head to be welded, then bring the two parts to welding heat and make a butt weld. If the work is done quickly, the surplus high-carbon steel can be cut off with a hot set (Fig. 9-4A) and the part that is left can be hammered or ground to shape. That

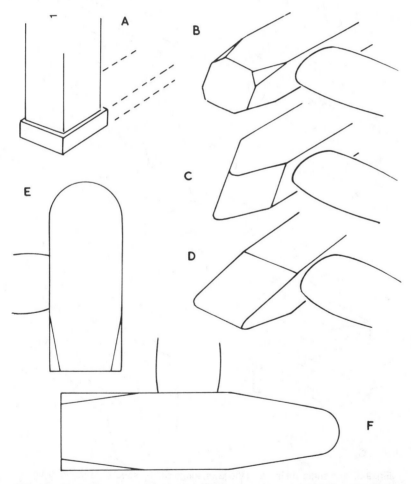

Fig. 9-4. Hammer heads made by a smith start as square bar: (A) hot set; (B) flat face; (C) narrow peen; (D) straight peen; (E) full-size ball peen; (F) narrower end.

type of weld is not easy to make satisfactorily. It is better, at least for early attempts at hammer making, to make the heads entirely of mild steel or high-carbon steel.

Although it is possible to shape hammer heads so that they compare with those you can buy, it is more common to forge smith's hammers so that they are basically square. Bring the flat face to an octagonal outline (Fig. 9-4B) and either make the other end the same or take it to a narrow peen across (Fig. 9-4C) or straight (Fig. 9-4D). The end can be forged and ground to make a full-size ball peen (Fig. 9-4E). Because it is most often used for riveting, however, a narrower end might be better (Fig. 9-4F). A hammer need not balance exactly across the handle, but one side should not be much heavier than the other. To allow for this, any taper at one side—as with the smaller ball peen—should be taken further from the hole than the face on the other side.

The hammers described here are those the smith will use himself, but any tool catalog will show that the variety of hammers for various crafts and activities is very large. These often only show minor variations, but the user for one craft would not accept the slightly different version used in another craft. A smith can make the most of hammers and other tools used by other craftsmen. A pick is just a hammer head with a point. A carpenter's hammer with a claw at one side is very similar to a cross peen, taken thinner and split. Some hammers are much lighter than those used by a smith. Making them from smaller section bar would provide practice for a beginner before moving on to the same work in heavier sections.

Whatever the hammer, the hole for the handle is nearly always the first job. This has to be shaped. When it is satisfactory, the other work to make a hammer head is a straightforward process. If the other shaping was done first, the distortion due to punching the hole would affect shapes already forged.

To make a basic hammer head, use square bar. For use in the blacksmith's shop, the section would be from ¾ inch up to 2 inches across. It might be smaller for other hammers.

The hole through the hammer head has to finish elliptical. The size depends on the hammer, but it must be big enough to accommodate a handle that will be strong enough. A handle that is too slim will break where it enters the head. An examination of other hammers will provide a guide to the size hole needed. In general, the length of the ellipse should be about the same as the width of the bar, and the width of the ellipse should be more than one-third and maybe as much as half the width of the bar. Sizes will also have to be related to available punches and drifts.

Mark a length of bar with center punch dots indicating the center of the hole and the eventual length (Fig. 9-5A). Leave the rest of the bar as a handle. The first step is to make a hole. Use a round punch on the bright red or yellow heated steel. Be careful to keep the punch upright. Work on the face of the anvil. Penetrate from one side, reheat as necessary, and cool the punch in water. Go about one-fourth of the way through from the first side, then turn the rod over and punch back from the other side until the center is knocked out. At this stage, the bar will have bulged each side of the hole (Fig. 9-5B).

Dress the sides of the bar on each side of the hole by hammering the red-hot steel. Besides bringing the sides back to width, this will enlarge the hole. The next step is to open the hole to the intended final shape by driving through one or more elliptical drifts. The drift should have as its body the section you want, but the end will have to be tapered to enter the hole (Fig. 9-5C). When the drift of the final size is through so

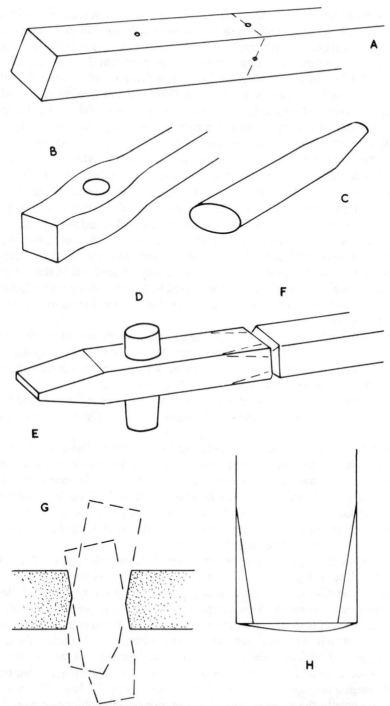

Fig. 9-5. A hammer head is shaped and punched on the end of a bar: (A) center and eventual length; (B) bulge; (C) tapered end; (D) the body is parallel; (E) draw out the end; (F) hammer the corners; (G) tilt slightly; (H) slightly dome the working face.

that its parallel body is in the hole, leave it there (Fig. 9-5D) until other forging has been finished and so that the hole is kept in shape. There will have to be additional dressing of the sides of the head where the drift has caused bulging.

While the drift is in place, heat the steel and draw out the end for the ball, cross, or straight peen (Fig. 9-5E). Use a set to cut partly through all the way around where the head has to be cut from the bar. Check the shape of the head before parting off completely. The corners can be hammered or left for grinding later (Fig. 9-5F). Drive out the drift. If it can be tilted slightly each way as it is knocked through, the hole will be waisted slightly so the handle spread with its wedges will have a better grip (Fig. 9-5G).

A flat face is not the best for most hammering, and it is better to slightly dome the working face when grinding it (Fig. 9-5H). The head can be ground all over, but if this is not done, the two peens should be ground on a high-carbon steel head. This removes any of the surface that has become decarbonized. It also brightens the steel so tempering colors can be seen.

The bulkiness of the hammer head means it takes and holds heat for a long time. The slow cooling needed for annealing will take much longer than thinner tools. The heat retention is an advantage when hardening and tempering. Both can usually be done with one heating. Bring the hammer head to redness all over. Then quench each peen by turning and dipping, without letting the center of the head go in the water. Brighten the part of the steel toward each peen and watch the oxide colors moving from the center to the ends. When the color you want reaches the end, quickly quench that side and the head completely when both are done. Exact colors are not critical, but tempering has to be taken far enough to leave the ends of the head as hard as possible without risk of chipping. A deep yellow or brown should be satisfactory.

SETS

If you are making other tools with wooden handles, the methods are similar to those for hammers. A set hammer is almost the same as a basic hammer. Because it does not have to be swung, the handle can be round and the hole made to suit (Fig. 9-6A). Use a round drift through the hole while hammering out bulges. The bottom part of the tool should be a true square with a flat face. What comes above it should not project (Fig. 9-6B) outside the lines of the square. Otherwise the edges might be fouled when being used in deep recess. Above the handle, the square can be given a slight taper and the top be ground around for hammering (Fig. 9-6C).

Hot and cold set can be forged in a similar way with holes for round handles (Fig. 9-6D). Make the hole first while using the bar as a handle, then draw down to the cutting edge (Fig. 9-6E). A cold set needs more strength behind the cutting edge than a hot set so it should be made slightly more obtuse. In any case allow some thickness on the end for grinding (Fig. 9-6F). If the tapered faces are slightly hollow, sharpening during long use can be taken further back before the tool gets so thick that it has to be scrapped or reforged. Make the top similar to the top on a set hammer. Tools that are to be hit should be left soft at the top, but the working ends should be tempered to a dark yellow for most purposes.

FULLERS

Flatters and fullers are better made with wrap-around handles, although they can be

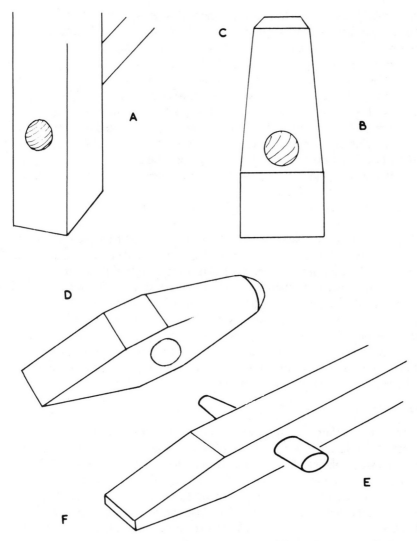

Fig. 9-6. Punches and sets can be made like hammers: (A) round handle; (B,C) slight taper; (D) a set with a round handle; (E) draw down to the cutting edge; (F) allow for grinding.

made with holes for wooden handles. Sets can also be grooved for wrap-around handles, but a set hammer is better with a hole.

A small fuller can be made by upsetting the end of a bar to get sufficient metal there to forge to shape (Fig. 9-7A). Except for very light work, the tapered part of the finished tool should not be thinner at the top than the rod above it (Fig. 9-7B). The width that can be obtained depends on how much is built up by upsetting (Fig. 9-7C). Work on the end of a rod and forge the end to shape. Be sure to make an allowance for grinding. Above that, use a fuller to make grooves to hold the wrap of the handle. If the basic rod is square, the hollows need only come across the corners (Fig. 9-7D), but with round or octagonal material, hollow all around. Make the hollows wide enough for a double

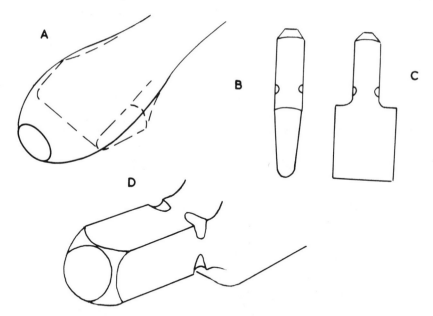

Fig. 9-7. Enough metal to make a fuller is obtained by upsetting. (A) upset the end; (B) taper; (C) width depends on upsetting; (D) hollows.

width of the rod. The handle usually has a ¼-inch diameter. Above the hollows, shape the part to be hit much like you would a set hammer.

The other way to make a fuller is to start with a bar of about the same section as the finished dimensions are to be. Reduce the end, first with fullers, and then by drawing out to the size needed (Fig. 9-8A). Because weight in the tool is an advantage, the upper part need not be reduced very much. Hammer or swage it to shape. Cut off from the bar and draw out to a suitable taper while holding the other end with tongs (Fig. 9-8B).

Grind the taper, at least in its lower part, and grind the working edge to the curve required. A template for checking it can be made by drilling a hole through a piece of thin steel, then cutting it across (Fig. 9-8C). Finish with a fine grinding wheel or by rubbing around the curve with abrasive paper. Leave the top of the tool soft, but temper the end to a dark yellow or brown color.

SWAGES

A top swage can be made by either of the above methods. Upsetting is not only suitable for a small tool with a narrow groove, it is useful for rounding drawn-out nails and similar things (Fig. 9-8D). Reducing the top part from a thicker bar is more suitable for large swages. Make them the same way as fullers, except omit the tapering and grind the bar level after cutting off. The groove can be made by raising the swage to a yellow heat and hammering it onto a bar of the required diameter (Fig. 9-8E). Repeat this until the bar is about halfway into the swage. By then the surface will have become uneven. Further grinding or filing will leave a groove that is slightly less than a semicircle. The top swage and its partner bottom swage together should not quite make a complete circle in their sections. Otherwise it will be impossible to completely round a rod.

177

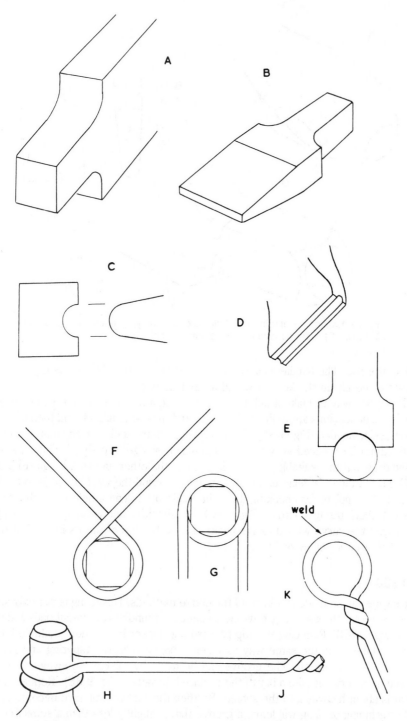

Fig. 9-8. Swages start like fullers. Iron handles are closely twisted: (A) reduce; (B) cut; (C) a template; (D) upset; (E) raise the groove; (F) pull ends; (G) continue around; (H) use a vise; (J) twist; (K) make the eye.

To make tightly wrapped rod handles involves fitting in two stages. Heat the middle of the ¼-inch rod evenly for a length equal to about six times the diameter it is to fit. Have the tool held in a vise. Put the middle of the rod against the near side of the tool and pull the ends across away from you (Fig. 9-8F). Continue around, still pulling on them, back to the near side (Fig. 9-8G) so that you can squeeze them together with tongs or the vise (Fig. 9-8H), all in one heating. The other ends of the rod can be heated and twisted together (Fig. 9-8J) or welded. A combination of twisting and welding will make an eye for hanging (Fig. 9-8K).

Most of the top tools described with handles can be made in lighter form for directly holding in the hand. A cold chisel, which is really a cold set without a handle, is described in Chapter 8. Fullers and swages can be made in a similar way for directly holding light work.

BOTTOM TOOLS

The tools that fit into the hardie hole of the anvil and act as partners to the top tools are made in a similar way, except that they must have square parts to fit easily into the hardie hole. Forge this part first. Use a fuller around the bar and then draw out the end (Fig. 9-9A). If the bar is considerably bigger than the final square piece, there might have to be several heatings. Use a set hammer to square both ways into the angle (Fig. 9-9B). Once the square has been brought down to a size to pass into the hardie hole, hammering the bar down onto the anvil top will get the shoulder to match (Fig. 9-9C). The square shaft should be long enough to pass right through with a little extra length. It might have a slight taper, so when the tool is put into place it goes in easily, but finishes without much play.

The overall sizes of a hardie need be no more than the maximum width it is expected to cut (Fig. 9-9D). Always allow sufficient bearing surface at the bottom to take the thrust of the hammer blows. Fullers are usually paired with the upper handled one. Make the operative part of the bottom fuller the same size as its partner (Fig. 9-9E).

A spreading fuller is useful if the end of a rod has been split and has to be opened to an equal V shape. It is made much like a rounded fuller, but its upper edge has a triangular section, usually with a 90° top (Fig. 9-9F).

Swages are not only circular. Other shapes can be made by forming grooves by hammering onto rod of other sections. For drawing out an accurate square from a larger section, the grooves could match in a diamond shape (Fig. 9-9G).

Although the top swage usually only has one groove, its partner might be given two or three grooves so that one bottom swage matches more top swages. Making the extra grooves brings the problem of keeping one in shape while making the other. Rather than drive the swage on the rods, it is easier to see how the work is progressing if the swage is made to fit the hardie hole. Then drive steel rods into the yellow-hot steel (Fig. 9-9H). As with a single groove, allow for grinding and get the grooves an even depth across the swage.

Besides matching top and bottom swages, the bottom swage might also have to be a partner for a top fuller when thinned steel has to be made into a curve with a gouge section. Keep this in mind when you are making tools. Some fullers should have their curves ground so that they can be used over swage grooves, with an allowance made for the thickness of metal between. For smaller sizes, it might be sufficient to make

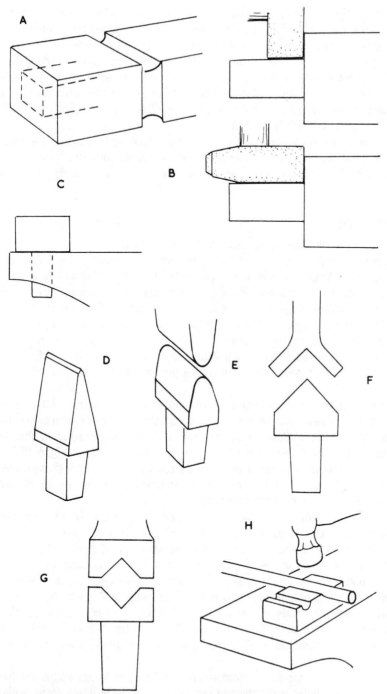

Fig. 9-9. Tools to fit in the hardie hole have the square end made first. Then the top is shaped as required: (A) draw out; (B) use a set hammer; (C) hammer the bar down; (D) overall size; (E) match fuller sizes; (F) triangular edge; (G) diamond shape; (H) drive the steel rod.

matching hand fullers that can be held directly in place.

For a smith who is working alone, a problem arises when he has to control a top swage over the bottom part of the anvil, as well as hold the work in place and swing a hammer. Similar problems arise when a fuller has to be held. Several arrangements can be made so the top tool is attached to the lower one to relieve the smith of the need for a third hand. If the top and bottom swage have similar outlines, there can be guide pieces to keep one in the correct relation to the other (Fig. 9-10A). The guides can be sheet metal pieces screwed on.

Another arrangement has the upper and lower parts on long arms hinged together (Fig. 9-10B). A similar method uses a spring instead of a hinge (Fig. 9-10C). A spring can be made from a piece of round high-carbon steel. Use ½-inch diameter steel for the average size swages or other tools. It must be long enough for handling and long enough to keep the curve away from the heat. About 30 inches should be adequate. At the center, flatten enough to wrap around something about 4 inches in diameter. This is the spring and it should be tempered to a purple color.

Have the top and bottom tools in an annealed state and drill them slightly undersize. Grind short tapers around the ends of the spring arms. Heat the tools to redness and drive them onto the spring ends. The steel will have expanded on heating and should go on easily. When it cools the joints will shrink and tighten. Alternatively, use flat steel for the spring and weld to the tools.

A similar idea can be used to position a punch over a bolster. This is particularly useful when punching square or other shaped holes. Having a bolster underneath ensures a clean outline to the hole, but when using it freehand it is difficult to locate correctly.

The bolster could be part of the spring and the punch could go through a hole in the other part without being attached rigidly to it (Fig. 9-10D).

STAKES

Most of the heavier work is done directly on the anvil, but for fine and light work there is often an advantage in having something standing above the anvil to hit on. The special needs of nail makers have been mentioned, but when anything has to be shaped with small section steel, a tool generally called a *stake* can be mounted in the hardie hole or a wood block. Some stakes are more like slender anvils and they are easier to buy than make. However, many stakes can be made.

An anvil stake is like a bottom swage, but without the grooves. It could be low or it could stand 2 or 3 inches above the anvil (Fig. 9-11A). It need not be square, but could be made from round rod or have one corner of the square ground off. There could be one or more rounded edges.

A bick iron or horn can be T-shaped (Fig. 9-11B and 9-12). It can be built up by welding a bar across the end of an upright, then forging and grinding to shape. Another version is made from one bar bent over (Fig. 9-11C).

A saddle is a piece of stout plate, possibly a 3-×-½-inch section bent over (Fig. 9-11D). Forge it over the anvil face so that it can be put over and used for chopping on when the work is unsuitable for putting across the table of the anvil. The saddle prevents the set or other cutting tool from hitting the hard anvil and damaging itself or the anvil. If the saddle is turned around, it can be placed on the anvil for working on something divided (Fig. 9-11E) that is too narrow to go anywhere else.

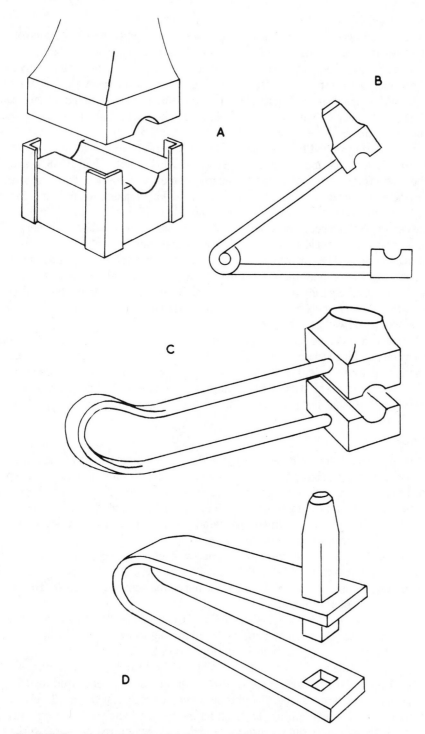

A

B

C

D

Fig. 9-10. For single-handed use it helps to make fullers and punches that have the two parts joined: (A) guides; (B) hinged; (C) spring; (D) bolster.

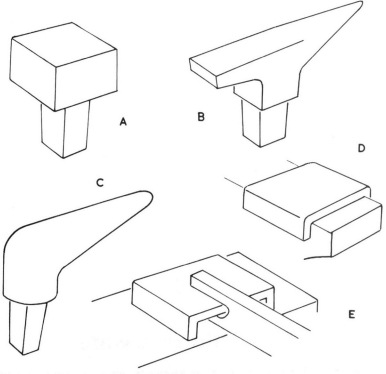

Fig. 9-11. Some small supplementary anvils can be made to fit the hardie hole (A,B,C) or stand on the anvil face (D,E).

Fig. 9-12. A bick iron mounted in a block of wood.

10

Domestic Hardware

In modern homes, most of us are surrounded by things that have been mass-produced. We live in an age where individually-produced, one-of-a-kind items are rare. There is not necessarily any virtue in individual production; in many cases the mass-produced item might be both better and cheaper. A definite advantage in mass production is that replacement parts can be easily obtained. There are standardized screw threads, where nuts made will be certain to fit any bolt made to the same standard. Not so long ago a nut might fit its own bolt, but would not suit any other. Its head was forged to a size decided by the smith, who also made a wrench to suit.

Although mass production has its advantages, there is still an attraction in having one-of-a-kind items. Projects that have been made by hand using the one-off method can be very beautiful. It is also nice to be able to say that there is nothing else quite like it.

There was a time when utilitarian items such as hinges, handles, and catches had to be made by the blacksmith. There were no quantity items in plastic or metal, and no hardware store where they could be bought. If a house builder needed brackets to support shelving or gutters, the blacksmith made each item to suit the intended purpose. There also was close cooperation between woodworkers and smiths in building such things as carts and wagons.

Most smiths had an appreciation of design and were not content to turn out something that was merely functional. Fortunately, iron has a long life and it is possible to see examples of individual smithing in old European or early American houses. Nearly all of these things have a beauty of proportion or decorative touches added by the smith that are not necessarily a functional part of the item. These old examples are useful guides for modern blacksmiths who might have become accustomed to mass-produced items.

The attraction of blacksmithing is being able to make something that is definitely different and that is an expression of artistic ideas. In some items, artistry might be of primary importance (see Chapter 11). Even when the item must serve a practical purpose, there is scope for giving it those touches that mark it as an individual product worth having for its own character.

CATCHES

Door and gates can be held closed or open with many sorts of devices. One such device is a hook and eye. In its basic form, a piece of rod is made into a hook to swing on one eye and engage with another (Fig. 10-1A). The eyes are U-shaped pieces like staples that are shouldered to go through backplates and riveted at the back (Fig. 10-1B). In small sizes, the ends are most easily formed by filing. Rod ¼ or ⁵⁄₁₆ inch can be reduced to about ³⁄₁₆-inch diameter. Have the ends projecting above the vise jaws. Put a washer over each end and use the file around the rod while resting on the washer (Fig. 10-1C). If possible, use a file with a safe edge (one with no teeth on it). For larger rods, the round ends can be accurately forged to shape with swages. The backplates can be simple circles or rectangles, but the outlines can be decorated. Even in the small sizes, the plate can be ⅛ inch thick. This is enough to make scalloped edges (Fig. 10-1D) by hitting with a ball peen hammer while the edge is red hot. Drill for two screws as well as for the ends of the U-shaped staple pieces. Countersink for the screws on the front and for the riveted ends on the back (Fig. 10-1E).

Make the ring end of the hook resemble a small eye by bending back enough rod and hammering it to shape (Fig. 10-1F). The finished ring should be an easy fit on its staple. In the smallest sizes, this will have to be quite a tight curve; the end of the beak might not be small enough to shape it. In that case, curve as far as possible on the end of the beak, then close the ring around a tapered punch held in the vise.

Put a point on the other end and bend that back before curving to make the hook (Fig. 10-1G). Notice that the point curves outward slightly. Fit the hook onto its staple and rivet that to its plate. Rivet the other in the same way. Fill the countersinks to make secure rivet heads. It will probably not matter if the rivet heads stand slightly above the surface for greater strength, because they will press into the wood to which the plates are screwed.

An attractive hook made from square rod and given rounded ends is shown in Fig. 10-2A. Allow some extra length at what will be the hook end. This will give you something to hold, without using tongs. Allow enough length for making the ring and make a twist in the part that will remain square. Round the part for the ring by hammering the corners of the square (Fig. 10-2B). You will probably be able to get an approximately circular section by hammering. For a large hook (over ⁷⁄₁₆-inch bar) swages can be used to finish the end. Forge that part into the ring to fit the staple.

Cut off the other end and draw it out to a round taper. Do not make it too thin. The main taper should be to about half the thickness of the bar. Take the end down to a rounded finish (Fig. 10-2C), and shape that into the hook. The hook looks best if the shaping of both ends is done in line with a pair of sides of the square section.

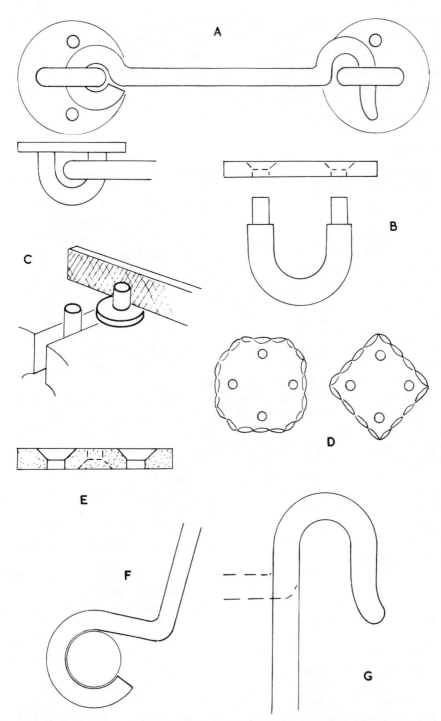

Fig. 10-1. A hook and staple can be made plain or decorated: (A) the basic form; (B) U-shaped piece; (C) use a file; (D) scalloped edges; (E) countersink; (F) bend and hammer to shape; (G) curve to hook.

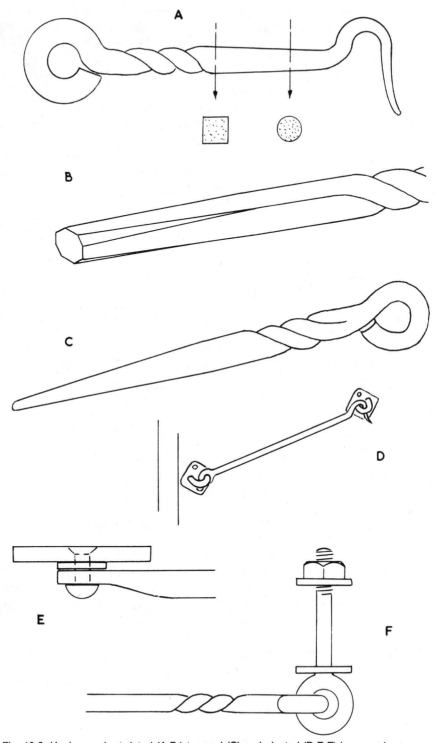

Fig. 10-2. Hooks can be twisted (A,B,) tapered (C) and pivoted (D,E,F) in several ways.

For most purposes, the hooks need not have much reach, but a long arm might be needed to hold a door back to a post. It is possible to decorate the rod with more than one twist, or it could be given a dog-leg shape instead of being left straight. When a hook is out of use, it hangs down. A long one might swing and mark the door. To prevent this, make a second staple for the hook end to go in across the door. The hook might also function as a door handle (Fig. 10-2D).

In some places, it is better if the hook pivots without swinging. To allow for this, flatten the end instead of forming a ring, and drill for a rivet. Put a thin washer between the parts to provide some clearance (Fig. 10-2E).

If attaching the parts with wood screws would not be enough strength, use bolts. Instead of staples, make eye bolts. Forge a ring on the end of a rod to go through the ring on the hook. Cut this off at a sufficient length to to through the woodwork, and make a thread on its end for a nut (Fig. 10-2F). Make a back plate to go under the nut at the other side. When making the eye bolt where the point of the hook will go, allow enough clearance for the point to drop in easily. It should not be necessary to force it in.

A variation on the hook and eye is a hasp and staple. It is used with a lock to hold a chest lid closed (Fig. 10-3A). The staples can be riveted to plates that are held with wood screws, or one or both of them can be eye bolts. It would be difficult to upset enough of the end of a round rod to make the flat part of a hasp. It is better to start with flat bar of the correct section and draw down its end to make the round part that forms the eye.

Punch the hole first, at a suitable distance from the end (Fig. 10-3B). It can start round and be followed through with an oval punch or drift. Leave the final drift in while hammering the sides of the bar straight after they have bulged during punching. However, the comparatively thin metal will not hold its shape as hammers will, so the drift might have to be knocked out while the bar is flattened, and then replaced if more work is needed on the sides. The sides of the bar need not be finished straight and the bulging can be regarded as a decorative feature.

Draw out the end of the bar and forge it to a ring to engage with its staple or ring bolt (Fig. 10-3C). The other staple has to be a size that will go into the punched slot and project far enough for a padlock to be fitted (Fig. 10-3D). A ring bolt could be given an elongated eye for the same purpose (Fig. 10-3E).

Instead of using a flat plate for the hasp, it could be made entirely of parallel round rod, with an oval piece to go over the staple (Fig. 10-3F). Welding the oval eye might be advisable for a large hasp, but for most purposes it could be left as bent.

A hasp made from flat plate could be given a bent end for lifting (Fig. 10-3G). This might be developed into a decorative feature (Fig. 10-3H), but it should not project much or it will interfere with a hanging padlock. If the eye is made by bending round rod, it is possible to give clearance for a finger to lift the end without interfering with passing the padlock through: Curve the eye (Fig. 10-3J).

If a lock is unnecessary and the hasp and staple are only there to keep a lid closed, a tapered peg can be positioned through the staple, made by drawing out a piece of rod so it fits tightly. The end can be flattened and drilled to take a cord or chain (Fig. 10-3K).

LATCHES

A hook fastener allows a certain amount of play. If a door or gate has to close and be

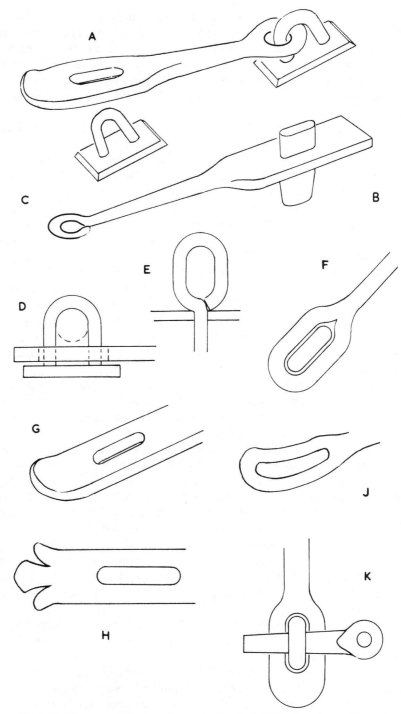

Fig. 10-3. A hasp and staple can be used with a lock; (A) hook and eye; (B) punch the hole; (C) draw out the end; (D) project the staple; (E) an elongated eye; (F) an oval piece; (G) a hasp; (H) decorative feature; (J) curve the eye; (K) flattened end.

held reasonably tight, the traditional form of fastener made by a blacksmith is a latch (Fig. 6-9). In its simplest form, a latch is operated from one side of the door only—the side from which the door can be pushed closed. If the latch is to be worked from the other side of the door, there has to be a lever through the door. This is usually incorporated into a plate with a handle for pulling the door closed. The sizes for a typical latch are shown in Fig. 10-4. They might have to be modified to suit a thicker door or a longer reach.

A latch that is a piece of flat bar $7/8 \times 1/8 \times 3/16$ inch will do for a small door. Nick the sides with a hardie or set, and round the end (Fig. 10-5A). Much of this could be filed, but for a forged look it is better when hammered. Drill for a rivet. There has to be a handle for lifting the latch. It could be made from the head of a coach bolt, shouldered and riveted (Fig. 10-5B). If a lathe is available, it could be turned. However, it is more in keeping with the design to forge a knob on the upset end of a rod and rivet this on (Fig. 10-5C). There is no need for a knob on the latch if there is to be a lever through the door from the other side. Some old latches are decorated with crossed lines, which can be cut on lightly with a set (Fig. 10-5D).

The plate on which the latch pivots need only be big enough to take two screw holes, or it could be made larger and decorated much like the back plates for hooks. The latch must swing up and down easily so that it drops into the catch plate by gravity. Using a plain rivet might make the pivot too tight. It is better to use a round-headed rivet— which keeps its full diameter through the latch—and a washer. Then it is shouldered to a smaller size for riveting through the plate (Fig. 10-5E). In the suggested size bar, this could be a $5/16$-inch rivet with its end filed to fit a $1/4$-inch hole.

The guide is made of two parts. The back is flat and a joggled front piece is held to it by the wood screws driven into the door (Fig. 10-5F). The opening should provide sufficient space for the latch to lift clear of the catch plate and be wide enough for unrestricted movement. To ensure matching, make both parts too long at first, then cut and file them to match. The front part can be hammered to shape, one bend at a time, by using a flat bar as a punch (Fig. 10-5G). Another way is to start the bends, but have a bar of the correct section to fit inside and another of the same thickness to use outside. With the bar red hot, hammer the shape on the face of the anvil (Fig. 10-5H).

The important part of the catch plate is the projection. This has to be shaped so that if the door is slammed, the latch hits the slope and rides up to drop into the recess. Forge and file this shape on the end of the bar (Fig. 10-5J), then cut down the recess. It can be chopped out, but it will have to be filed. Therefore, it might be simpler to do this work with a hacksaw. The back of the catch plate should have a slot punched in it, and the end of the other piece filed to go through it for riveting (Fig. 10-5K). Drill for wood screws.

In some door jambs, it might be better for the catch plate to go into the edge of the door post instead of on its surface. In that case, it can be one piece of flat plate with screw holes (Fig. 10-5L).

That completes the parts for a latch that is to be operated from one side of the door. Screw the parts to the door so that the latch projects enough, and so that the guide has the lower part of the opening level with the lowest position the latch has to go. Try the catch plate temporarily in place to find the best height to mount so that the latch will close properly.

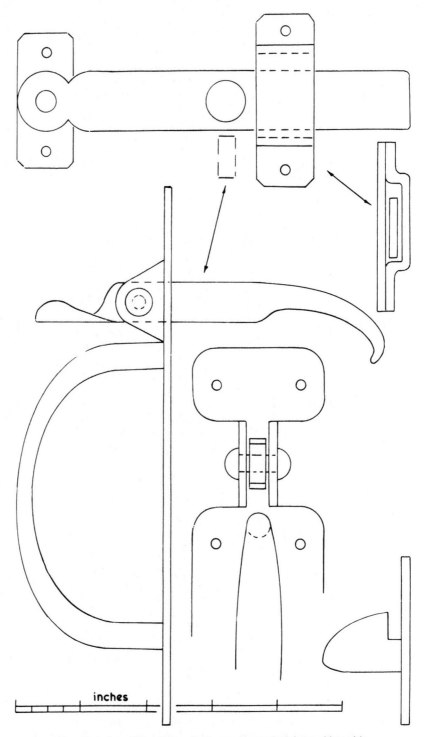

inches

Fig. 10-4. A traditional door latch can be worked from either side.

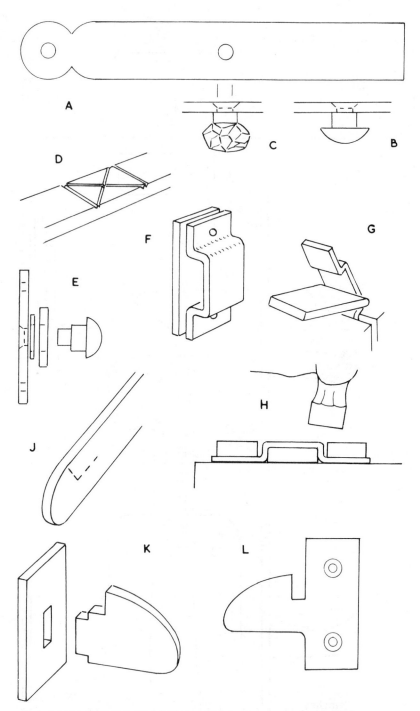

Fig. 10-5. A latch can be plain or decorated and it is controlled by parts made from flat bar: (A) round the end; (B) shoulder and rivet; (C) forge and rivet a knob; (D) cut lines; (E) rivet; (F) joggled front piece; (G) hammer to shape; (H) use the face of an anvil; (J) forge and file; (K) back of the catch plate; (L) flat plate with screw holes.

The important equipment for the other side of the door is the lever. To match the sizes suggested for other parts, this could be made from bar ⅝ × ⅜ inch. One end has to be made into a palm to be pressed by the thumb while the fingers are holding the handle. Upset the end of the bar to provide enough metal for shaping. Then spread a flat palm with rounded edges (Fig. 10-6A). Hammer this to a curve, over the beak of the anvil, in a swage, or over a bottom fuller. Get a shape that will be comfortable to press (Fig. 10-6B).

The other part of the lever has to be tapered and curved, but before doing this, check the thickness of the door. Your palm should project about 2 inches from the surface of the door and the bar should go through the thickness of the door parallel before starting to draw out. The upper edge of the lever has to lift the latch, and the lower edge rests on the bottom of the slot in the door. Further out, it is curled down to provide a grip for lifting on that side.

Cut off the bar and draw out the end to a tail, finishing about ³⁄₁₆-inch square. Form an attractive downward curve with enough curl in the end for a finger grip to lift the latch (Fig. 10-6C).

The lever is supported by two cheeks on a plate that also has the loop handle. It would be possible to rivet, weld, or braze the cheeks to the plate, but they are shown made from the plate by cutting and bending. The back plate shown is 8 × 2 × ⅛ inch. Mark the position of the slot for the lever and punch this (Fig. 10-6D). Make it undersize at this stage; leave working it to size with files until after raising the cheeks.

Mark the shapes of the cheeks and saw their edges (Fig. 10-6E). Position a bar horizontally, with a square edge and a thickness the same as the gap between the cheeks is to be. With open-mouth tongs, hammer and squeeze the cheeks into shape (Fig. 10-6F). File them to shape, and mark and drill through for a ¼-inch rivet that will form the pivot. File out the slot to give an easy clearance for the lever and sufficient room for it to move up and down. Drill the lever and try its action.

The handle for pulling the door is a loop. In its simplest form it could be a piece of ⅜- or ½-inch rod bent to shape. However, it looks better and is more comfortable to hold if it is worked to an elliptical cross-section at the center, while remaining round at the ends (Fig. 10-6G). Shape this section in the straight bar by hammering, then form the handle shape and cut off. File down the ends for riveting. Leave marking the rivet holes in the back plate until after shaping the handle. It is easier to modify their spacing than to alter the handle to suit holes already there. Have the upper part of the handle close to the lever so that it is easy to reach with the thumb (Fig. 10-6H).

The basic back plate is shown as straight-edged with rounded corners. It can be modified to a more ornamental outline, and it can be hammered all over to avoid a plain-looking surface. If the door is being equipped with forged hinges, the plate can be given a matching outline. Styled leaf outlines are found on medieval doors (Fig. 10-6J). The same motif can be carried onto the smaller plates, guide, and catch plate.

Lightly rivet through the cheeks and lever. Make sure all sharp edges are taken off all parts that hands will touch. The part with the handle has to be located on the door so that the lever goes through and comes under the latch fairly close to the guide. First fit the latch and the parts that go with it on the door and jamb. Drill a small hole through the door, below the latch, at the place where the top of the lever has to come. Use this as a guide for marking out the slot through the door, which is best cut from both

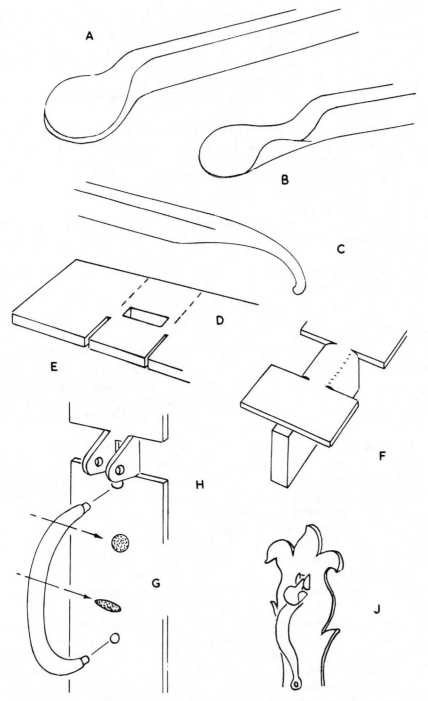

Fig. 10-6. The handle and latch fit through a backplate which can be decorated: (A) flat palm; (B) shape; (C) curve; (D) punch a slot; (E) saw edges; (F) shape the cheeks; (G) round the ends; (H) the handle is close to the lever; (J) a leaf outline.

sides. When the slot has been shaped satisfactorily, it will help you position the assembly on the other side of the door.

DOOR BOLT

Doors and gates can be secured from one side by a bolt, either as the only fastening or as an addition to it. A horizontal bolt can be short, but for large doors with bolts going up and down, extension handles can be used for convenience. These also provide the smith with a chance to decorate the work.

The basic door bolt has a bolt sliding in two keepers, with a stop piece projecting to limit movement each way. The bolt then goes into a similar keeper on the door post. The amount the bolt has to open and close determines the spacing of the keepers on the door (Fig. 10-7A). The bolt could be square (Fig. 10-8) or round. Square is better for bolts with extension handles (Fig. 10-7B). If round is used for a short bolt, it can be turned to bring the knob against the door when it is not being moved (Fig. 10-7C).

Sizes will vary according to the bolt. If it is ½ inch across, keepers can be made from ¾-inch bar and the back plates can be ⅛ inch thick. For a large and heavy door, a more massive construction would look better, and be stronger. With a ¾-inch bolt the bar for the keepers could be nearer to 1 × ³⁄₁₆ inch.

Choose the rod for the bolt first and use this or a piece off the same rod to shape the keepers. A plain keeper need not be cut to length first. The end of a rod can be heated and shaped before cutting off. Open the vise jaws to a little more than the thickness of the bolt and twice the thickness of the keepers. Put the heated bar across the vise and hammer the rod over it (Fig. 10-9A). Knock the rod down until it is level and the ends can be turned back (Fig. 10-9B). Thicker bar can be difficult to bend easily in this way. In that case, use a bar with a rounded end as a punch to start the hollowing (Fig. 10-9C). When a sufficient depth has been reached, lever open the ends and finish to size with the rod in place.

If square bar is used, the keepers for a small bolt can be made over the vise in the way just described. For heavier sections, you might have to make each bend separately as described earlier for other joggled bars. In any case, true the keepers around a bar of the same size on the anvil (Fig. 10-9D). Make three matching keepers. They can be riveted to the backplates, which are then screwed to the woodwork. Alternatively, the woodscrews can go through them and the backplates rather than using rivets. The woodscrews should be large enough so they don't work loose as the bolt is used. For most purposes it is probably better for the smith to make the parts as riveted units, with separate holes for mounting screws.

In a simple bolt, the backplates are plain rectangles (Fig. 10-9E). Give the end of the rod for the bolt a slight taper (Fig. 10-9F) so it will enter the keeper on the post, even if the door or gate has fallen slightly. The other end has a bent part for handling. Any decoration of the end should be done before bending. A knob is most often used (Fig. 10-9G). Upset the end, either by bouncing it on the anvil or by hammering it while gripped in the vise. From this thickened metal, hammer a ball. It could be a sphere, an oval, or any shape you fancy. Thin the bar slightly below the ball by hammering over the beak (Fig. 10-9H). Make this part round, even if the bolt is square. Finally, bend out enough to give a grip that is clear of the door.

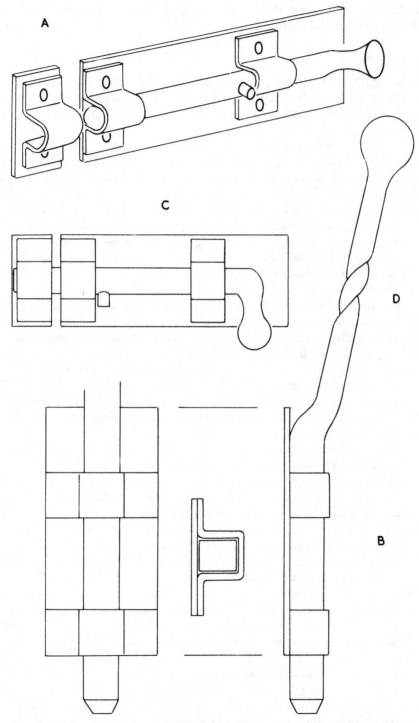

Fig. 10-7. A door bolt can be made of round or square rod: (A) space the keepers; (B) extension handle; (C) short bolt; (D) true the keeper.

Fig. 10-8. A square door bolt with a shaped handle and the backplate split at the end and shaped.

The stop is a small peg in the bolt. If screwing equipment is available, drive it in like a bolt (Fig. 10-9J). A piece of rod might have its end threaded to match a thread in the hole, or a bolt could be used and cut off after driving. It might be strong enough to shrink the peg in a plain hole. Drill a hole slightly undersize, then heat the bolt to redness so the steel expands. Drive in a piece of cold rod. Cool the work and cut off the excess peg. Another method would be to shoulder down the peg to fit a smaller hole taken completely through and countersunk. Then the peg goes through and is riveted.

Check the action of the bolt. See that the movement is as required. Adjust this by positioning the keepers on the backplate to suit, then drill and rivet them in place.

For a long bolt with an extended handle, sometimes call a *tower bolt*, check the length needed to suit a person standing by the particular door. The assembly is the same as for a short bolt, except for the handle (Fig. 10-7D). Crank the rod just outside where it comes in the closed position. It could remain parallel, but it looks better if drawn out slightly to finish with a knob. It need not be straight (Fig. 10-10A). If it is drawn out square, there can be a twist in it (Fig. 10-10B).

The end of this or a short bolt does not have to be a round knob. The end can be flattened and given a roll for a different effect, (Fig. 10-10C). This would be particularly appropriate on a wrought-iron gate (see Chapter 11)

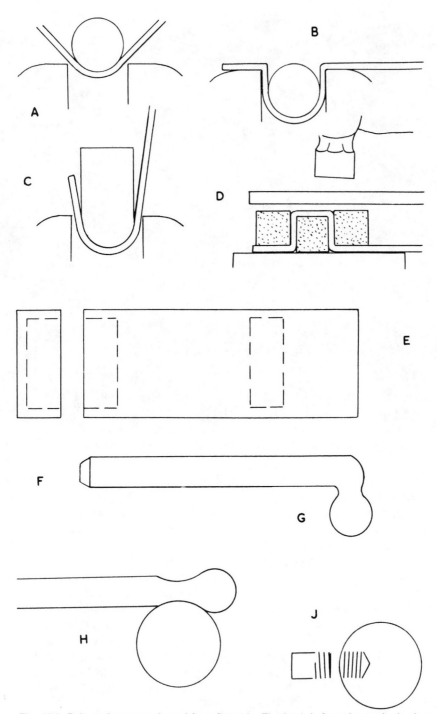

Fig. 10-9. Bolt retainers are shaped from flat strip. The knob is forged over the beak of the anvil and a stop is screwed in: (A) hammer the rod over the bar; (B) knock the rod until level; (C) hollow; (D) true the keepers; (E) backplates; (F) taper; (G) use a knob; (H) thin the bar; (J) drive in a bolt.

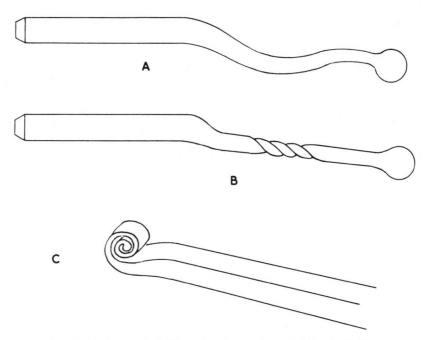

Fig. 10-10. A tower bolt (A) can be given a decorated handle (B,C).

The bolts as described are plain, but if you examine examples on old doors, you will find most to have shaped outlines, or they might be hammered all over. Even if the backplates start as straight-edged, working over them with a large ball peen hammer will give an attractive surface. Heavier blows toward the edges will provide a scalloped effect (Fig. 10-11A). This can be done on the ends of the keepers as well (Fig. 10-11B). However, leave the edges straight that face each other between the door and post.

The outlines can be chopped to curves with hot or cold chisels, either as wavy edges or in leaf patterns. Keepers can be made with spread shaped ends (Fig. 10-11C). Parallel bar can be split and opened (Fig. 10-11D), but if you want larger ends the keepers would have to be cut from wider plate (Fig. 10-11E). Split ends can be dealt with after the keepers have been shaped around the bolt. Wider pieces, however, will have to be made first and the bending around the bolt carefully centered.

DOOR HANDLES

A door handle does not have to be incorporated into a latch. The loop handle shown with the latch could be made separately, or a more complicated handle intended for separate use could be used in its place with a latch.

If a handle is to be used horizontally, it should be symmetrical. This would apply to drawer or chest handles. If the handle is to be vertical on a door, it looks better if both the handle and its backplate are wider or heavier at the top. Whatever design is chosen, the loop should be long enough for a hand to enter easily, and the grip should be comfortable. Curves always look better than straight lines, so either the whole thing should be in curves or the important parts should be curved to draw attention away from straight lines.

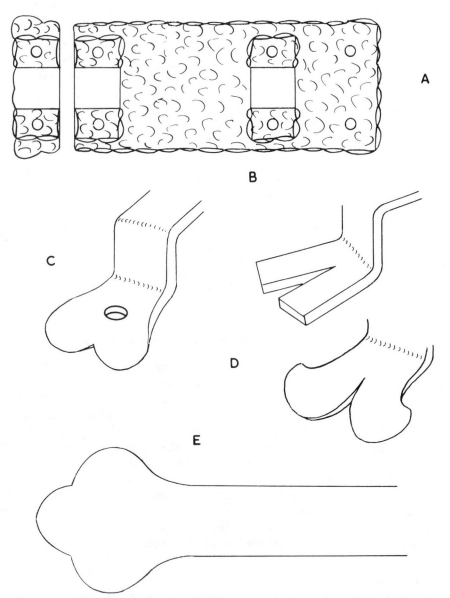

Fig. 10-11. To decorate a door bolt, part can be hammered and shaped: (A) a scalloped effect; (B) scalloped ends; (C) spread shaped ends; (D) split and opened bar; (E) a wider designed end.

For most doors a suitable handle can be made from ⅛- or ⅟₁₆-inch sheet steel, with the parts riveted and woodscrews used for mounting.

The first handle has a shaped outline (Fig. 10-12A). Draw half of it full-size on paper and turn it over the centerline to get the plate symmetrical. Cut this to shape with chisels and file the outline true. If the steel is to remain smooth, make the outline accurate. If it is to be heated and hammered all over and the edge thinned by heavier blows, there is no need to start with quite as accurate an edge.

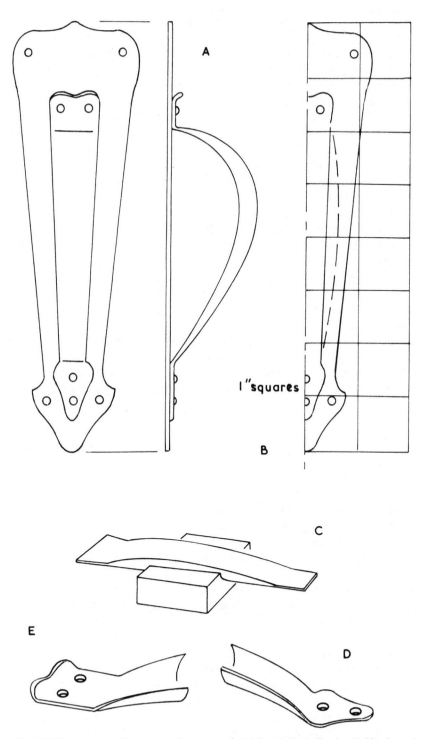

Fig. 10-12. A door handle can be given a comfortable grip by hollowing it: (A) shaped outline; (B) draw to size; (C) heat and hollow the grip; (D) bend the ends; (E) roll back.

The handle is made of sheet the same thickness. Draw its outline before shaping (Fig. 10-12B) and cut this out. Do not drill rivet holes yet. Heat the steel and hollow the part that will be the grip in a suitable swage (Fig. 10-12C). With a further heating, pull the grip to shape over the beak while using two pairs of tongs. Keep the heat adequate because there has to be some stretching of the edges. The hollow made by the swage will probably flatten in parts. True this again, either in a swage or by hammering lengthwise over the beak. Do not worry about the ends at this stage. Check that you have a smooth curve that will be looped out far enough for gripping when finished. Getting to what you consider to be an attractive curve is more important than matching the handle exactly to any preliminary drawing you have made.

Bend back the ends. The bottom can finish flat (Fig. 10-12D). The top can be flat or the divided end can be rolled back (Fig. 10-12E). Drill for rivets and screw. Check that the backplate comes flat on the door when finished.

The backplate for the other handle (Fig. 10-13A) has its corners rolled and the outline curved. Chop it out of sheet with enough at the corners for rolling (Fig. 10-13B). Hammer the edges thin. They can be allowed to spread or kept parallel, depending on the pattern you want. When red hot, it will probably be possible to roll a corner with round-nosed pliers. If not, roll a corner by hammering over the edge of the anvil, as previously described for the ends of bars. In any case, make the rolls tight and the same as each other (Fig. 10-13C).

The handle has a similar hollowed loop around the curve, but the top finishes square, while the bottom is divided (Fig. 10-13D and E). There is only one rivet at each position, but the screws to the door go through the ends as well as the backplate. Most strain usually comes at the top of a handle, so more screws go through there.

HINGES

Hinges with catches, latches, bolts, and handles form part of what are sometimes collectively known as *door furniture*. There are several ways of providing a pivot on which a door can swing. Pegs can go parallel to the framing, but it is more common to have some form of hinges. Hinges can be produced in many ways. Modern doors swing on mass-produced hinges, but in earlier days individual smiths had their own ideas about how hinges should be made (Fig. 10-14).

Some hinges produced by early smiths have lengthy straps across the door. These give ideas for decoration, ranging from basic cuts and shapes to elaborate representations of leaves and flowers. The knuckle of the hinge around the pin might not need to be very big, but the parts of the hinge on both door and post can be. On many old doors, this large part also served to hold the boards of the door together. In some instances, the hinges went around the frame to brace joints.

Most hinges are made so that the two leaves encircle the pin, with alternate pieces forming the knuckle. The methods used in modern manufacture follow those devised by blacksmiths many centuries ago. The parts of a modern hinge knuckle are divided into an uneven arrangement of equal widths (Fig. 10-15A). The number of parts depends on the length of the knuckle; it is more logical to use the same amount on each flap. This shares the load more equally and is seen on some older hinges. With three parts, the central one would be wider than those on each side of it (Fig. 10-15B).

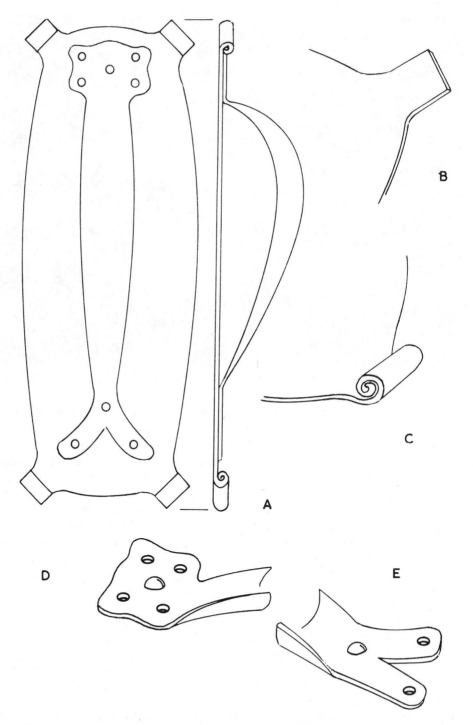

Fig. 10-13. A handle backplate can have rolled corners: (A) backplate, (B,C) roll corners; (D,E) the top finishes square while the bottom is divided.

Fig. 10-14. An old door hinge with welded scrolls, split and shaped end, and punched line decoration.

A cast hinge will have the knuckle formed in the metal (Fig. 10-15C). Simpler hinges are made from sheet metal wrapped around the pin (Fig. 10-15D). A better sheet metal hinge has the wrap attached to the flap (Fig. 10-15E). This is obviously stronger for the same thickness metal, but a single wrap is satisfactory if the steel is thick enough. Another construction seen in some medieval hinges has the metal thinned and carried behind the visible part of the hinge far enough for screws or nails to go through it (Fig. 10-15F). The pin through a hinge knuckle is often machined level in a manufactured hinge, but in an individually made hinge, it adds strength if a little extra is left on each end for riveting (Fig. 10-15G). It is not always easy to decide how thick to make the pin. In modern hinges, it is often no thicker than the metal used for the flaps. It has to share the load without bending or breaking, and it is easier to forge good knuckles if the pin is thicker. A reasonable choice for the pin is about twice the thickness of the metal used for the flaps.

For ease in handling, a strap hinge is a good choice for a first hinge (Fig. 10-16A). Use a bar about $1\frac{1}{2} \times \frac{1}{8}$ inch, and do not cut this off until the knuckles have been formed. Make hinge knuckles over a mandrel of the same size rod as you will use for the pin. It is unwise to use the pin itself, because it will almost certainly be damaged. If the mandrel has an eye forged on its end (Fig. 10-16B), it is easier to grip and pull out.

Start bending the end of the hot bar over the end of the anvil (Fig. 10-16C). The pin will be $\frac{1}{4}$ inch in diameter. Estimate that you are leaving about this much as you make the curve and work on the face (Fig. 10-16D). As more of the curve is made,

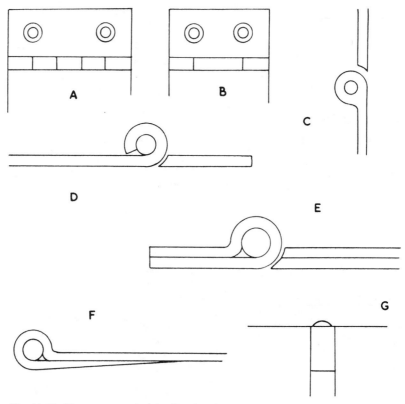

Fig. 10-15. Hinges are made from flat plate in several ways: (A) hinge knuckle; (B) the central part is wider; (C) cast hinge; (D) simple hinge; (E) more complex hinges; (F) the metal is thinned; (G) extra on each end for riveting.

insert the mandrel and continue closing the bar around it (Fig. 10-16E). It can be hit against the edge of the anvil (Fig. 10-16F), but final closing is better done with the edge of a piece of steel (Fig. 10-16G) used as a punch. Pull the mandrel out and make the knuckle on the end of the other bar.

Mark the cuts on the parts that will have the outer sections of knuckle. Saw down these lines, chop out the waste with a cold chisel, and file the opening to shape. Use this as a pattern to mark the other knuckle, and cut that to shape ((Fig. 10-16H). Try the parts together. If the hinge is to be a back flap that swings from the closed position to 90° the other way (Fig. 10-16J), the slots have to be cut away deeply. If, as is more common, the hinge has to go from closed to flat, the bottoms of the cutouts are neater if filed at an angle that follows the curve of the knuckle (Fig. 10-16K).

If a hinge is to be made with a double thickness, it can still be formed on the end of a bar and cut off after shaping. If it is a broader one, sheet steel must be folded around. Have the mandrel ready and heat the steel to redness. Bend back enough for a flap over the mandrel (Fig. 10-17A). If it is a suitable size to go in the vise, squeeze the flat parts together there (Fig. 10-17B). If not, use a flatter or set hammer to do the same on the anvil. In any case, flatten so that the knuckle is to one side (Fig. 10-17C).

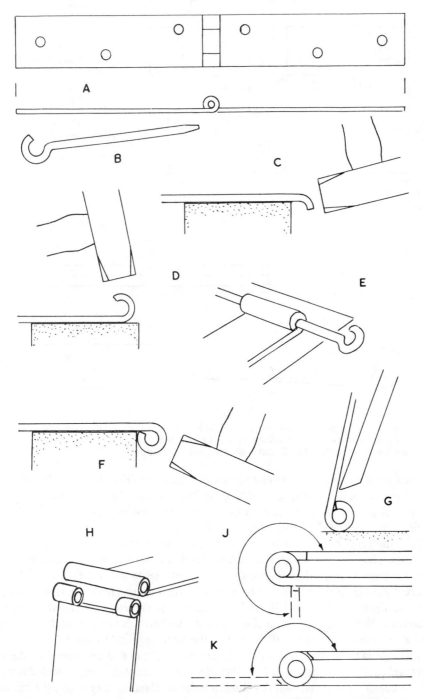

Fig. 10-16. The knuckle of a hinge is rolled around a pin and cutouts are arranged according to the amount of swing the hinge is to have: (A) strap hinge; (B) mandrel with eye; (C) bend; (D) curve; (E) close the bar; (F) hit against the edge of the anvil; (G) final closing; (H) cut to shape; (J) back flap hinge swings 90°; (K) follow the curve of the knuckle.

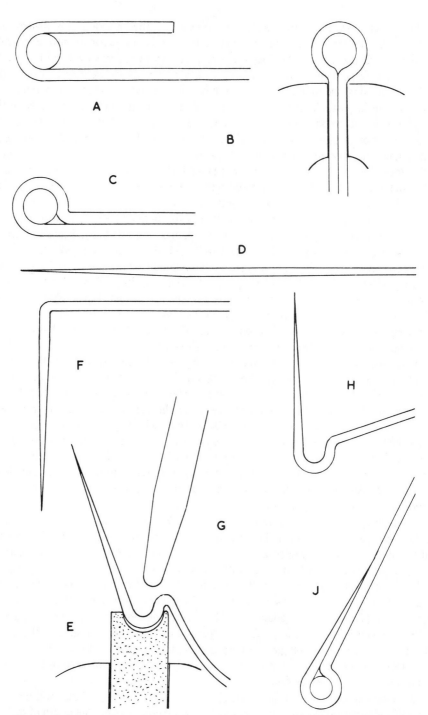

Fig. 10-17. The metal of a hinge can be double thickness and the back can be tapered: (A) bend to make a flap; (B) squeeze in a vise; (C) flatten; (D) thin to a feather edge; (E) use a stake to make a curve; (F) bend to a right angle; (G) drive the steel into the groove; (H) finish to more than a semicircle; (J) close the hinge over the mandrel.

Do the same with the other part. Cut the spaces in the knuckles. It is always better to start with the half that has outside parts. If there is any error in cutting, it will be less obvious. If there are to be five or seven parts, work progressively with a fine file. The parts should go together tightly at first because they will soon wear against each other.

You can follow the method used in medieval hinges: With a part tapered in thickness behind the main part, thin the end for a length sufficient to make a feather edge (Fig. 10-17D). It would be possible to fold around the pin mandrel, but because thinner steel tends to bend more easily, it might be difficult to get a satisfactory result. Another method uses a stake or grooved tool like a small swage, but with the curve at one side coming to the edge (Fig. 10-17E). The curve in it should match what is to be the outside curve of the hinge knuckle. This can be used with a cross peen hammer or there could be a matching punch to suit the curve inside the hinge material.

Bend down the tapered part and enough of the parallel part to go around the pin, so that it is at right angles to the rest of the hinge (Fig. 10-17F). Have the grooved tool standing as high as possible in the vise. Hook the hinge steel over the tool with the tapered part across it. Use the cross peen hammer or the punch to drive the steel into the groove (Fig. 10-17G). Except for the thinnest steel, this must be done hot. Get as much curve as you can by lifting the long part as you hit. Finish with a semicircle (Fig. 10-17H). Put the mandrel in and close the hinge over it (Fig. 10-17J). Make sure that screw holes will be placed to go through the tapered part. If any help is needed in keeping the parts tight, put a rivet through centrally.

Once the methods of making knuckles have been mastered, many kinds of hinges become possible. Strap hinges can be straight and parallel, as in the example used, but they are more often tapered and can be hammered or otherwise decorated (Fig. 10-18A). A T-hinge is the same on one side, on the other there has to be enough screw holes for fastening to a narrow part (Fig. 10-18B). A hinge with flaps that has the same width as the knuckle is a butt hinge (Fig. 10-18C). If this is extended to provide a greater spread of screw holes, it is an H-hinge (Fig. 10-18D). If it is extended from the knuckle, it is a parliament hinge (Fig. 10-18E) and is used where a door has to swing clear of obstructions. An L-hinge (Fig. 10-18F) has an extra leg to go around the corner of a framed door (Fig. 10-19 and Fig. 10-20).

Some hinges only have a stout pin, called a *pintle* on one part, and the loop or knuckle on the other part drops over it (Fig. 10-21). The rudder of a boat is hinged in this way, and the other part is call a *gudgeon*. However, that name is not used for steelwork ashore. Wrought-iron gates are often hung in this way, with loops on the gates dropping over pintles on the posts (Fig. 10-22A). It is then possible to lift a gate off, although this might be prevented with a nut screwed on the end of a pintle. For use with field gates, the pintle can be provided with a spike (Fig. 10-22B) or welded to a backplate (Fig. 10-22C) that is screwed to the gate post. A strap goes at the other side (Fig. 10-22D) and this can also be called a strap hinge. If a gate is to be hung on two pintles, it helps to make the bottom one longer. The strap can be located on that first, instead of having to try to line up at two places at once.

A pintle can be just a parallel rod. However, if it is for a gate that will have to be lifted off and replaced frequently, it is better to keep it parallel for the depth of the strap, then draw it out to a slight taper and round the tip (Fig. 10-22E). A strap can be wrapped around and welded (Fig. 10-22F), or the pintle can be shouldered to a smaller diameter

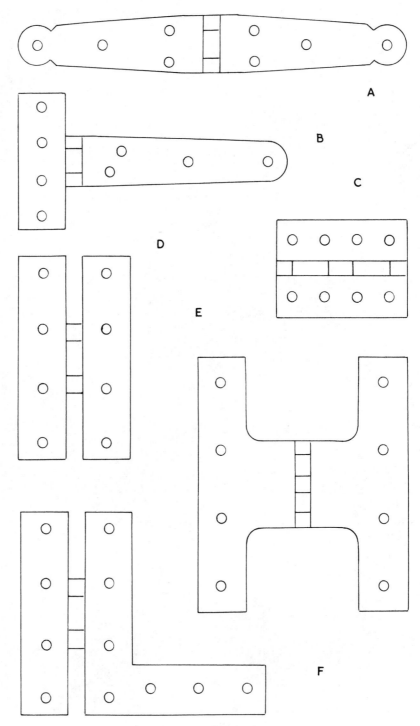

Fig. 10-18. Hinges are arranged with their leaves to suit the arrangement of screw holes:
(A) strap hinge; (B) T-hinge; (C) butt hinge; (D) H-hinge; (E) parliament hinge; (F) H-L hinge.

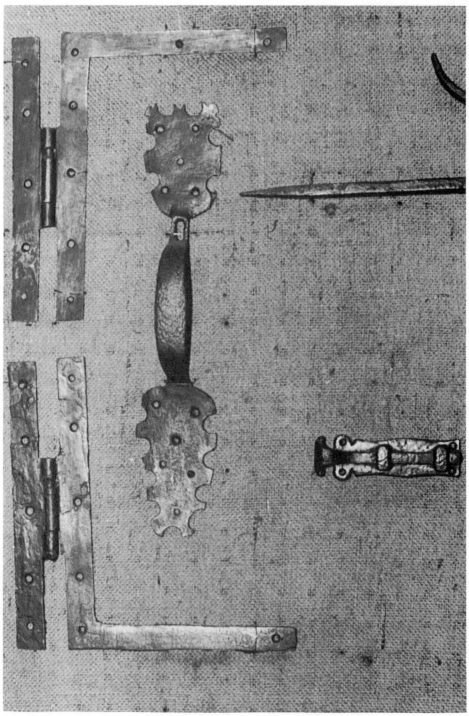

Fig. 10-19. A pair of L-hinges and a door handle.

Fig. 10-20. A forged L-hinge carried across several boards of a door.

Fig. 10-21. In this gate hinge a loop on the gate fits over a pintle on the post.

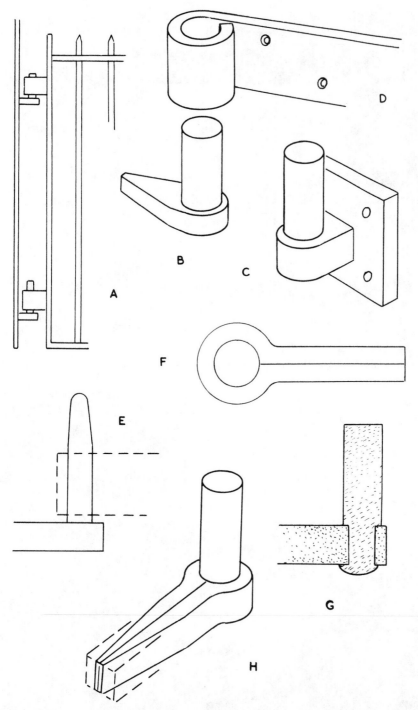

Fig. 10-22. Stout hinges can pivot on pintles: (A) wrought-iron gate; (B) field gate; (C) welded to a backplate; (D) strap hinge; (E) taper and round the tip; (F) welded strap; (G) pintle shouldered and riveted; (H) draw to a point.

and riveted through the strap (Fig. 10-22G). This can also be brought to welding heat and hammered together. If it is to be a spike, the two sides can also be welded and drawn down to a point (Fig. 10-22H). Another way is to start with a solid rod for the point and punch a hole through it to take the pintle.

The strap is made in the usual way, with a knuckle that will fit easily over the pintle. Use a mandrel slightly bigger than the pintle. When the hinge is put into use, have a washer on the pintle to minimize wear between the two parts.

Hinges can be decorated in many ways. Long straps provide opportunities for various decorations. A parallel strap can have its ends split and pieces notched in the sides (Fig. 10-23A) with a set or chisel. These parts can be curled and shaped so that the straight outline disappears (Fig. 10-23B). Fullers can be used to stretch the outline to curves (Fig. 10-23C). With much forging to shape in this way, the strap looks best if finished with dents from a ball peen hammer (Fig. 10-23D). Some medieval hinges also have punched patterns over the surfaces, but even in reproduction work it is possible to overdo decoration. The art is in knowing when to exercise restraint. Punched holes for rosehead nails might be most appropriate for reproduction hinges, otherwise drill and countersink for screws.

Hinges have been both practical and decorative features in furniture and housing for a very long time. It is interesting to examine the work of old smiths and see the difference of fashion and methods. Some examples of wrought-iron Jacobean hinges are shown in Fig. 10-24. Notice the unequal widths of knuckle parts so that the same amount of metal is used from each side. In the originals, the outlines would have been obtained partly by forging and partly by sawing and filing to shape. Edges are nearly all beveled, and surfaces are smooth. Countersunk screws came into use during Jacobean times.

WALL HOOKS AND BRACKETS

Wall hooks are readily available as mass-produced metal and plastic articles, but there is a character about individually produced versions. A smith can easily make a variety of hooks.

A basic hook (Fig. 10-25A) starts as a flat bar. One end is drawn out to make the hook (Fig. 10-25B). The hook is then curved and the top is rounded. An alternative method is to start the other way with round bar, which is flattened (Fig. 10-25C). To enhance the appearance, additional work can be done on the back and the hook.

The rectangular outline of the back can be broken up by hammering over the edge and the surface (Fig. 10-25D). The end can be split and curled outward (Fig. 10-25E). This will have a functional advantage in spreading the points of attachment to the wall. A simple curve to the hook can be improved by giving it a swan's neck shape (Fig. 10-25F).

If the tip is left thick and then upset, before the hook is curved, it can be given a round knob (Fig. 10-25G). Leave hammer marks showing. For ease in slipping a coat loop over the end, make the knob more oval, with the smaller curve outward (Fig. 10-25H).

Another way of dealing with the tip is to draw it down finely and curl it (Fig. 10-25J). If it would be better for the tip to be wider to prevent things from coming off, flatten and curl the end (Fig. 10-25K). Some old wall hooks have heads on the end. This is not easy to do, but a knob can be converted to an animal's head by careful hammering and use of punches and files. A double hook can be made with different heads on the ends (Fig. 10-25L).

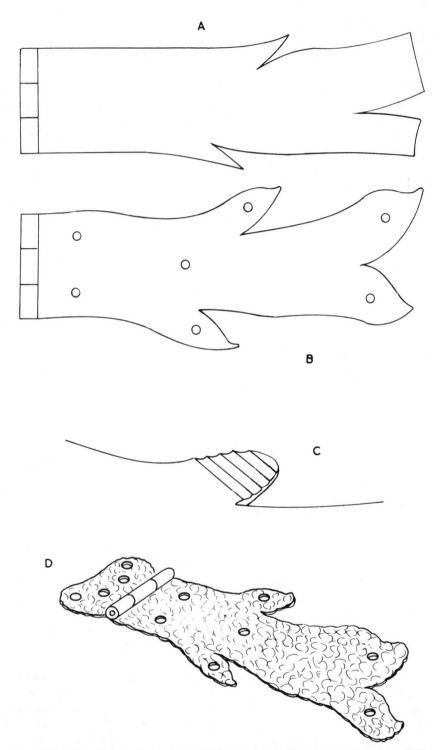

Fig. 10-23. Large hinges can be decorated by splitting (A,B) and spreading edges (C.D).

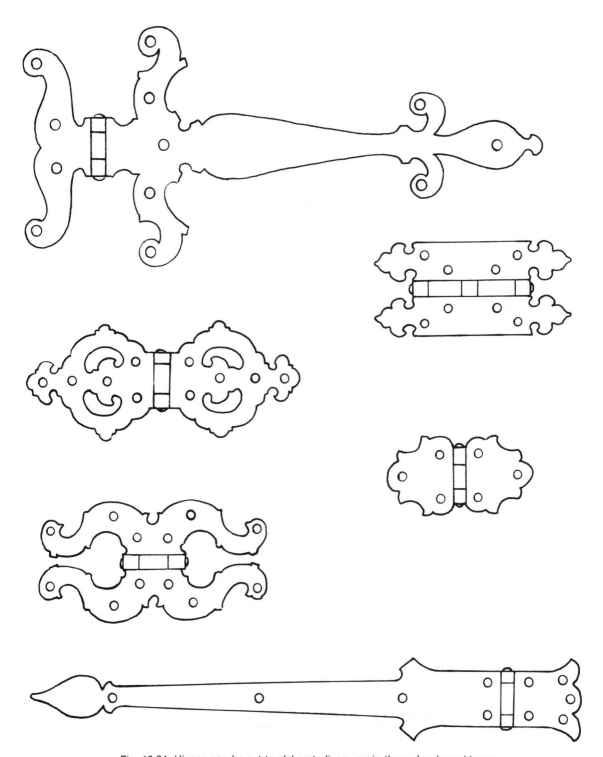

Fig. 10-24. Hinges can be cut to elaborate lines—as in these Jacobean hinges.

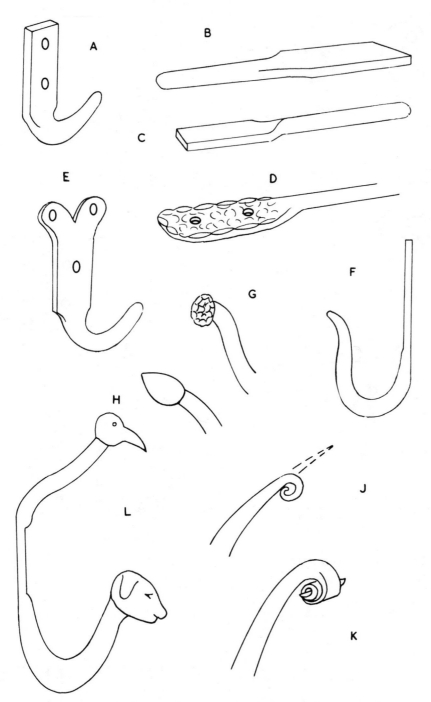

Fig. 10-25. Hooks can range from basic shapes to elaborately decorated ones: (A) basic hook; (B) draw out one end: (C) flatten the other end; (D) hammer the edge; (E) a split and curl; (F) swan's neck shape; (G) round knob; (H) oval knob; (J) curl the tip; (K) flatten and curl; (L) double hook.

The simplest shelf bracket is a bar bent at right angles (Fig. 10-26A). If made of stout enough bar, there will be no need for a strut. Even this can be given some character by decorating. If the bar starts quite thick, most of this can be drawn out toward the end and the bracket has strength and stiffness where required. It also has a more delicate look than one made from a parallel bar.

As an example, start with a ½- × -¾-inch bar. Mark where the corner will come, and leave the bar its full section for about 1 inch on each side of that. Draw out the thickness to about ¼ inch. The width can be allowed to increase gradually (Fig. 10-26B), or the sides can be tapered and a broad thin end formed (Fig. 10-26C). With flatter bar, 1 × ⅜ inch, the drawn-out parts can be kept the same width. Decoration can be provided with cuts from a set (Fig. 10-26D). When making any shelf bracket, be careful not to make the angle less than 90°. Even if exactly that, a shelf might look as though it is sagging forward. It is always best to finish a bracket slightly open when tested with a square (Fig. 10-26E).

Making an unbraced bracket means using fairly heavy bar. For many purposes, it might look better and be just as strong to use lighter bar and provide a brace. The basic form is made from strip, with the brace bent and held with rivets (Fig. 10-27A). Appearance is improved if the angle of the brace differs from 45°. Because the upright leg of a shelf bracket is usually longer, the brace or strut will come closer to being upright (Fig. 10-27B).

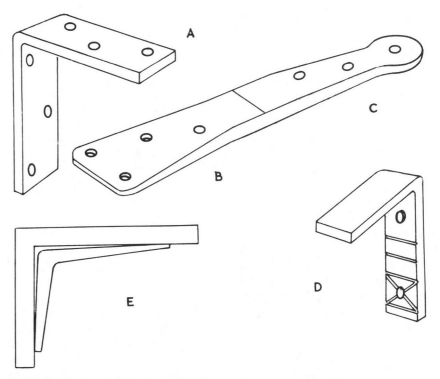

Fig. 10-26. Brackets can be tapered (A,B,C) and decorated. They should usually be slightly wider than a right angle (E,D).

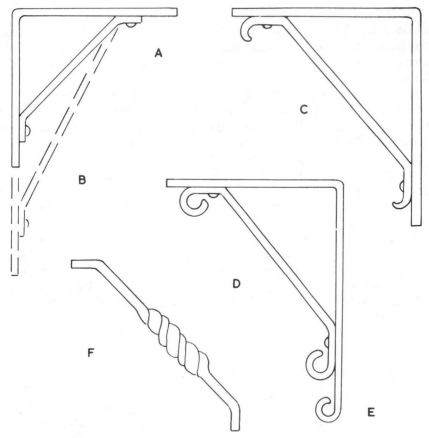

Fig. 10-27. Struts to shelf brackets allow decoration by twisting: (A) basic form; (B) strut; (C) ends can be curled; (D) looped curl; (E) shape one end; (F) twist.

For decoration, the ends of the struts can be curled by lifting a drawn-out end (Fig. 10-27C) or by making a larger loop (Fig. 10-27D). A matching shaping can be given to one or both ends of the bracket (Fig. 10-27E). The center of the brace should not be thinned in any way, because that would weaken it, but if it is very long it can be made to look better by twisting it (Fig. 10-27F). Do this before shaping the ends since twisting reduces the overall length.

Another bracket can be used for hanging a gong or a flower basket (Fig. 10-28A). The back can go upward, with both the horizontal part and strut riveted to it. The upper part does not have to be horizontal, so there is scope for trying the effect of curves (Fig. 10-28B). In Fig. 10-28C, the back strip is drawn out at the ends and split so there are single curls. The other two parts can be slightly narrower and their riveted ends are neater if reduced slightly in width (Fig. 10-28D). A hook on the horizontal part can be a curl similar to those on the back (Fig. 10-28E), or it can be drawn out round and made into a deeper hook (Fig. 10-28F), with its tip finished in any of the ways suggested for wall hooks.

An interesting exercise is to include a circle between the other parts (Fig. 10-28G). To do this accurately, make a drawing—preferably in chalk on an iron plate—so the parts

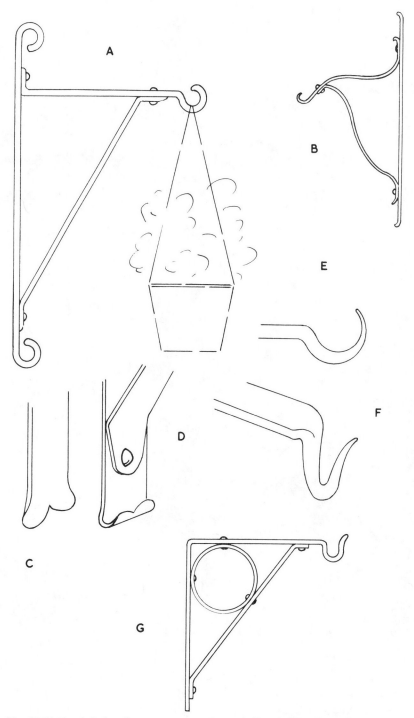

Fig. 10-28. Brackets for other purposes can be made like shelf brackets: (A) bracket for hanging a basket; (B) use curves; (C) the back strip is split; (D) rivet ends; (E) hook; (F) deeper hook; (G) decorative circle.

Fig. 10-29. This bracket with scrolls supports an outside light.

can be tried on it. To allow for final adjustments, form the vertical and horizontal parts and make the circle. Bring these parts together. Get the actual length between bends on the strut from this—even if the assembly differs slightly from the original drawing. Otherwise you might find that the circle does not touch at all three points. Brackets can be elaborated into other designs (Fig. 10-29).

FOOT SCRAPER

Before the days of paved surfaces, a foot scraper was a common item outside most house doors. The worst of the mud could be scraped off before boots were wiped on a mat. A scraper might still serve a practical purpose when gardening boots have to be wiped. Also, a blacksmith could put a scraper outside the entrance of his home as an indication of his craft and skill.

The important part of a boot scraper is the horizontal bar. The bar should be wide enough for any boot. Its top should be thinned, although not to a knife edge, in order to get under caked mud. What else is incorporated depends on the artistic ideas of the blacksmith. The design will be affected by how the scraper is to be mounted. There could be spikes placed in a stone wall or a concrete step, or there might be wood screws or spikes set in wood. For an authentic appearance, smith-made spikes or nails with rose heads would be best.

In Fig. 10-30, the parts can be joined to wood in both directions, but for a stone wall the back strip could be omitted and spikes taken directly into the stone. If the floor is stone or concrete, a spike could be forged on the scraper, particularly if the concrete is laid at the same time the scraper is fitted.

Make the scraper from a steel bar (Fig. 10-31A). Shoulder the ends to make tenons and taper its center either by hammering or grinding, but leave the ends at the full section where they will come against the uprights (Fig. 10-31B). Let the tenons be too long at this stage. Their section should suit a stock punch; you might have to make one to suit.

The back is a straight bar (Fig. 10-31C) that goes just above the point where the front piece is riveted. For attaching to wood, split the end so that screw or nail holes are far enough out for the hammer or screwdriver to miss the front part (Fig. 10-31D). Where the scraper comes, punch a hole (Fig. 10-31E). The sides of the bar will bulge. They can be hammered back parallel while the punch is left in the hole, but the curved outline could also be left as a decorative feature. It will probably be satisfactory for the upright to finish at ground level, but it could continue with a spike or be bent horizontally and formed like its top end for spikes into the ground (Fig. 10-31F).

The front piece is the main decorative feature that shows the smith's skill. Start with bar of the section of the largest part. Have a full-size drawing with which to compare the work as it progresses. For the leg that will take the scraper and be made into a foot, bring the section down to a rectangular section (Fig. 10-32A). Then spread the foot. It could be thinned and bent (Fig. 10-32B). Another way of dealing with it is to have it too long and partially shape the foot. Then heat to an upsetting temperature and hammer the bend while the leg is in a vise in order to spread at the bend. By building up thickness there, it is possible to forge a foot that is flat underneath and shaped around the leg without any bend being apparent (Fig. 10-32C).

Reduce the part that will come against the wall to a section that will take rivets or spikes (Fig. 10-32D). Draw out the part that makes the curved sweep. Try to avoid a straight taper in the length. Let it be slightly bulbous and work to an elliptical cross-section (Fig. 10-32E). The inner surface can be flat, but it is just as easy to make curved because it comes against the anvil when a hammer is used on the other side.

Deal with the top in a similar way, but it will look better if its greatest width is somewhat less than that of the main sweep. Curl the end (Fig. 10-32F) and shape that

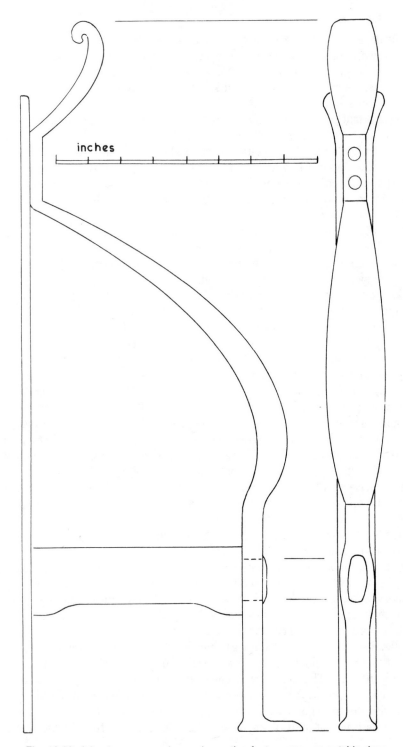

inches

Fig. 10-30. A boot scraper makes a decorative feature near an outside door.

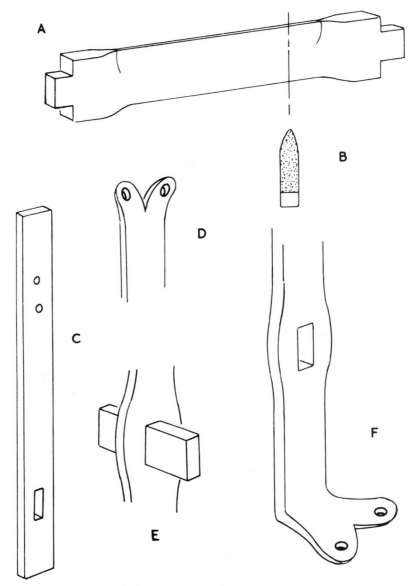

Fig. 10-31. Parts are punched and shaped to be joined with tenons: (A) steel bar; (B) shoulder the ends; (C) straight bar; (D) split end; (E) punch a hole; (F) finish.

part. Use a fullsize drawing as a guide to the curve for the sweeps of both parts, and the angles and positions of the bends for the flat parts.

Check the height and position of the tenon of the scraper and punch for it. Rivet the parts together. The end of the front tenon looks best if the spread end stands above the surface (Fig. 10-32G). File the end of the tenon so there is just enough projecting for spreading a suitable head. The other end can be dealt with in the same way if a projecting head can sink into the wall or woodwork. Otherwise, countersink the punched hole by filing.

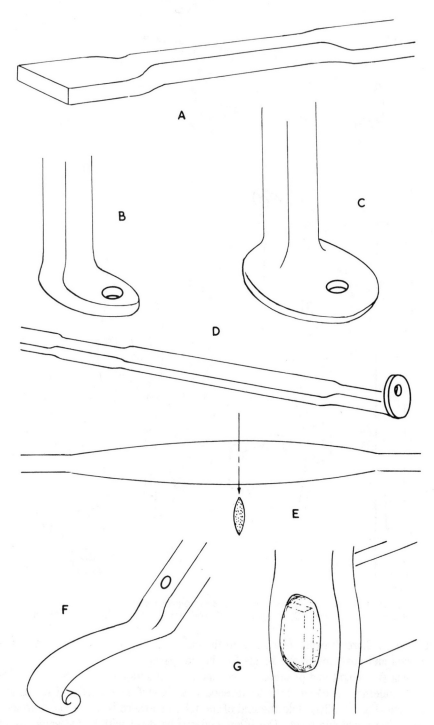

Fig. 10-32. There is scope for decoration on the top and feet of the scraper: (A) the foot is rectangular; (B) thin and bend; (C) forge a foot; (D) reduce; (E) slightly bulbous; (F) curl; (G) front tenon.

11

Decorative Ironwork

Much of the skilled and artistic work done by blacksmiths in the last few centuries can be seen in gates, railings, grills, church screens, and similar objects where the assembly was a mass of individually shaped parts joined together to make a pleasing pattern. In some cases, the blacksmith's work was linked with cast iron. There are a great many surviving examples of work executed entirely by the smith at his forge with quite simple equipment. His skill and creativity were his most important tools. He could not call on precision machinery, and any jigs used were made by the blacksmith himself as needed.

The material was iron, and the type of work is collectively called *wrought*-iron work. The work wrought in this instance is used in the sense of meaning worked, although the material was also called wrought iron.

Some modern wrought-iron gates and similar things are very different from the traditional work. They are made of bars all of a uniform section. The majority of parts in a traditional piece of wrought-iron work, on the other hand, are tapered and twisted and changed section in their length to get the effect the smith wanted. The scrolls of modern work are not very thin and are all identical, showing that they were pulled cold around standard shapes, probably in a machine. Although such gates and other assemblies might be attractive, they are machine-age imitations of the products of real craftsmen.

Like many seemingly complex things, a gate or length of railings is built up from a series of comparatively simple steps. If the steps are understood and each performed properly, the final assembly should be very satisfying. Although the assembled construction might be quite heavy, the individual parts are not. There are some stages where a helper is essential, but much of the work can be done single-handedly. The amount of heat required at any time is not great and a small hearth should be adequate. It is always easier to work on a large anvil, but if the work is schemed to suit, much of the shaping can be done on a small anvil. For some of the details, such as twisted leaves, a small anvil might actually be better than a large one.

Much of the work involves applying techniques already covered in earlier chapters. If you think about what is happening to the steel when you hit or bend it, almost anything is possible as you direct your blows to get the best effect and the maximum result from each action.

Look at examples of wrought-iron work made by a blacksmith. If you cannot find an actual gate or similar object, examine photographs. Old churches might have a gate or screen. After you have enjoyed the object as a whole, look at some of the details. Try to visualize how various pieces were made. Notice how the parts are joined. See how sections have been changed, how the smith has thinned sections down to make ornamental twists and twirls. Look at the ends of scrolls (Fig. 11-1) and other parts. There are a large number of ways of shaping the ends before curling them. Think out the shape that was made before the end was rolled tightly. Finishing an end in the form of a leaf is common (Fig. 11-2). Note how the bar is thinned, shaped, and twisted or crinkled in leaf form. Look for the leaf veins that have been cut in it (Figs. 11-3, 4, and 5).

SCROLLS

The tip of a scroll (Fig. 11-6, Fig. 11-7 and Fig. 11-8) in blacksmithing is always given some sort of decoration, usually in the form of a tight roll on the end of the drawn-out bar. A machine-made modern scroll has the bar of the same thickness throughout and no rolled end. Some ways of dealing with the ends have previously been described, but these and others are summarized in this chapter.

Most decorative work of this sort is done with flat-sectioned bar. Round rods and square sections also have their uses but most work is done with a bar that is about twice as wide as it is thick. Practice with a bar of this section. First make sure you can draw it down with an even taper almost to a chisel end (Fig. 11-9A). Get as good a shape as you can under the hammer, but use a flatter if necessary. You should be able to get a graceful taper over a long length as well as a short length.

It is possible to curl the end almost entirely by hammering. Have the end at a yellow heat and use a light hammer while the bar is held across the anvil face. Hitting progressively with glancing blows on the end should curl the thin metal tightly (Fig. 11-9B). There might have to be occasional moves to the flat of the face to straighten and maintain the thickness, but it should be possible to get a tight curl on a light bar with one or two heatings. The thin end loses its heat quickly, but it also takes up heat quickly. Be careful not to leave it in the fire too long that the end melts off.

A tight curl is not always wanted throughout; it usually looks best if the inner curl is close. Afterwards the small scroll can become more open (Fig. 11-9C). Hit further back to make the curves longer (Fig. 11-9D).

Some smiths make snub ends with solid centers (Fig. 11-9E). Besides being considered more attractive, the snub helps in the early stages of making a large scroll. To make a snub end, have rod of suitable size and cut it almost through at a length slightly more than needed. Start a curve on the bar, then heat both parts to welding heat and

Fig. 11-1. A candle sconce shows applications of simple scrolls.

227

Fig. 11-2. The scrolls in this gate have their ends flattened to make stylized leaves.

hammer them together (Fig. 11-9F). Snap off the unwanted rod. The welded piece of rod can be hammered on the ends, or might have to be filed or ground later.

In much wrought-iron work, the ends of scrolls are not parallel. They can be wider than the bar, whether welded to a snub or the thin end curled alone. If the end is drawn down in the width as well as the thickness, the scroll end gets narrower (Fig. 11-9G). If it is flaired out toward the end, an interesting effect is achieved (Fig. 11-9H). It could be narrowed and then flaired so a narrow neck leads up to the roll (Fig. 11-9J).

A scroll can be just a part of a circle, or it can go around several turns in a spiral. Skill comes in getting the curves even and in keeping distances between the turns the same or at a regular rate of increase. This is complicated by the fact that in many assemblies there are a large number of scrolls that should be the same. Machine-like perfection is not wanted, but there should not be great differences between scrolls that are designed to be the same. Much of the skill is in the eye and hands of the smith, but there are some tools to help.

One tool is a block of steel that fits in the hardie hole and is called a *halfpenny snub end scroll*. The curve in the side is about the same as an old English halfpenny (pronounced ''haypnee'') and about 1 inch across. It is used with somewhat heavier bar than can be hammered across the anvil, and the tapered end is formed with a curve on it (Fig. 11-10A). It can be used with a tapered end, but it is particularly suitable for a bar with a snub end (Fig. 11-10B).

Fig. 11-3. The welded ends of gate rails have been flattened so the iron can be formed into lifelike leaves.

Fig. 11-4. Sheet steel is formed into leaves around a drawn-out flamelike center in each decoration.

Fig. 11-5. Leaflike shapes are used to enhance the appearance of the supports for a rail.

Fig. 11-6.   These old scrolls appear to have been made by a smith without the aid of a scroll iron, because they are uneven in shape and thickness.

Another tool is a *scroll starter* (Fig. 11-10C). It can be held in the vise or provided with an end to fit the hardie hole. The steel has its end curled so as to hold the thin end of the starter, then the hot steel is pulled to the curve.

To get a number of scrolls to match, a smith can make a scroll iron or tool (Fig. 11-10D). This is a scroll made of steel stout enough not to pull out of shape when bar is pulled around it. The center of it is thinned and curled to take the prepared end of the work. It also eases engaging the hot steel, which can be locked on there and quickly pulled around as far as the required scroll has to go. Not every scroll made has to go the whole way. Usually the scroll tool end is turned down and either fits the hardie hole or is held in a vise.

Scrolls can be worked with a scroll fork and a scroll wrench. The scroll fork stands with its end upward in the hardie hole or vise, and the scroll wrench is used to lever the curves in the hot steel (Fig. 11-10E). With the horizontal action, it is possible to see how the shape is coming and make adjustments even after you have passed a particular point.

Fig. 11-7. This church gate shows how scrolls and leaves can be built up into a very effective whole design.

Fig. 11-8. The top of the previous gate showing how the design rises to an apex with flame effect at the peak.

Scrolls are best tackled boldly, with the whole length of the shape heated and pulled or hammered around quickly. In wrought-iron work, many scrolls are enclosed in other parts, so they have to be carefully worked to match a drawing. This is particularly so if both ends of the same piece are scrolls, the same or opposite ways (Figs. 11-10F and 11-11). If the end is free from anything around it, exact sizes are not so important.

COLLARS

Although the main structure will have more substantial joints, the decorative parts between the primary parts are held to them and to each other with straps or collars. Collars are sometimes welded and they are made from bar of lighter section than the parts they are to join. A collar can go around parts of similar size (Fig. 11-12A) or they might have to accommodate a stout part of the framing with the thinner scroll bar. To forge collars, use a bar of the same section that has to be enclosed. Double back a piece of scroll bar (Fig. 11-12B) or hold together thick and thin of other sizes. Usually there are a large number of collars in an assembly and it is easier to make them all at the same time.

A collar could have the ends meeting in a butt joint (Fig. 11-12C), but it is more usual to cut them diagonally (Fig. 11-12D) or to overlap the ends (Fig. 11-12E).

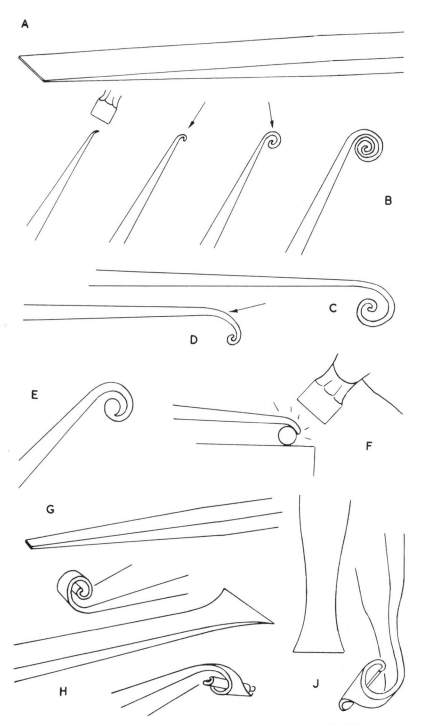

Fig. 11-9. In decorative ironwork, tapered ends are decorated by scrolls: (A) draw down and taper; (B) curl; (C,D) styles of curls; (E) snub end; (F) heat and hammer; (G) the end is drawn down; (H) flair the end; (J) narrow neck and roll.

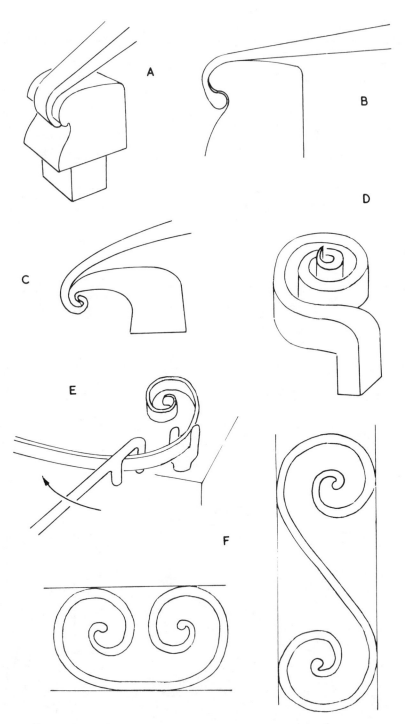

Fig. 11-10. Tools the smith can make help in shaping scrolls to exact sizes: (A) form a curve; (B) snub end; (C) scroll starter; (D) scroll iron; (E) lever curves while in a vise; (F) matched scrolls.

Fig. 11-11. Two identical pairs of snub-end scrolls fit between gate parts and are held with a collar.

Cut across the end of the bar diagonally, if that is the type to be made. Roll the former on the bar to get the length needed, and partly cut through there with a set. Heat the bar and hammer the end around the former, almost to completion, then snap off the surplus bar. Hammer the collar to shape, but while it is still hot, spring it open to come off the former (Fig. 11-12F). When it is put in position on the parts it is to hold, hammer it around hot and squeeze it tight with tongs, pliers, or a hand vise.

For overlapping ends, draw out the ends to a length that will go around (Fig. 11-12G). Because it is difficult to hold a short piece, form it in the vise. Hammer one leg in the vise (Fig. 11-12H). Then make the other leg around a former (Fig. 11-12J) and put the former on the anvil to close the overlapping ends (Fig. 11-12K). As with the other type, spring open the collar so that it can be put in its final place and squeezed tight.

SQUARE CORNERS

In good-quality wrought-iron work, corners are square or sharp. If a bar is bent, the iron curves around the neutral axis of its section, with the inner edge compressing and

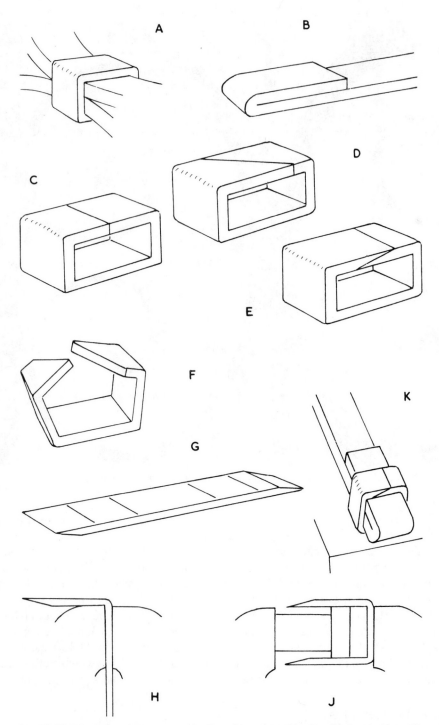

Fig. 11-12. Decorative parts are usually clipped together: (A) collar; (B) doubled bar; (C) butt joint; (D) diagonal cut; (E) overlap the ends; (F) open collar; (G) draw out ends; (H) hammer one leg; (J) position the other leg; (K) close the ends.

the outer edge stretching (Fig. 11-13A). A curve is apparent. For many purposes this does not matter, but in most wrought-iron work structures the corners are sharp. If the corner of a rounded bend is hammered, it can be made sharp outside. However, the section of the bar will be reduced (Fig. 11-13B).

To get a square corner while retaining at least the full thickness on the corner (Fig. 11-14), the steel has to be first upset there. Usually the part has a taper going away to a scroll and care must be taken to avoid damaging this. The corner should be dealt with before the scroll is completed. The work is best done in the vise. To protect the tapered part from the vise jaws, make vise clamps from iron wrapped around (Fig. 11-13C).

Have everything ready and heat what will become the corner to welding temperature. Grip the tapered part in the vise jaws and bend the corner into a loop that stands up slightly (Fig. 11-13D). Hammer this hard so the metal will flow towards the corner. There might have to be another heat to build up sufficient thickness there. At this stage, aim to build up steel where you need it. Do not try to square the corner yet. When there is sufficient steel, move the work to the anvil and hammer the corner square (Fig. 11-13E). Do not hammer so much that you spread the metal you have gained. Finish with a thin corner.

QUATREFOILS

A grill can be made with flat bars crossing each other (Fig. 11-15A). To bring them into line they have to be offset over each other, either by keeping the bars straight one way and doing all the offsetting the other way (Fig. 11-15B) or by taking half out of each bar (Fig. 11-15C). In many old European churches and castles, the spaces in the squares are decorated by parts cut from the bars to form quatrefoils (Fig. 11-15D). The points might touch, be joined with collars, or twisted sideways to overlap.

The process is simple in principle, but it is not so easy to get an even result. The pattern should be drawn on a steel sheet and the cuts marked on the steel with center punch dots. Each part of the quatrefoil pattern is cut and bent from the sides of the bars forming the grill.

It is possible to deal with light bar while it is cold, using cold chisels and cold sets. But for stouter steel that has to be heated, do the cutting with hot sets. The end of each slice can be a diagonal cut from a straight-edged tool, but it is better to have a set or chisel sharpened to a curve like a gouge (Fig. 11-15E). Make the curved and straight cuts from both sides, so that the parts curve away (Fig. 11-15F). Shape the pieces over the beak of the anvil or a piece of rod of the diameter you want. At the same time, hammer out any unevenness due to chopping out. There might have to be some slight adjustment to the points when the grill is assembled because the final shape cannot be matched until they are together. With the thinner sections it should be possible to alter the shapes cold with a wrench or tongs.

That is the basic way of dealing with quatrefoil, but there are a great many variations, some that are very elaborate. One piece can be cut inside another, the piece cut away might be cut again, or the parts that join might have another between them. All could be held with collars. An arrow gripped in this way is common in medieval grills.

A similar technique can be used on a single bar, such as might stand up in an assembly or provide the central decoration at the top of a gate. This starts as a broad bar and

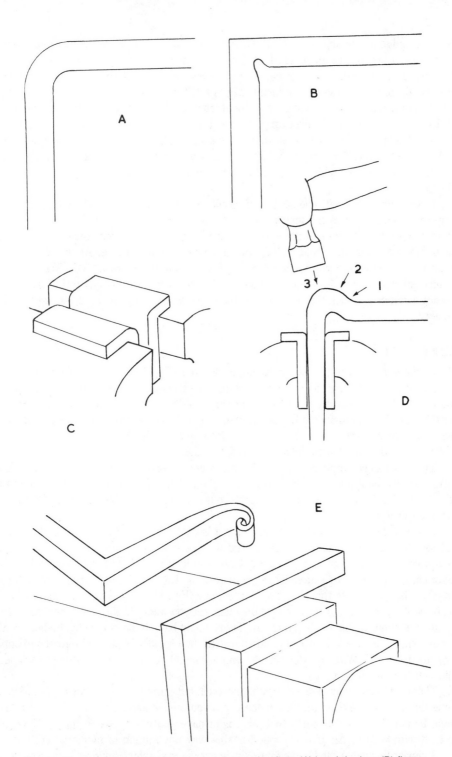

Fig. 11-13. A square angle needs the bend upsetting first: (A) bend the bar; (B) flatten the corner; (C) vise clamps; (D) bend to a loop; (E) hammer the corner square.

Fig. 11-14. The main parts of this decorative feature have been formed with square corners, then tapered to form snub-end scrolls.

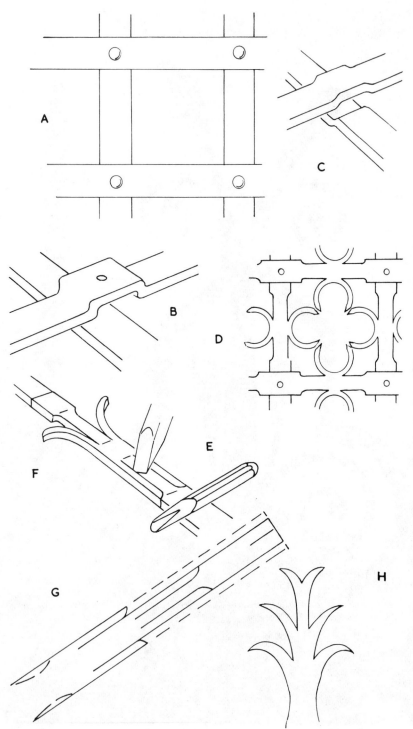

Fig. 11-15. Grill parts are bent over each other (A,B,C) and can be cut to make decorations (D,E,F,G,H).

parts are cut from it like the branches of a tree (Fig. 11-15G). They can be curved outward, then the end split and curved (Fig. 11-15H).

LEAVES

Many decorative touches in wrought-iron work are based on nature. Leaf forms are a popular and effective decoration. The most satisfactory ones are in iron, but mild steel can also be shaped.

If there are several upright round or square rods in a gate (Fig. 11-16), the tops can be finished in a flame shape (Fig. 11-17A). The rod could be drawn out into a flat taper one way only, or the whole rod could be given a round taper. Curving the flame shape is then done over the beak of the anvil with a fuller in a swage, or by pulling to shape with scroll wrench and fork—depending on the thickness (Fig. 11-17B). To look right, the point should finish in line with the straight part of the rod, so that the waves of the flame go to each side of the centerline but come back to it.

For fine detail work on leaves, a blacksmith uses several stakes and other tools that are also used by sheet metalworkers. The smith might also do some work cold on a lead block, using hammers with shaped ends. In some wrought-iron work the leaves are made separately from sheet iron and welded on. Welding thin metal to thick requires skill, because it is very easy to burn away the thin steel or destroy its shape by hammering. Because welding by oxy-acetylene was not available, we have to admire the skill of those medieval smiths.

It is easier to forge a leaf on a bar. This is done by hammering it thin. Some blows can come from the flat hammer peen, but where the leaf has to be spread in all directions, use the ball peen. When it has to be spread more in one direction than the other, the hammer to use is the cross or straight peen (Fig. 11-17C). Have the steel red hot. Be careful not to continue hammering once it has become black because the steel might split or break away at the edges.

Get the outline as near as possible to the shape you want; there will have to be some filing. Mark the veins in the leaf with a veiner, which is like a blunt chisel (Fig. 11-17D). No leaves in nature are absolutely flat, so the steel ones have to be shaped. If possible, have a few actual leaves available to serve as guides. There should be some hollowing in the width, which can be started with a fuller in a swage. There should be some curving in the length, and the edges made wavy. In many cases the shaping can be done with pliers (Fig. 11-17E).

DESIGNING

There are plenty of examples to use as patterns, but the greatest satisfaction comes in producing your own designs. Work full-size on paper first. Main outlines and frames will have to be drawn correctly with pencil and straightedge. When you come to draw the scrolls and other decorative features, use a felt-tip pen or something similar to make bold lines for your flourishes and curves. Single lines will do; there is no need to try to draw the thickness of the steel in these parts. Stand back and look at what you have drawn. When you have a pattern you like, transfer the drawing to a piece of sheet steel so the hot steel parts can be put on it for testing as the work progresses.

Do not be too ambitious at first. For one thing, a large project will require an assistant almost all the time. A small gate or screen would be a good choice (Fig. 11-18). Make

Fig. 11-16. The intermediate uprights have been drawn out to a flat taper and twisted. The main central square upright has been given matching twists.

the main structure first. Check it for squareness. This is best done by comparing diagonals. See that the structure is flat, when it is put down, for the other parts to be made and fitted to it. Make all the decorative parts and their collars and see that they fit in and to each other before finally securing any one part.

Forgework can be combined with cast iron and sheet metal (Figs. 11-19 and 11-20).

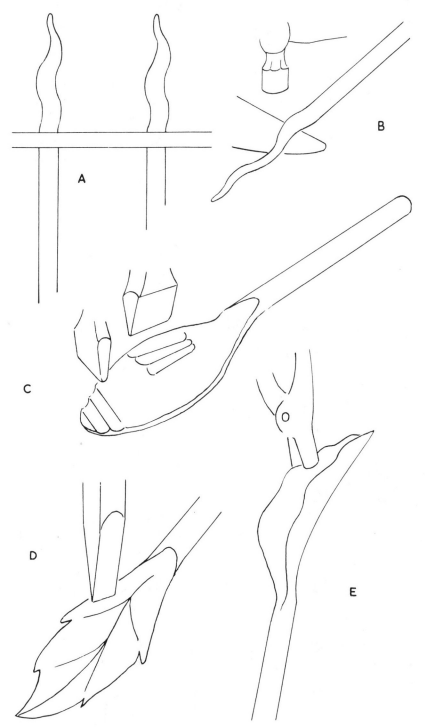

Fig. 11-17. Rail tops can be given a flame shape (A,B). Leaves are made from flattened iron (C,D,E).

Fig. 11-18. Patterns can be sketched and need not be fully detailed.

Fig. 11-19. This gate top uses cast leaves and dragon, along with a painted shield, to enhance the many forged parts that make up the whole design.

Fig. 11-20. Besides cast leaves added to the forged parts, this gate top also has pierced sheet metal decorations.

12

Finishing

If left unprotected, iron will corrode. Moisture from the atmosphere combines with iron to form iron oxide, which is more familiarly known as rust. Because there is moisture in even the driest air, rusting will occur anywhere. However, it will be more pronounced in places with high humidity or near water which is evaporating into the atmosphere. Salt accelerates corrosion, so rust is a particularly severe problem near the coast and on boats.

This applies to all alloys containing iron. Although pure iron corrodes, the comparatively slight first rusting might seal the surface and prevent or delay severe deep rusting. This means that untreated iron might last a long time without suffering severely. Mild steel does not have this characteristic, and if nothing is done to protect it, rust will eat the surface so that the shape is altered, and eventually the material will disintegrate.

There are alloys in which various metals have been combined with iron to minimize corrosion. Some of those form steels with small parts of other metals and carbon to make the steel something like pure iron in its ability to form a thin layer of rust that prevents further corrosion. Other steels have been alloyed to produce so-called stainless steels, which certainly do not corrode in normal circumstances. However, there are some chemicals that will attack them. Unfortunately, making alloys from iron also makes most of these materials unsuitable for forging. If they can be forged, the subsequent heat treatment that is required requires elaborate equipment.

PLATING

Another way to protect an iron surface is to plate it with metal that has a good resistance

248

to corrosion. Zinc or other metal could be used that provides protection without improving appearance much. This is called galvanizing. Nickel or chromium, which produce the bright, glossy appearance on automobile parts, could also be used. However, sometimes the plating can be porous and rust finds its way through. Plating methods are not common to blacksmithing, except in cases where a project might be galvanized by a specialist. It could not be done in the blacksmith's shop.

Any normal product of the blacksmith's shop needs protection. Tools and other things used frequently are prevented from corroding seriously because they are handled and used so often. If they have to be left unused for long, they can be wiped with an oily cloth. Lanolin is a good protectant for tools that have to be stored for a long period.

Polished steel will usually resist corrosion better than the black surface, so a scriber, punch, or chisel that has been brought to a high finish towards the cutting end might rust on the handle part before the smooth part.

The best long-term protection is paint, but if you don't want a painted surface, the simplest treatment is oil or wax or a combination of the two.

REMOVING SCALE

Scale should be removed. Heating to a high temperature will burn off scale, but that is inappropriate for a finished piece of smithing. Knocking the steel against the anvil during the last heating will remove some scale. Any that is left is best removed with a wire brush. This could be a hand powered wire brush. Brushing will have a burnishing effect, but the following treatment with oil or wax will restore an even coloring.

Although scale may be removed mechanically, mainly by wire brushing, there are some areas that are deep and intricately worked, in which scale can remain. If a rust preventative treatment is to be effective, scale also has to be removed. Quenching hot steel in brine loosens and removes much of the scale. For complete removal the project is subjected to pickling in an acid bath.

Of course, all strong acids are dangerous, whether concentrated or diluted. They will attack many things, including their containers. Glazed earthenware makes the best container and it should have a wooden cover. Have an alkali ready to neutralize any acid that gets on clothing, skin, or anywhere else it should not be. Baking soda or ammonium hydrate are suitable, followed by washing with water.

Make up a pickling bath by pouring acid into water. **Caution: Never pour water into acid**. This would cause it to spurt dangerously. An effective pickle is made by adding one part sulfuric acid to ten parts water. Phosphoric acid can be used in the same proportion. Hydrochloric acid in a rather stronger proportion is most effective. A solution of one part sulfuric acid and one part hydrochloric acid to 16 parts water, makes a particularly potent acid bath.

The length of time to leave the steel in any of these baths has to be found by experience. Remove the item and examine it until you see that the scale has gone. Keep your hands away and use tongs, which are washed in water after use. Follow descaling by washing off the acid with plenty of water and treating with the alkali to neutralize any remaining acid, before another wash and drying.

In the simplest protective treatment, rub the steel with a cloth soaked in linseed oil, then return the work to the fire to warm it. The oil will carburize. Remove the warm article and rub it with oil again, then leave to cool. Wipe off excess oil, and the surface should remain free of rust for some time—then the treatment can be repeated. You can do the same with beeswax. Have a block big enough to handle, so you can give a first rub, followed by another on the hot steel.

It is even more effective to combine wax and linseed oil. Proportions are not very critical, but about 6 cubic inches of wax to 1 quart of linseed oil makes a suitable mixture. Warm the linseed oil and flake the wax with a knife. Stir until all wax has melted. Apply this in the same way as suggested for oil alone. It is possible to use almost any oil or wax, so you can experiment and make a corrosion preventative to your own formula.

Steel which has been given the oxide colors used as a guide for tempering high-carbon steel has a better resistance to corrosion than untreated steel. This applies to mild steel—which cannot be tempered, but will still produce the oxide colors—as well as to tool steel. The oxide colors are only visible on a polished surface, so the treatment is only suitable for something that can be made bright and smooth. However, it has possibilities on an uneven surface, such as is produced by hammering all over with a ball peen hammer. The raised parts are wire brushed and made bright with abrasive or by polishing, leaving the hollows black. If a power polisher is used, remove any remaining polishing wax with a solvent and dry the steel.

Hold the article above a flame. It has to heat slightly and slowly where you can see the colors form. A single gas flame is better than a fire. The series of oxide colors will appear and you can stop at the color of your choice. If you wish, a part can be heated differently so the graduated colors are seen. Remove the steel from the flame when you have the color you want. There is no need to quench mild steel in water. Rub it with oil or wax, but do not return it to the fire because that would remove the color. This finish is described as *patination*.

Rust-inhibiting fluids can be obtained from automobile suppliers, and they can be used on steel with no further treatment or as a preliminary to painting. Follow the instructions on the container. In most cases, the fluid neutralizes any rust that is present. It forms a layer of its own corrosion that seals the surface and prevents any further moisture attack.

PAINTING

For outside work, it is best to finish steelwork with paint. This puts on a protective skin that is not everlasting, but it can be renewed as necessary. If it becomes damaged and moisture gets through to the steel, rust will attack and creep from the opening under surrounding paint—particularly if the steel was not originally cleaned and properly primed. Unfortunately, a coat of paint hides some of the texture of your forgework.

Treat steelwork that is to be painted to remove scale and rust, then apply the first coat of paint soon afterward. Rust will attack again if a surface is left unprotected. A small amount of rust attacking in this way can be neutralized by the priming treatment or a coating of a rust-inhibiting fluid. If rust is allowed to continue, it will spread under the paint.

Paint intended for wood and other materials can be used, but it must be applied over a suitable steel primer. Using paint directly on the steel or over a primer intended for wood will result in loose paint that soon comes away. The special steel primer has an etching action that eats into and grips the surface. Follow the manufacturer's instructions, but usually a thin coat has to be left to dry for some time before following with other paint. These primers are in colors that bear no relation to the final paint color. Primer colors are due to their chemical composition. However, the very different color allows you to see that you have a good coverage when you apply further coats of paint.

In general, steelwork does not lend itself to bright colors. If there is no reason for picking a particular color, black is always a good choice because it is close to the natural look of forged steel. For the first treatment, use a matte undercoat over the special primer. If that does not obscure the color of the primer, apply another coat of the same paint before going onto the top coat. A gloss top coat is the most durable because the constituents that provide the gloss also make a tough finish. Be careful not to get an excess of paint anywhere. Paint running into thick blobs in a recess is more likely to come away than paint applied thinly.

Varnish is not a finish to put on steel. Because it is transparent, the surface cannot be primed first, and varnish applied directly to steel would not adhere very well and would soon chip away. Decorative steelwork for use indoors, could be painted black. If you particularly want the texture of the smithing to show through, treating with clear lacquer is a possibility. There are special lacquers made for treating polished silver and gold. They would be suitable, but a cheaper general-purpose clear lacquer should be satisfactory.

SECTION 2

METALWORKING

13

General Metalworking

Through most of the history of civilization the blacksmith was the only metalworker in most communities. In larger towns there might have been specialists like locksmiths, or those who worked precious metals. But in the rural communities, if anyone needed anything in metal, it was the blacksmith who did the work. This meant that the average blacksmith was an adaptable craftsman who could leave his forge and do work at the bench ranging from small locks to large agricultural machinery.

As long as horses provided transport and power, the smith was kept almost fully occupied dealing with horse-drawn vehicles and farm equipment. The smith had a never-ending job as a farrier, keeping the horses shod. The coming of the automobile changed that. As the use of horses diminished, so did the need for the blacksmith's traditional craft. World War I and the demand for war weaponry required general engineers. Also, tractors reached a stage of efficiency and reliability so that they were able to do more than horses. Little traditional blacksmithing was needed to accompany these new advances.

A great many blacksmiths were put out of business in the years following the war. Many blacksmiths found places in industry but the work was quite different. Other smiths kept their hearths and anvils, but broadened their scope to include the maintenance of agricultural equipment or the servicing of automobiles.

It is with this background in mind that modern smiths should approach the craft today. While blacksmithing might be the primary craft, a great many projects that involve smithing, either as the larger part of the work or as a base on which other work develops, call for skills in other branches of metalworking to complete the work in hand. Consequently, any modern blacksmith should also be able to augment his forging by being able to do other work in metal. A project made using a variety of skills can be enjoyable for both the maker and the user.

Much of the metalwork associated with blacksmithing is done with hand tools or portable electric tools. If blacksmithing is the main activity, it is unlikely that heavy metalworking equipment would be necessary. The following chapters deal with the basics—metalworking that can be done with simple equipment, in association with blacksmithing or as an extension of it.

When working hot steel it is impossible to use close measurements; much measuring is done by eye. Herein lies much of the skill in blacksmithing. You can obtain a pleasing and correct shape without the use of many measuring instruments or gauges. The smith sees development of a curve or taper under his hammer and knows that it is right. For many things made by a blacksmith it would not matter if there was an error of ⅛ inch or more from the intended size. However, work on a lock or a clock will need much closer tolerances if it is to serve its purpose. These items have to be checked with such measuring instruments as a micrometer and a vernier. Obviously, some things made by benchwork do not have to be any more accurate than those made at the anvil, but when you are cutting shapes by sawing and filing, the craftsman should always be aware of the precision possible.

METALS

Much work on the bench is done with mild steel; it is the basic constructional metal or alloy. Information on it is given in Chapter 2. For blacksmithing, it is mostly used in bars (rectangular sections) and rods (round sections). Wide lengths up to about ⅛-inch thick are called strip, while larger areas are sheet. Smaller rod that is supplied in coils is wire. In addition to these, there are angles and other preformed sections. It is worthwhile accumulating a stock of mild steel parts from discarded machinery, domestic equipment, and similar things. Providing it is not badly rusted, it can be used again successfully.

When buying steel and other metals of easily measured dimensions, there is no difficulty in quoting sizes in feet and inches (or metric measure). For thin sheets and strips or finer wire, the actual measurements have to be checked with a micrometer and might have to be quoted to three places of decimals of an inch. There have been several schemes for quoting thicknesses by gauge number, to avoid referring to decimal thicknesses. Unfortunately there is no universal standard and you need to know what gauge system is being used to check thickness. Some gauge systems are: American or Browne and Sharpe, Stub's, Birmingham and British Standard Wire Gauge. Some gauges are used for one metal and a different gauge for another. Because of this, it is always wiser to quote actual measured thickness where possible. In all the gauge systems, the lower number indicates the thicker metal. In most systems, 8 gauge is about ⅛ inch while 20 gauge is about 0.035 inch—a useful thickness for light sheet metalwork.

Metals and alloys are often referred to as ferrous or non-ferrous, meaning that they do not contain iron. The stainless and high-carbon steels are the only ferrous metals, in addition to mild steel, that will normally be used. All the other metals are non-ferrous.

COPPER

Copper is soft reddish metal, obtainable in sheet, rod, and bar form. It is often used for electrical work. It can be annealed by heating to redness and left to cool, or by quenching in water. It is then extremely soft and ductile. It hardens with age slightly, but the only way to get it to maximum hardness is to work it, usually by hammering. Copper is mainly used for its decorative qualities and for its good electrical conduction, but it is not strong enough for assemblies that have to take much load.

ZINC

Zinc is unlikely to be used as a metal today. It is grey and can be obtained in sheets. It can be annealed with a little heat, too much will melt it. Boiling water is sufficient. Zinc has a good resistance to corrosion and is used to make a protective coating over steel. Galvanized iron is actually mild steel coated with zinc. Galvanizing leaves a rather rough surface; a smoother finish is obtained by smooth zinc plating.

BRASS

Brass is one of the most popular non-ferrous metals or alloys. It is an alloy of copper and zinc, proportions vary. The type alloyed for good machining qualities cannot satisfactorily be annealed, but the rolled forms of strip, sheet, bar, and rod can be heated to redness and left to cool. Quenching quickly can cause cracks. It does not anneal as soft as copper, but it can be shaped in a similar way and hardened by hammering. Brass has good resistance to corrosion, but in a salty atmosphere the zinc in the alloy could be eaten away, which would allow the metal to disintegrate. Brass will melt at temperatures obtainable at a smith's hearth, so with simple equipment, it is possible to use it for casting.

Another form of brass is sometimes called spelter and is used in brazing. The alloy is melted with a flame and fused to the surfaces being joined. This process can also be called hard soldering, but hard soldering actually uses silver solder, which is a copper/zinc alloy with a little silver added. It requires a lower melting point. The melting temperature can be varied according to the proportions of the alloy. It is possible to make one joint using an alloy of a lower temperature near another without fear of the first joint parting.

TIN

Pure tin is an expensive metal, so it is not used alone. It has been used as a coating for iron and steel sheet to make the tinplate on cans and other things. Tin is a safe metal to use with food and it has a good resistance to corrosion. Before plastics took over, tinplate was used for many kitchen items. A tinsmith was a worker in tinplate, not pure tin.

BRONZE

Tin can be alloyed with copper—much like zinc. The result is similar. The color is usually a rich golden shade, depending on the proportions. In sheet form, it can be shaped into bowls and other things like copper can, but with greater strength. Like brass, it can be annealed with heat and hardened by hammering. That form of copper/tin alloy is called gilding metal. In rod or bar form it is called gunmetal. The old "brass cannons" were actually copper/tin alloys, usually with small quantities of other metals added. Many modern bronze items are basically copper and tin with small quantities of rarer metals included to give special qualities. While still known as bronze, they can be prefixed by the name of an important added metal, such as *phosphor bronze*. Special types of bronze are mostly cast and can be machined, but they are not intended to be bent or otherwise shaped. Most bronze has a very good resistance to corrosion.

LEAD

Lead is the heaviest of the common metals, and many of its uses are connected with its weight. It is an unattractive soft grey metal that is not strong enough to retain much detail. Its melting point is low enough for it to flow at temperatures obtained with a gas flame or fire. Consequently, it can be used for casting, particularly to give stability to something made from a lighter material. Lead alloys easily with many other metals and some, such as antimony, can be used with it to lower the melting point and make a stronger casting. Lead is also alloyed with tin to make soft solder, which is the common joining material in electrical work and other assemblies. The melting point is lower than that of either metal independently: enough heat can be provided by a copper bit, heated electrically or by a flame.

ALUMINUM

Aluminum is very light in weight and silvery white in color. It is easily melted and can be cast with simple equipment. Pure aluminum is soft, although it is possible to specify the degree of relative hardness required. Resistance to corrosion is good and the metal is safe to use with food. Much aluminum available is actually alloyed with other metals to give special qualities, particularly strength and hardness.

Aluminum anneals with heat and can be work-hardened, but the annealing temperature of 350° is much lower than that of other metals. Too much heat will ruin it. One shop method of getting the right annealing temperature is to rub the metal with soap and heat only until the soap turns black. Aluminum is the one common metal that cannot by joined with lead/tin soft solder. There are special aluminum solders, but in general it is better to design aluminum constructions so rivets or other fastenings are used instead of solder.

14

Measuring and Holding

Accuracy of finished work depends on careful marking out, in a way that can be seen and does not allow mistakes to occur due to misreading. Usually, marks are best made with a scriber the smith can make. Its scratched line cannot be accidentally erased. The only place a scriber is not advisable is on a surface that will be polished or that would otherwise be marred by the scratch.

A measurement from an edge is most easily made accurately by using a steel rule with the measurement on the rule over the edge, and the scriber drawn across the end of the rule (Fig. 14-1A). If a series of measurements have to be taken, make them all from one mark rather than from each other. This will reduce the possibility of making an overall error. For instance, a series of marks at 2-inch intervals are better made at 2 inches, 4 inches, 6 inches, and so on from one point, rather than at 2 inches from each other. However, spacing from one to the other could be used as a check.

Dividers are also useful for stepping off equal spacings (Fig. 14-1B). If a length has to be divided into a number of equal parts and it is not a length easy to divide arithmetically, make a series of steps with the dividers at experimental settings until they are right. This will give a perfect result. Locate the exact spots by swinging the dividers to make short arcs across the base line (Fig. 14-1C).

A fine center punch, often called a dot punch, can be used lightly to make a small impression at any point that has to be marked. If the cone of the punch point is no more than ⅛ inch across and the angle a little more acute than the usual 60°, exact location is easy to see and accuracy is ensured. If the same location will also be drilled, enlarge the dot with an ordinary center punch. If a position has to be marked, locate it with crossing

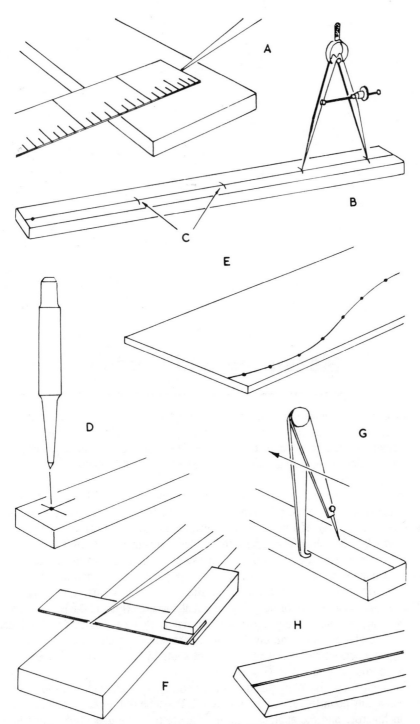

Fig. 14-1. Use a steel rule (A) to measure, step off with dividers (B,C) and mark positions with a center punch (D). Use dots as a guide (E), mark right angles (F), set the calipers (G) and use two lines as a guide (H).

scriber marks and use the dot punch at the crossing (Fig. 14-1D). If a shaped outline has to be followed, a series of light dots is a good guide (Fig. 14-1E). If circles have to be drawn, use the divider, but have a dot punched for the center leg or it might wander.

Mark right angles to an edge with a try square (Fig. 14-1F). Use the try square to check a finished angle. Look toward light, otherwise you might assume that the angle is accurate when it is not.

Odd-leg calipers are marking instruments. The pointed leg is a scriber (Fig. 14-2). If you want to draw a line at a particular distance from an edge, set the caliper and pull it along (Fig. 14-1G). If you want to draw a line along the center of a bar, use the caliper from both edges. If two lines appear, the distance is wrong. Quite often the two lines are a sufficient guide (Fig. 14-1H) for locating a series of center punch dots for screw holes or other instances where utmost precision is unnecessary.

Calipers are tools for comparing measurements. They are particularly useful for round objects, where it might be difficult to use a rule directly in position. The calipers depend on a friction joint or have a screw adjustment similar to the dividers. Outside calipers (Figs. 14-2 and 3A) can be set to span an external measurement, such as the outside of a cylinder. Inside calipers have their ends outward (Fig. 14-3B) and are used for internal measurements. Settings then have to be checked against a rule. However, in many situations the caliper can be checked against the part that has to be fitted, or a check with inside calipers can be tried against the outside calipers.

Accuracy by measuring with a rule or calipers depends on the vision of the user and even on the direction of view. "Errors of parallax" due to looking diagonally, or

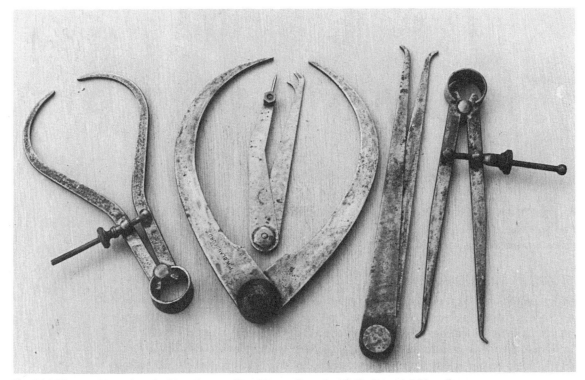

Fig. 14-2. Two outside and two inside calipers, with odd-leg calipers inside the large outside calipers.

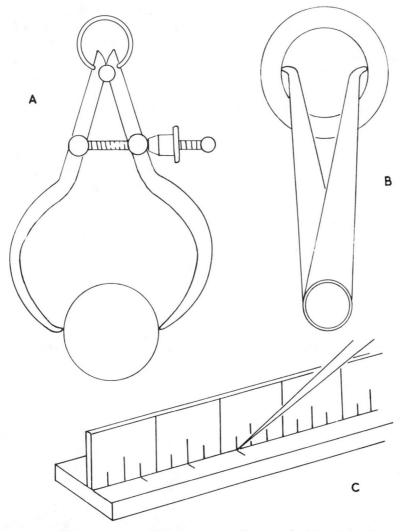

Fig. 14-3. Calipers measure outside (A) or inside (B) curves. Avoid error by using a rule on edge (C).

because of the thickness of the rule, are avoided by having the rule on edge, which brings the calibrations on it as close as possible to the thing being measured (Fig. 14-3C). Some rules are marked as finely as $\frac{1}{100}$ inch, but it is very difficult to read fine graduations.

FRICTION-JOINT CALIPERS

Inside calipers can be reversed for use on external curves, although not to the extent of calipers shaped for outside use. These calipers (Fig. 14-4A) can be used for inside curves up to about 5 inches or outside curves to about 2 inches. They are made of $\frac{1}{16}$-inch steel plate and depend on friction in the pivot to hold them to any set size.

It would be possible to cut the shaped ends, but it is easier to make them straight and forge them to shape. Cut both pieces with straight tips (Fig. 14-4B). Do not cut

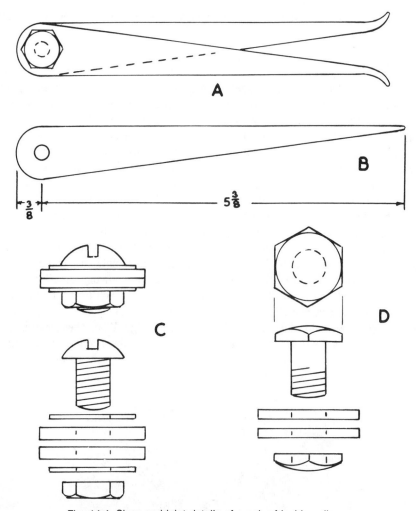

Fig. 14-4. Sizes and joint details of a pair of inside calipers.

to points, but leave a small curve. Bend the ends. The exact curve is unimportant, providing both pieces are the same.

The simplest pivot is made with a ¼-inch screw through washers and with a nut at the far side. A standard nut could be cut thinner for a neat finish (Fig. 14-4C). Allow for the end of the screw projecting slightly through the nut, so it can be riveted lightly to prevent loosening. If you have used flat steel plate there should be sufficient friction between the arms: if you want more, put a thin fiber washer in the joint.

If you have the use of a lathe, a neater joint can be made with screw and nut turned from ½-inch hexagonal bar. Put a clearance hole through one arm, but allow for a thread in the other arm, then the nut outside will act as a locknut (Fig. 14-4D).

Turn the screw with quite a thin domed head and a ¼-inch shank. Turn the nut to match the appearance of the screw head. Thread the screw sufficiently to fit into the lower arm and the nut. When assembling, tighten the screw with a wrench to get the required friction, then tighten the nut to lock it. Bend the tips sideways so they will meet when the calipers are used on an outside curve. They will spring over each other when you change to inside use.

MICROMETER

The engineering tool used for making measurements with greater accuracy than is possible by eye is a micrometer, usually a micrometer caliper. The micrometer caliper works in a 1-inch range and reads to $\frac{1}{1000}$ inch. One tool reads from 0 to 1 inch, another reads from 1 inch to 2 inches, and so on (Fig. 14-5). The caliper is in a form such that the gap is adjusted by turning a screw and the size is read on the barrel enclosing the screw (Fig. 14-6A). The screw is very accurately made and the standard pattern has 40 threads per inch, so if it is turned 40 times it has moved 1 inch, and one turn of $\frac{1}{40}$ of an inch is 0.025 of an inch. An engineer might describe this as "25 thous," meaning 25 thousandths of an inch. If the screw is turned only $\frac{1}{25}$ of a turn, the gap in the caliper will have increased or decreased by $\frac{1}{1000}$ (or 0.001) of an inch.

That is the principle, and calibrations are arranged so these things can be read. The screw is inside a barrel, but its head is in the form of a thimble that travels over the barrel as it is turned (Fig. 14-6B). The barrel has a scale showing a mark at each $\frac{1}{40}$ inch, or each complete turn of the thimble, with a figure at each fourth mark ($\frac{1}{10}$ inch or 0.100 inch), so each mark is 0.025 of an inch (Fig. 14-6C).

The thimble has 25 equally spaced marks around its edge. When the caliper is closed, the one marked 0 is level with the line along the barrel. When the thimble is turned so the next mark is level with the line, the gap is 0.001 of an inch. At one more mark, it is 0.002 of an inch or $\frac{2}{1000}$ of an inch (Fig. 14-6D). That is about the thickness of a hair.

Fig. 14-5. Sliding combined inside and outside calipers and a 1-inch micrometer caliper.

264

As you can see, the actual measurement is not read as a single figure. A simple sum is necessary and it is usually mentally calculated. There are three things to add: the number of figured line exposed (each 0.100 of an inch), the number of unfigured lines beyond that (each 0.025 of an inch) and the number of marks around the thimble edge (each 0.001 of an inch). The example in Fig. 14-6E) can be interpreted as follows:

One numbered turn (tenth)	0.100 inch
Two more unnumbered turns (fortieths)	0.050 inch
Seventeen thimble divisions (thousandths)	0.017 inch
Total	0.167 inch

Other examples can be computed in the same way.

VERNIER

A vernier is a different method of making fine measurements, and it is not limited to 1-inch steps like a micrometer. The principle is used in many instruments, but a common type serves as inside and outside calipers with a sliding head on a calibrated stem (Fig. 14-7A). The ends of the jaws are a known thickness (often 0.25 of an inch), so their total can be added to the reading obtained on the scale when you use the tool as an inside caliper. Outside measurements are read directly.

The marks on a vernier scale are read from one small scale sliding alongside another. Marks that coincide indicate the measurement. A simple vernier to read to hundredths of an inch will show the principle. The main scale along the stem is calibrated in inches and $\frac{1}{10}$ of an inch (Fig. 14-7B). This can be any length. On the sliding jaw there is another scale. When zero on one jaw is against zero on the other scale, the jaws are touching.

The vernier scale on the sliding head is $\frac{9}{10}$ inch long, but is divided into ten equal divisions. Each of these divisions is 0.09 of an inch (Fig. 14-7C). This means that a division on the sliding scale is 0.01 of an inch less than a division on the main scale. It is this fact that allows the particular vernier to be read to $\frac{1}{100}$ of an inch.

If a measurement is to be taken by adjusting the jaws on an object, the reading has to be computed in steps like using a micrometer. The number of whole divisions on the main scale before the zero on the sliding scale each represent 0.10 of an inch. Look along the sliding scale until one mark can be seen to coincide with a mark on the fixed scale. The marks from the zero are in one-hundredths. In Fig. 14-7D:

Five whole marks on the fixed scale	0.50 in.
Seven marks on the vernier scale	0.07 in.
Total	0.57 in.

If the caliper has been opened to more than 1 inch, there would be the number of whole inches to add in as well.

The same principle is used in a vernier to read to thousandths of an inch. The main scale is divided into numbered tenths, then these are divided into four (0.025 of an inch each). The vernier scale is 0.60 of an inch long and divided into 25 parts. Each of these parts is 0.024 of an inch or 0.001 of an inch less than a main division. Like the micrometer and the one-hundredth vernier, tenths are noted. Any fortieths and further thousandths

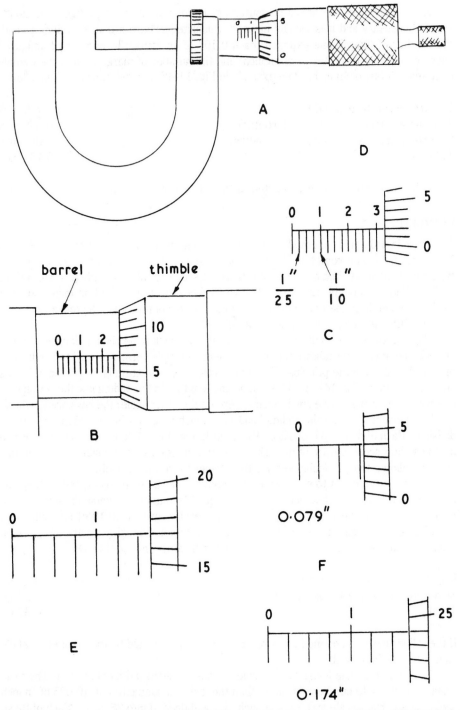

Fig. 14-6. A micrometer has its barrel and thimble calibrated to read to one thousandth of an inch: (A) the gap is adjustable; (B) the thimble travels over the barrel; (C) each numbered mark is 0.100 of an inch; (D) 0.002 of an inch; (E,F,) see text for explanation.

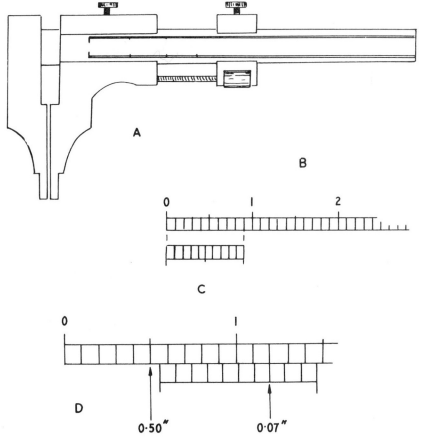

Fig. 14-7. A vernier gauge (A) uses two scales (B,C) sliding against each other. Marks are in one-hundredths (D).

are found by checking along the vernier scale to find marks on it and the main scale which coincide. The number on the sliding scale is the total of single thousandths.

In both cases, the thickness of the jaws must be added for an inside measurement if there is not a second scale for this. Some verniers are calibrated on the other side metrically to read to fiftieths of a millimeter.

VISES

The blacksmith's leg vise can be used for general metalwork. Precision work, particularly over different thickness ranges, is more easily done with a parallel-action machinist's vise. It need not be as large as the leg vise, which can be up to 6 inches or more across the jaws. A parallel-action machinist's vise with 3- or 4-inch jaws will be large enough for most benchwork. This bolts to the top of the bench and should be arranged to overhang enough for the fixed jaw face to come a little further out than the edge of the bench (Fig. 14-8A). Have the bench top thick (as much as 2 inches) and bolt through. Wood screws would soon loosen. A modern machinist's vise will withstand fairly heavy hitting, but if it is to remain accurate it is better to do all hammering on the leg vise.

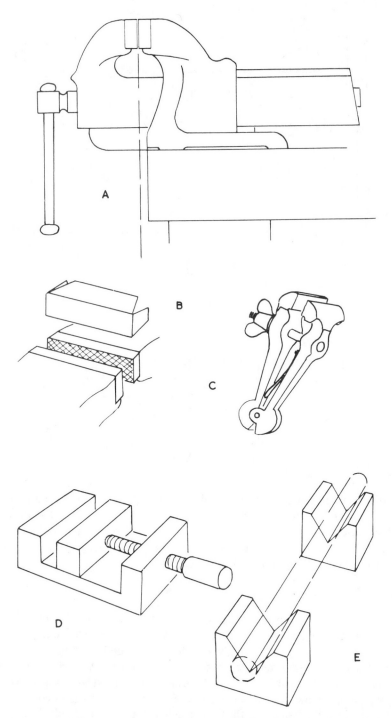

Fig. 14-8. A vise overhangs the edge of a bench (A) and can be fitted with clamps (B). Hand vises; (C) bench vises (D) and V-blocks (E) will hold work for machining.

A machinist's vise has hardened steel jaws with teeth cut in them. Make vise clamps from brass or other soft metal to protect polished metal from the teeth (Fig. 14-8B). Some vises have a quick-release action by pulling a lever to open a split nut.

Hand vises are used for holding small work. The better ones have a parallel action, but the simplest is hinged and works in the same way as the leg vise—with a butterfly nut on a bolt to provide tightening (Fig. 14-8C). Besides gripping small things to file or manipulate in the hand, a hand vise makes a good handle for a piece of metal being held under a drill in a press.

A machine vise can be used for holding work in a drill press, and for other occasions when it is convenient to have metal held on the flat top of the bench or elsewhere (Fig. 14-8D). There are several versions, but all have fixed and moving jaws over a flat base that can bolt down.

A problem arises when dealing with round rods that have to be marked out or drilled. V-blocks (Fig. 14-8E) are made in pairs, and rods can be rested across them. In better types, the sides of the blocks are grooved to take the ends of clamps. The clamps have screws that press down on the rods and hold them in place.

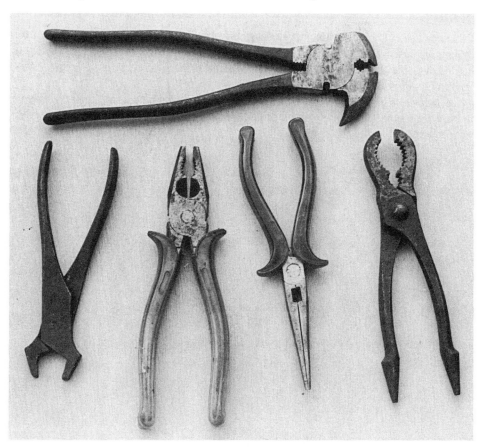

Fig. 14-9. Fencing pliers that combine several functions, nut pliers, common pliers with insulated handles, long-nose pliers, and gas pliers for gripping pipes.

PLIERS

Pliers have regular uses in benchwork. Examination of a tool catalog will show that there is an enormous range of pliers available (Fig. 14-9). Most useful are those with broad flat jaws, that are stout enough not to flex when gripped tightly. These will do many things, from picking up small items to closing folded sheet metal and pushing rivets through holes. Many pliers have cutters in the jaws near the pivots, and there might be wire cutters at the side. Thin-nosed pliers are for getting into awkward places, while round-nosed pliers are useful for twisting loops in wire.

Gas pliers have jaws hollowed across with teeth pointing inward. They are useful for gripping and turning round objects.

Pliers or wrenches that can be adjusted and then locked on with a lever can be used as hand vises as well as pliers.

Sizes of pliers to choose depend on the work to be done. There are some delicate ones for watch repairs, but for the usual benchwork an overall length of about 8 inches should be satisfactory.

CLAMPS

C-clamps used in woodworking have occasional uses in holding metal parts together for drilling or during assembly. A toolmaker's clamp has two jaws and two screws across it. The one near the gripping end pulls in and the other pushes out with a levering action. Such a clamp is commonly used for general woodwork.

Much clamping is done in a vise or by using bolts through holes in the parts. Where there are no holes, two bars can be drilled for bolts and the parts drawn together between them.

15

Cutting and Shaping

If benchwork is being done in the same place as the forge, some pieces can be cut to length on the anvil with the hardie and sets. Most general metalwork cutting and shaping will have to be done to the cold metal on the bench. Work on the anvil using hand tools is inappropriate to most non-ferrous metals in any case.

The basic cutting and shaping tools are saws and files. Thinner metals can be cut with snips and cold chisels.

SAWING

Unlike woodworking saws, metalworking saws have blades that are discarded when blunt or broken. Metalworking saws are not resharpened. Hacksaws are the general-purpose metalworking saws. Blades are usually about ½ inch wide, with teeth on one edge and holes at the ends to engage with pegs in a hacksaw frame (Fig. 15-1A). The teeth are designed to cut on the push stroke and they are set in alternate directions to make a cut wider than the thickness of the blade, so the saw does not bind in a deep cut.

Hacksaw blades are made in several lengths, but for most purposes, 10 or 12 inches work well. Teeth coarseness is described by the number of teeth per inch: 18, 24, and 32 are common. Hacksaw blades are made of high-carbon steel, but makers also supply blades made of alloy steels to give special qualities. Blades made of *high speed* steel indicates a hard, long-wearing steel. However, some of these steels are brittle, and an unintentional twist during sawing could shatter a blade. Better high-speed steel blades have graduated hardness, softening towards the back, which gives flexibility and toughness. Other blades are described as unbreakable or flexible, which should be

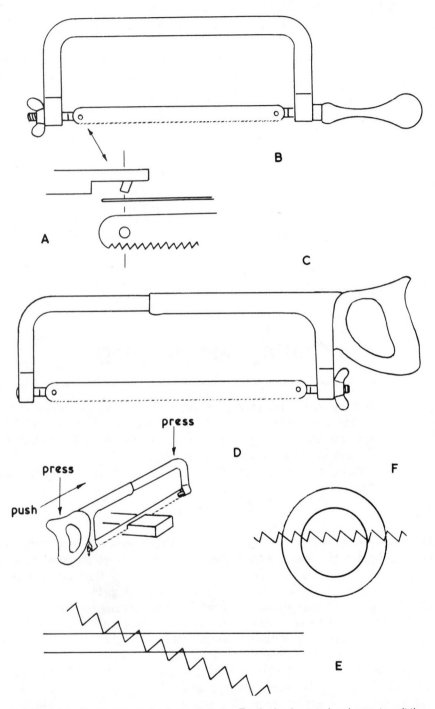

Fig. 15-1. A hacksaw cuts on the forward stroke. Teeth size have to be chosen to suit the work: (A) the peg engages a hacksaw frame; (B) the blade is held by a butterfly nut; (C) piston-grip handle; (D) apply pressure and push; (D) cut at an angle; (F) most tube can be cut with a hacksaw.

regarded as relative terms only. Keep a stock of blades because they do not have a very long life.

The simplest hacksaw frame has a bowed rigid back and a straight handle attached to a rod with a peg. At the other end, the rod is screwed with a butterfly nut to tension the blade (Fig. 15-1B). This is the basic frame and one would not be difficult to make. A straight handle is not the most natural way to control a saw. Most manufacturers produce frames with pistol-grip handles, usually on a frame that can be adjusted in length to accommodate different sizes of blades (Figs. 15-1C and 15-2). Details vary. Usually a butterfly nut at the handle end tensions the blade, and the rods are square sections that turn in any of four positions. The blade can be set across the frame as well as in line with it.

In woodworking, it would be considered wrong to put your second hand on the far end of the saw. But in cutting metal, it is usual to hold the far end of the frame to provide extra control and put on pressure (Figs. 15-1D and 15-3). To position a cut accurately, start by making a small groove with the edge of a file. Metal is best cut with a slow, heavy stroke going the full length of the blade. Keep enough pressure on for the teeth to be always cutting. If they merely slide over the metal, they will quickly blunt. Fast light cuts are not as effective as steady cuts with good pressure. Have enough tension on the blade to keep it taut. It should not flex in use, but pulling it tight could cause breakages.

Coarser teeth should cut faster than fine ones. For general work in cutting fairly thick mild steel, 18 teeth per inch is suitable. The finer teeth are particularly intended

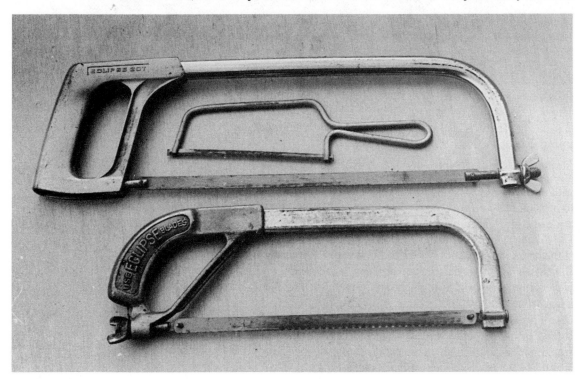

Fig. 15-2. Two type of standard hacksaw frames and a small frame for fine work.

Fig. 15-3. One hand, with the first finger along the handle, controls a hacksaw. The hand at the other end applies pressure.

for thin metal. It is a good rule to try to keep at least three teeth cutting. Obviously, if the metal is so thin that it is less than the spacing between teeth, you cannot cut straight across. One way of dealing with thinner metal is to cut at an angle so more teeth are in use (Fig. 15-1E). Thin-walled tube can be a problem, but 32 teeth per inch will deal with most tubes (Fig. 15-1F).

Turning the blade sideways in the frame allows a long cut parallel with an edge. There are special deep frames made for greater clearance. Handles are available that hold blades with a short end projecting to get into openings. Blades used in this way are less liable to break if arranged to cut on the pull stroke. Some small frames and very fine blades are made for delicate work. A jeweler uses metalworking fretsaws in a sprung frame.

Power sawing has to be done slowly. Many sawing machines are really adaptions of the hacksaw, using a slow reciprocating stroke. Circular saws for metal are uncommon. A bandsaw for metal has to run very slowly in comparison to a woodworking bandsaw. It would not be possible to substitute a metal-cutting blade for a wood-cutting one in a normal machine without making provisions for stepping the speed down considerably. There are abrasive discs that can be mounted in place of a circular saw and used for cutting off metal. They are particularly valuable for cutting off hardened steel, which would not respond to any saw blade. Hardened steel can be held against the edge of a grinding wheel in order to cut notches around it. Then it is snapped off.

SHEARING

Much sheet metal can be cut in the same way scissors cuts cloth. For example, when using a cold chisel across a vise, the vise jaw acts as one shearing blade and the chisel is the other (Figs. 15-4A and 15-5). It is possible to cut through thick, hard metal in this way, and moderate curves can be followed by altering the position of the metal in the vise between cuts.

For thinner and softer metals, it is more common to use snips. They are usually sold as tinner's or tinman's snips. Snips have short blades and long handles to provide leverage. The handles can be straight (Fig. 15-4B) or given eyes like scissors (Fig. 15-4C).

Straight blades will cut large sweeping curves as well as straight lines. For tighter curves, there are snips with curved blades. The best choice, if buying only one pair, is combination snips which are narrow and suitable for curves or straight lines. Overall lengths are from 8 to 13 inches, and there are small versions for delicate work. Some snips are made with alloy steel blades for cutting hard metals and there are others with toggle action for greater leverage.

When using hand shears or snips, both sides of the cut will have to be bent slightly to give clearance for the snips. Tilt the snips slightly. The newly cut edge is often sharp, so be careful you do not cut your hand. One side of the cut—that over the lower blade—will remain true, but the other will buckle slightly. It is possible to get snips hinged opposite ways to allow a choice of which is to be the good edge, but it is usually sufficient to arrange the important part to the left when using the normal right-handed snips.

A bench shearing machine is useful for cutting across large sheets, although it will also deal with smaller work. It is able to cut thicker material than hand snips will, and it can have a hole through the jaws to cut rod. There are several versions, but basically the machine has a straight jaw to the left and a curved jaw to the right to pivot when pressure is applied with a lever (Fig. 15-4D).

For cutting wire and thin rod, many pliers have notches in the side to cut the wire with a squeeze on the handle. In another arrangement, the cutting edges meet, as on top cutters (Fig. 15-4E), where the blades are not far from the pivot point and provide considerable leverage. The cutters extend wider than the body of the tool so wire can pass along the side. Side cutters (Fig. 15-4F) are a similar tool, but with the cut angled. Both types can be used for cutting off the ends of rivets and similar things, as well as for cutting wire.

FILING

After metal has been cut, the edges have to be brought to exact size, which is usually done by filing. A file is to metalwork what a plane is to woodwork. A file is a piece of hardened steel with grooves cut in it so as to raise cutting edges. If it has a set of single cuts, the tool is called a mill file. It is more usual for a second set of cuts to cross the first, so the intersections form teeth instead of broad cutting edges. If teeth are raised individually, the tool is a rasp and not a file. Rasps are used on wood and horses' hooves, and are unsuitable for metal.

The length quoted as the size of a file excludes the tapered tang that goes into a handle. There are a great many sizes of files, and most types range from 4 inches up to 18 inches or more. For general use 10 inches is a good choice.

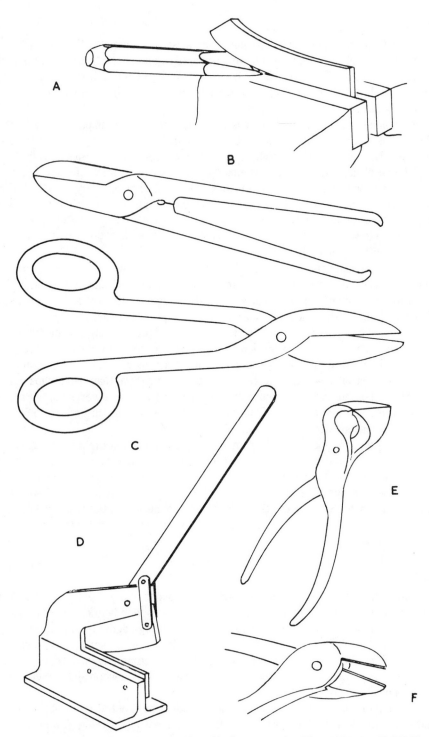

Fig. 15-4. Sheet metal can be cut with a chisel across a vise (A) or with snips (B,C,E,F) or shears (D).

Fig. 15-5. Sheet metal can be sheared across vise jaws with a cold chisel.

Files are given different *cuts*, meaning coarseness of teeth. From coarse to fine the cuts are: rough, bastard, second, smooth, and dead smooth. However, files are often only available as bastard and smooth, and these serve most purposes. "Cut" is relative to length. For instance, a bastard 12-inch file is actually much coarser than a bastard 6-inch file.

Most files have at least one flat surface, but if you ask for a flat file, it will have two flat surfaces and be tapered in the width (Fig. 15-6A). If you want a parallel flat file, it is called a *hand file* (Fig. 15-6B).

A half-round file has flat and curved surfaces, but the curve is not exactly a half circle in section as the name indicates (Fig. 15-6C). A round file is parallel for much of its length, but tapers towards the point (Fig. 15-6D). There is only one diameter to each length. A small round file is called a *rat tail* file.

A file with a triangular cross-section is called a *three-square* file (Fig. 15-6E). Square files taper towards the point (Fig. 15-6F). Flat and hand files will have teeth on all four faces or one edge will be a smooth "safe edge." This is useful when working into corners and it is necessary to avoid cutting into the adjoining surface.

Single-cut mill files can be in hand or flat shapes. One type is made like a hand file, with rounded edges for sharpening certain wood saw teeth. Another single-cut file for a similar purpose has a tapered cross-section. A round file without a taper is used for saw sharpening. For woodwork hand saws, there are single-cut, three-square files in several sizes. One type is double-ended to reverse in its handle. Files of this type are also suitable for sharpening high-carbon steel tools that have been tempered soft enough for filing, such as woodworking drill bits. The single-cut file leaves a better cutting edge than would a double-cut file.

Warding files are small thin files the same shape as the hand file. They get their name because they are used to cut the wards of locks and keys, but they are useful for any filing in a narrow space.

Smaller files are called *Swiss pattern* or *needle files*. They are about 6 inches long with round ends that can be used as handles. Shapes follow the same patterns as larger files, with a few special sections. They are available in sets and are intended for watchmakers and other fine metalworkers, but are also useful for small cuts in general work.

Files tend to clog in use. This can be reduced by rubbing the cutting surface with talc (French chalk). There are occasions when the space between teeth will have to be cleared. This is best done with a wire brush that can be bought by length and nailed to wood, or bought already on a handle (Fig. 15-6G).

Like using a hacksaw, filing is most efficiently done with long slow strokes, using plenty of pressure. The teeth will soon blunt if allowed to slide across the metal without cutting. In all but the shortest files, one hand goes on the handle and the other is closed around the other end. Because the middle of the file gets worn first, teeth are better at the ends.

It does not matter if a saw rocks as it goes across, but usually when filing the intention is to get a flat surface. It is very easy to dip the file at each end of a stroke so that the surface becomes rounded. Spread your feet out and always stand so that your weight is on your feet, so you are not supporting part of your weight against the bench. Use your arms from the shoulders as well as the elbows. You will then acquire a rhythm

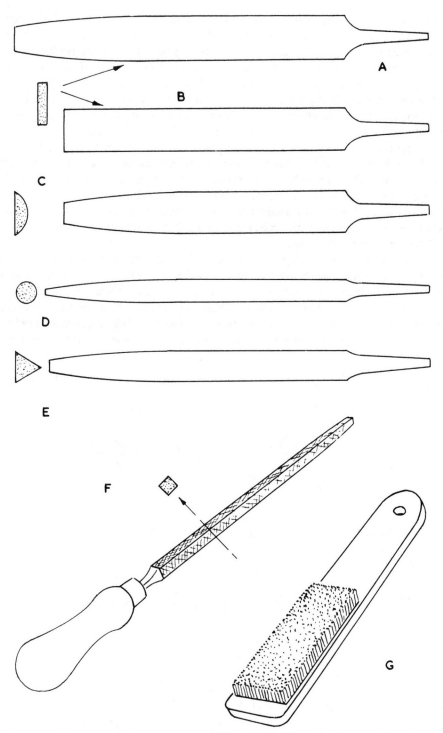

Fig. 15-6. Files are made in many sections (A,B,C,D,E,F) and can be cleaned with a wire brush (G).

that involves swaying slightly on your legs as your arms direct the file. With a little practice the file will follow a level path. Although a file only cuts on the forward stroke, slide it back over the surface. Lifting between strokes would destroy the rhythm.

If a long edge has to be filed, support it fairly low in the vise. If much is allowed to project, even a thick piece will judder or vibrate and leave a series of jump marks on the filed surface. It might be necessary to file straight across some parts, but the work is easier and more effective if the file is held diagonally and taken across so the cutting surface goes along as well as across the edge (Fig. 15-7A).

Filing in this way leaves marks diagonally across in a size that matches the cut of the file teeth. If a bastard file has been used to remove metal quickly, it should be followed by a file with a smooth cut—preferably at a different angle to the first strokes to achieve a smoother surface. There is another way of getting an even smoother surface by *draw filing*. Hold the file straight across the metal edge with a hand at each end and move it sideways along the edge (Fig. 15-7B). Using a smooth file in this way leaves very fine lines along the edge.

If there is a turned-over edge, it can be rubbed off with the tip of a file. If further smoothing is needed, use abrasive paper wrapped around a flat piece of metal or wood. The traditional abrasive for metal is emery, but there are other abrasives just as suitable.

Double-cut files serve for nearly all metals. For hard steel, as in saw sharpening, single-cut mill files work better. Lead and other soft metals and alloys quickly clog ordinary files. Single-cut files with coarse teeth in curves across the face are made for use on lead.

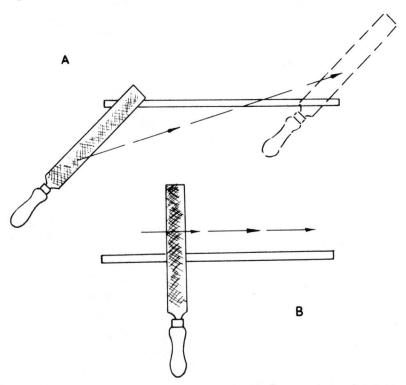

Fig. 15-7. The full file should be used along an edge (A). The edge is then finished by draw filing (B).

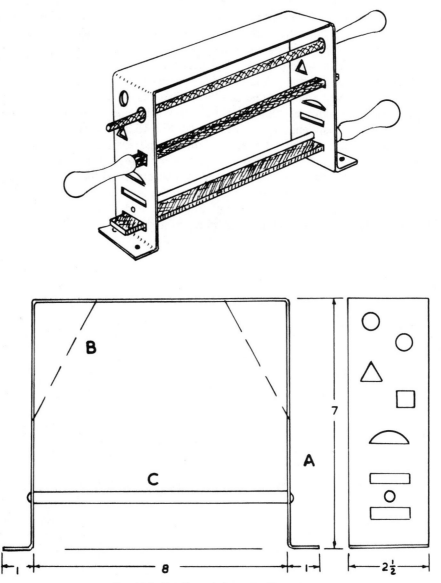

Fig. 15-8. Details and sizes of a file rack.

File Rack

If files are tossed together in a box or drawer they will soon blunt each other. It is better to put them in a rack. Several types are possible, including slotted shelves on a wall, but the rack in Fig. 15-8 is intended to stand on a bench and keep the commonly used files within reach. If you are new to filing, making the rack gives you practice in using various files. The sizes shown (Fig. 15-8A) suit 10-inch files, but you could include some shorter ones by making the top narrower (Fig. 15-8B). Sizes will depend on your files, so the arrangement should be spaced out to allow for them. You can enter files from opposite ends so the handles do not interfere with a compact arrangement.

The rack is mild steel sheet. For the arrangement shown, this could be 12-gauge or up to ⅛ inch thick. Cut a piece 24 inches long and 2½ inches wide. Mark on it the bend lines. Mark the file sections on what will be the opposite ends. Allow plenty of clearance, so the files can be pushed in and out easily.

Drill away much of the waste. A series of holes close together can be chopped through with a cold chisel, then a file entered and the outline shaped.

There might be sufficient stiffness in the rack if it is screwed to the bench or to a block of wood, but a stiffening rod could be used (Fig. 15-8C). This could be ⁵⁄₁₆-inch diameter with its ends shouldered to ³⁄₁₆ inch for riveting. Drill for it, probably above the bottom file position. Also drill holes in the feet for screwing down.

When you are satisfied with the holes and file sockets, bend the strip squarely on the bend lines. Check that it stands correctly with the ends upright.

Measure the length of the stiffening rod. Reduce its ends to fit the holes, allowing enough length to go through for the ends to be riveted.

Fasten the rack down with roundhead woodscrews.

16

Drilling and Screwing

Throughout the time that man has worked metals, he has mastered most techniques. However, for a long time, the weakest technique was making holes, particularly in the harder metals. The blacksmith punched holes and worked them to shape with drifts, but they lacked the precision that would give an exact fit on a cylindrical rod as required for an axle running in a bearing. The alternative, until comparatively recent times, was to use a flat drill that cut mainly by a scraping action and that required considerable force to get it through metal of any thickness.

Flat drills can be made with simple equipment. That is an advantage, since they can be made to special sizes. However, the only use for flat drills in a modern shop is for countersinking. To make a flat drill, flatten the end of the rod of high-carbon steel. See that the flattened part is central with the rod and thick enough to provide strength. It should be about ⅛ inch for drills that are ½ to 1 inch in diameter. It is proportionally less for smaller ones. Grind the two faces and the two cutting edges (Fig. 16-1A). The point where the cutting edges meet must be central. Rotate the rod to see if this is so, and regrind until it is right. Not only must this be central, but the cutting edges must be at the same angle to the centerline of the rod. For countersinking, the included angle is usually 60°. However, it could be between 60° and 90° (Fig. 16-1B).

Although the cutting edges could continue to the outside, the edges should be ground parallel if the drill is to be a particular size (Fig. 16-1C). This gives a better appearance to a countersink drill. Leave the grinding of the cutting angle to last. For brass, this should be about 12° (Fig. 16-1D). The scraping action produced by the vertical leading edge works well on brass, but on steel and most other metals there should be some

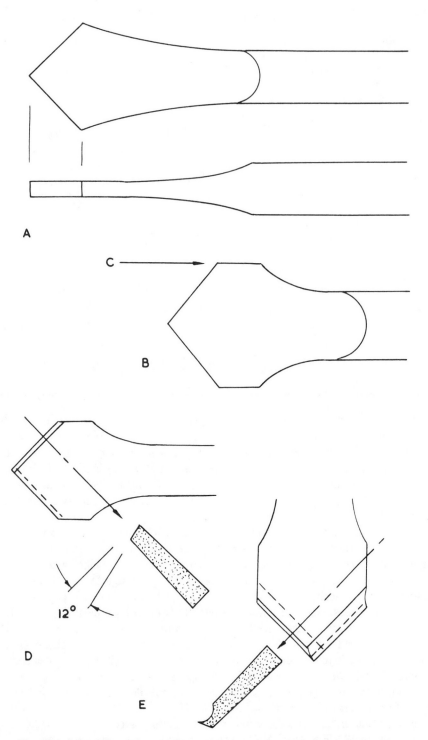

Fig. 16-1. A flat drill cuts by scraping and can be given a better angle by grooving: (A,B,C) grind the cutting edges to angle; (D) use this angle for brass; (E) grind a groove.

relief on the front. This can be made by grinding a groove across the edge (Fig. 16-1E). Harden and temper the end.

TWIST DRILLS

The flat drill was followed by a straight-fluted type, usually with three flutes to prevent the tendency to drill slightly eccentrically when cutting edges are opposite. Otherwise the cutting action was the same as a flat drill. Improvements came when Henry Morse twisted the flutes to make what has become the universally used twist drill. For nearly all drilling of metal, twist drills are the choice. Twist drills are made in all the sizes. In the smaller sizes, there are drills that differ only by thousandths of an inch. Sizes go up to much larger than would be needed in a small shop.

A twist drill has two cutting edges from which the flutes twist back to carry away the swarf (metal cuttings). The outside of the drill is parallel so that it is guided to cut straight when drilling deeply (Fig. 16-2).

The important part is the cutting end. This has to be ground to angles that combine to make the drill cut (Fig. 16-3A). A new drill comes correctly ground, but when it becomes blunt it has to be ground on an abrasive wheel. With the larger sizes, it is fairly easy to see the existing angles and hold the drill to keep them. However, with small drills there will be some chance involved in freehand grinding. There are drill grinding

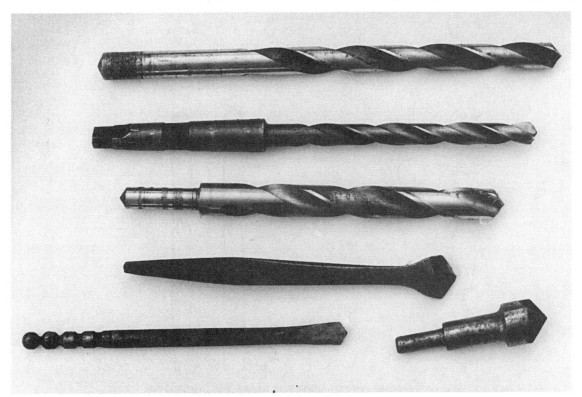

Fig. 16-2. A parallel twist drill, one with a Morse taper end and one with its end reduced, a flat countersink drill to fit a brace, a smaller flat drill and a power countersink bit.

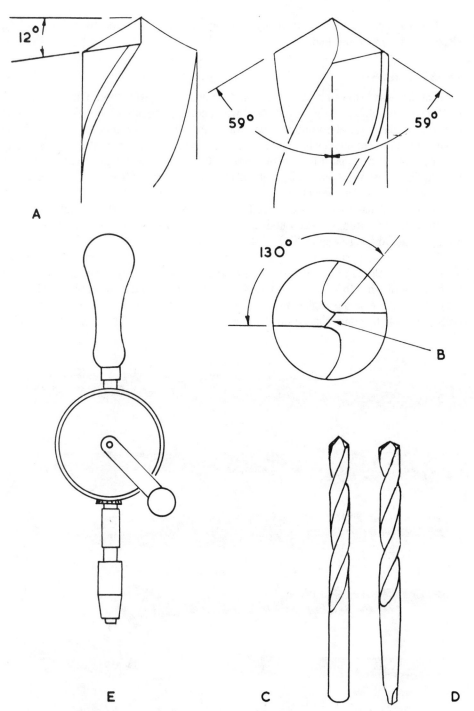

Fig. 16-3. A twist drill has to be sharpened correctly. Small sizes can be used in a hand drill: (A) cut; (B) center must be thick; (C) parallel shanks; (D) tapered shanks; (E) wheel brace.

jigs to hold the drill correctly against the stone, but most of these cannot take the smallest sizes. As with flat drills, it is important to keep the point in the middle and the cutting edges the same length and angle. Otherwise, the longer or leading edge does most of the work and the hole might finish slightly oversize.

The center of the drill must have a thickness in its web (Fig. 16-3B) to provide strength. This does not cut. With plenty of power to provide thrust, the center can be forced through. For limited power or hand drilling, it is better to put through a pilot drill to make a small hole to give clearance for the non-cutting web. A hole ⅜ inch or more in diameter could be started with a ⅛-inch drill. The flutes in any drill taper, therefore the web is thicker further from the point. If a drill is broken and resharpened further back, the thicker web at the point will be visible, and it is even more important to use a pilot drill for this. Such a resharpened broken drill might be better kept for use as a countersink.

Most drills today have parallel shanks (Fig. 16-3C) and are gripped with a three-jaw chuck. Other drills have tapered shanks (Fig. 16-3D) to fit special sockets and are used more in industry. Drills can also be obtained with square shanks to fit a carpenter's brace. Drills are of ordinary high-carbon steel or high-speed steel. High-speed steel keeps its edge much longer and is a better choice for power drilling. Lengths are standard, getting progressively greater as diameters increase.

HAND DRILL

Not much hand drilling is done today, although it has the advantage of preventing a small drill from going too far. The slow speed of hand work makes a countersink drill cut better. A carpenter's brace can be used with a countersink bit. For other hand drilling, there is a drill that is sometimes called a *wheel brace* (Fig. 16-3E). It can hold drills up to ¼ inch—or larger if it is designed with a handle to lean against and provide pressure.

It is better for most purposes to have an electric drill, preferably with a capacity to at least ⅜ inch and with speed variations. This can be used freehand. For accuracy, particularly in keeping a hole at right angles to a surface, mount the electric hand drill in a stand or use a stronger drill press.

Fortunately, drills are fairly tolerant of differences in speed. The work is more efficient if the speed can be adjusted to suit the diameter. It is the peripheral speed that counts. A point on the circumference of a large-diameter drill travels much further in one revolution than a point on a small drill, so the revolutions of the large drill should be less than those of the small one. A three-speed drill gives enough range, so drills near the chuck capacity should be driven at the slowest speed, small drills at the high speed, and others at the intermediate speed. Because the speed of an electric drill varies with the load, actual cutting speeds are usually lower than that indicated by the electric drill maker. Using too low a speed is better than too high a speed. With experience you will know when a drill is cutting at its optimum speed. As an approximate guide, a ½-inch high-speed steel drill in mild steel should revolve at about 500 rpm, and a ⅛-inch drill should revolve at 2000 rpm.

Drills are started with a center punch dot. Make sure this is large enough to take the non-cutting web of the drill, so that the point stays on the starting point and does not wander before it enters. Sheet metal should be supported, either on another piece of metal or a piece of hard wood. It is unwise to hold metal being drilled by hand. If precision is important, it would be better to hold the work in a bench vise or V-blocks, or in another appropriate manner. If it is something that can be held by hand, use a hand vise or the type of pliers that lock on. When a drill breaks through the far side of the metal it can snatch and jerk lightly held metal from your hand. The point of snatch also shows if the drill chuck has not been tightened sufficiently because the drill grips the metal and slips in the chuck. The chuck jaws will then damage the drill so that it will be difficult to mount accurately another time. Use the chuck key tightly. If there are several positions for it, use it in each to get maximum grip.

Drilling generates heat. If the drill is allowed to get too hot, its temper will be drawn and it becomes useless. There is no satisfactory way of heat-treating high-speed steel drills in a small shop. To keep the temperature down, accompany any drilling more than the occasional hole by lubrication. In production work special soluble oils are usually running continuously on the drill, but in a small shop a brush could be used to apply a little at a time from a container. Soapy water is also suitable for mild steel. Cast iron cuts without generating enough heat to matter. Kerosene can be used on brass and aluminum. Light lubricating oil can be squirted on from an oil can for occasional drilling.

SCREW THREADS

The principle of the screw thread has been known for a very long time. Archimedes in ancient Greece knew all about it. The practical problems associated with cutting internal and external screw threads to match prevented widespread use of nuts and bolts until quite recent times. Blacksmiths and engineers of only a century ago avoided screw threads if they could. If they had to make them, a nut would only fit the bolt it was made for. The Industrial Revolution brought standardization and the quantity production of screw threads became possible. Unfortunately, the users of screw threads never agreed on common standards. Today there is more of a standard, but there are still exceptions. Obviously, metric threads differ from those based on inches. Bicycle parts, for instance, are still made with different threads than other things.

Most thread forms are triangular, but these do not all have the same angles. There are other forms, mainly in larger sizes. For general use, triangular threads suit most purposes and screwing tackle is available to cut them. Threads are mostly known by diameter and a number indicating threads per inch. The diameter is that of the rod on which an external thread is cut. A thread described as $\frac{1}{4} \times 20$ means one cut on a $\frac{1}{4}$-inch rod with 20 threads in 1 inch of length. The hole in which a matching thread would be cut would have to start smaller (Fig. 16-4A). This is the tapping size. For the $\frac{1}{4}$-inch thread, the tapping size in most metals should be $\frac{13}{64}$ inch. It might have to be slightly larger in hard steel, and could be slightly smaller in softer metals. A table is usually provided with screwing tackle, indicating the size drill to use.

DIES

Screw threads on rod or bolts are cut with a die. At one time dies were in two parts, but now the common type is solid (Fig. 16-4B). There is a screw thread through a central hole and three or four holes that break into it provide cutting edges. The threaded part is ground away to provide a tapered entry for the rod to be screwed. The die is turned with a wrench, called a die stock. A round die is fitted in and prevented from turning with pegs or screws (Fig. 16-4C). Alternatively, the die has a hexagonal shape and the

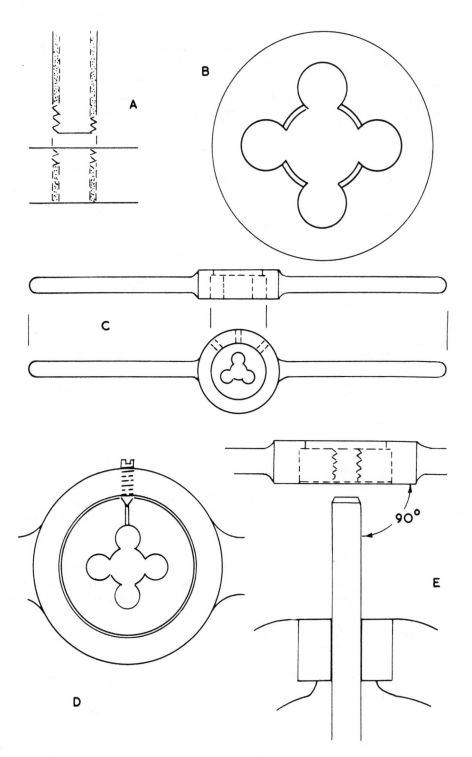

Fig. 16-4. Examples of screw threads.

stock has a matching recess. That type of die can be turned with a wrench-like nut for cleaning damaged threads or getting into places where there is no space for the stock. A split die gives limited adjustment (Fig. 16-4D). A pointed screw into the split can expand the dies slightly so a finished thread can be tighter in its nut.

Put the die in the stock with the tapered part of the thread outward. It helps to bevel around the end of the rod to help it enter the die. Have the rod pointing upward in the vise. Start the die on it with firm downward pressure and see that it is square with the rod (Fig. 16-4E). Turn the stock with both hands so the die screws onto the rod. Be careful not to wobble or threads at the end will break. Once you see the die is true, screw it down with a turning action and little pressure.

The die will remove particles of metal from the rod. With some metals, particles will clear easily. With others, a backward move occasionally will free the swarf. Use thin lubricating oil on a steel rod.

Cutting and shaping a thread is partly done by the cutting edges of the die, but there is also some squeezing by the shape of the threads in the die. Not all metals will take clean threads. Copper rod is difficult to screw because parts of the thread may break away. If a die is adjustable, spring it open for the first cuts, then reduce it for final cuts.

TAPS

Threads in holes are made with taps. A tap is a screwed rod with grooves along it to produce cutting edges (Fig. 16-5A). The end of the rod is square and fits into a tap wrench. The simplest wrench is a bar with a square hole in it (Fig. 16-5B). Others have two sliding parts to take many sizes (Fig. 16-5C). For small taps, there are wrenches with chucks (Fig. 16-5D).

Taps are classified by diameter and the number of threads per inch. They are made to suit many screw systems. The diameter refers to the outside threads, not the diameter of the hole. In each size a full set consists of three taps. A taper tap is ground so that the tip is small enough to go into a tapping hole, and there are only about two full threads at the top (Fig. 16-5E). A second tap has much less taper (Fig. 16-5F), while a bottom or plug tap has full threads to the end (Fig. 16-5G). There is some confusion because a tap with only a short taper on the end (second tap) can be sold as a plug tap.

Precautions must be taken when starting dies. Be certain to have the tap square to the surface and in line with the hole. Then start it with a firm pressure until it is obviously cutting into the metal. Lubricate if necessary and turn back to clear swarf occasionally.

If it is thin metal that is being tapped and there is not more than two or three threads in the thickness, running the taper tap fully in might be all that is needed. If the hole is deeper, follow the taper tap by the second tap. If that does not cut full threads all the way through, it has to be followed by the bottom tap.

The main use for a bottom tap is to cut a thread in a *blind hole*. A blind hole is one that does not go completely through. Although it would be possible to cut a thread absolutely to the bottom, swarf would have to be removed frequently and there would be a risk of the tap becoming seized in the hole. Consequently, it is common practice to drill deeper than necessary so you are certain that full threads go further than the end of the bolt will have to reach (Fig. 16-5H). A bottom tap is still used as the final stage, but it need not go to the bottom of the hole. If some swarf remains, it will not matter.

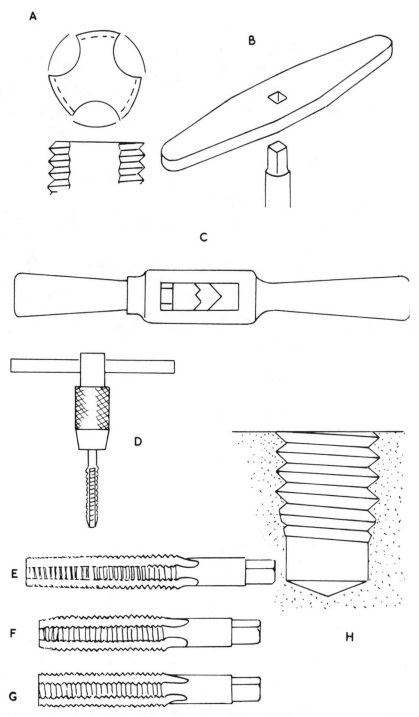

Fig. 16-5. A tap wrench is used to cut an internal thread: (A) grooves produce cutting edges; (B) a bar with a square hole; (C) sliding parts take many sizes; (D) wrench with a chuck; (E) a taper tap; (F) a tap with less taper; (G) plug tap.

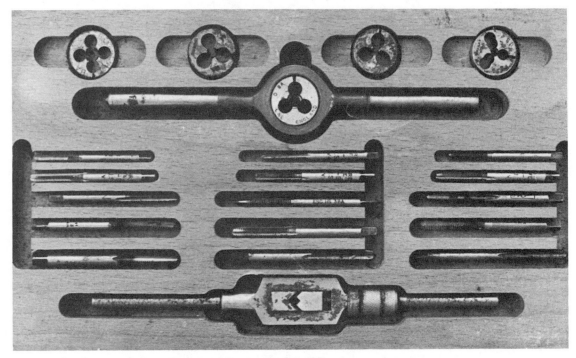

Fig. 16-6. Small taps and dies, with their stocks, in a fitted box.

In practice, there is rarely a need for all three taps in each size. Much can be done using the second tap. It can be started in a hole without the taper tap preceding it, and if a blind hole is made extra deep it will cut a thread far enough. Many sets of screwing equipment only include one tap of each size.

The general-purpose threads are fairly coarse. For greater precision in machinery, it is better to use a finer thread. For instance, instead of ¼ inch × 20 there is ¼ inch × 28 threads per inch. Another use for fine threads is in pipe work. A screw thread cut deeply into the wall of a tube might weaken it too much, but pipe threads are smaller and therefore shallower.

All normal screw threads are right-handed. They tighten when turned clockwise. Taps and dies to cut left-hand threads are available. If the action of a part would tend to loosen a right-hand thread, it can be made left-handed.

Sets of taps and dies are usually stored in their own compartmented box so they cannot be blunted by rubbing together (Fig. 16-6).

CLAMPS

Clamps of many types and sizes have uses in smithing and general metalwork. The type with parallel action will hold together parts being drilled or otherwise worked on. This is also an interesting project as an introduction to screwing techniques. The example (Fig. 16-7) has jaws 4 inches long, but the same methods could be used for clamps of other sizes. In use, the screw nearer the gripping ends pulls the jaws together. When fitting closely the other screw is tightened to push outwards and lever the ends tight.

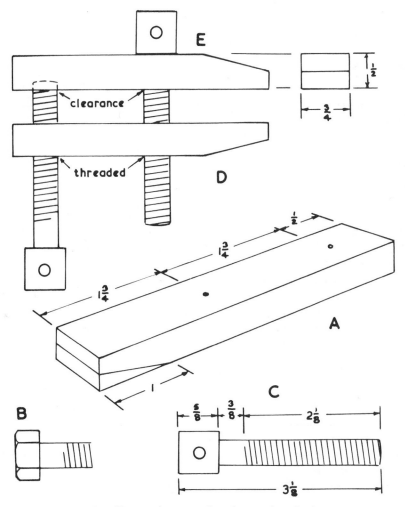

Fig. 16-7. Sizes and construction of an engineer's clamp.

Use parallel mild steel bar ½ × ¾ inch and mark out two matching jaws (Fig. 16-7A). Taper the gripping ends to half thickness, if you wish.

The two screws may be made from standard ⅜-inch bolts or screws with hexagonal heads (Fig. 16-7B), although if you have the use of a lathe they can be turned from ⅝-inch mild steel rod (Fig. 16-7C). Drill across the round heads so a ³⁄₁₆-inch rod can be used as a lever. This might be a loose piece, or you could fit 2½-inch lengths permanently in the heads.

Thread the screws to within ⅜ inch of the heads. It does not matter whether you choose a coarse or fine thread. A fine thread should give a more precise adjustment, but the difference is slight. Drill tapping size holes squarely through one jaw (Fig. 16-7D) and cut threads in them, then check the action of the screws.

In the other jaw, drill a clearance hole through at the position near the gripping end (Fig. 16-7E). At the other point, drill in ⅛-inch to provide a locating position for the end of that screw.

Assemble the parts, with oil in the threaded positions, and try the clamp action. With the sizes given, capacity is about 1½ inches.

NUTS AND BOLTS

There is no need for a mechanic to make standard nuts and bolts and other screwed parts, because they are available as stock items. However, you might want to screw special parts or lengthen threads on standard parts. Modern production is such that standards are close enough for a screwed part made in one place to fit the same made in another. This applies to other sizes, such as heads and the outside of nuts. Wrenches and other equipment for dealing with nuts and bolts have become standardized. Because there are still several standards in use, a mechanic needs to have a large number of wrenches.

It is correct to refer to a bolt only if it is threaded part of its length (Fig. 16-8A). It is called a machine screw if it is threaded to the head (Fig. 16-8B). Nuts and bolt heads intended to be turned with a wrench are square or hexagonal (Fig. 16-8C). If a head has a screwdriver slot, it is flat when countersunk level with the surface (Fig. 16-8D), round if it is curved above the surface (Fig. 16-8E) and oval if it is slightly domed above a countersunk part (Fig. 16-8F). If the head stands above the surface cylindrically, it is a fillister or cheese bolt (Fig. 16-8G). Carriage bolts (Fig. 16-8H) are intended for use with wood and have a square neck under the head to grip the wood. Stove bolts are long, thin bolts with screwdriver heads.

Nuts can be square or hexagonal. They match the size of heads of the same bolts, but are usually thicker. Locknuts are thinner. Their purpose is to stop the main nut from vibrating loose and they are often seen on top of the main nut. However, the correct place is underneath (Fig. 16-9A). After tightening down, two wrenches are used. One holds the top nut and the other is used to tighten the locknut underneath back against it.

There are many nuts that include something to provide stiffness and prevent loosening. It can be fiber or a distorted sprung thread in a raised part above the nut (Fig. 16-9B). Another way of locking nuts is to use an adhesive, which can be of an epoxy type. This prevents accidental loosening, but a wrench will still turn the nut.

Washers are put under nuts or bolt heads to spread the pressure. They can also be used for locking. One type has meeting ends sprung opposite ways (Fig. 16-9C) so they dig into the surface and the nut. Tab washers are used on machinery. One tab goes over an edge or into a hole, while the other is turned up a flat surface of the nut (Fig. 16-9D).

Castellated nuts are not so common now, but they are a positive way of locking a nut. They are used with a split pin (cotter pin) through a hole drilled in the bolt (Fig. 16-9E). This is a useful way of locking a nut to a bolt when there are moving parts being held and a nut locked by other means might loosen. Withdrawing the pin allows disassembly.

WRENCHES

As with nuts and bolts, there has been some standardization of wrenches. Experience has shown what length is most suitable for particular sizes. A reasonable length is needed to provide enough leverage, but too much might shear off a bolt or strip a thread. Too short a wrench might not get the nut tight enough.

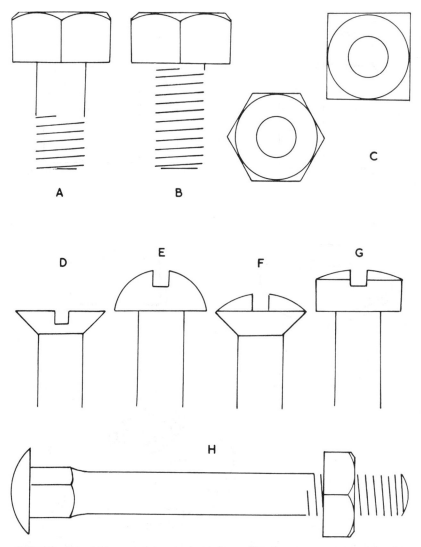

Fig. 16-8. Bolts and nuts can be square or hexagonal (A,B,C) and screws can have various heads (D,E,F,G) intended for use with a screwdriver. A coach bolt has a square neck to pull into wood (H).

The blacksmith who made individually matching nuts and bolts usually made an open-ended wrench to suit. This is still the common pattern of wrench: usually double-ended, either two sizes or the same size at different angles (Fig. 16-10A). When there is limited space to move a wrench, it helps to have the end set at an angle. If this is 15° and used on a hexagonal nut, the wrench can be moved as far as possible. Then it is turned over and moved again (Fig. 16-10B). By the time that move has been made, there should be another pair of faces ready to be gripped.

Where the wrench can be slipped over the bolt head or nut, a ring wrench (Fig. 16-10C) grips across the corners of a hexagon. Combination wrenches with one end open and the other a ring for the same size are worth having.

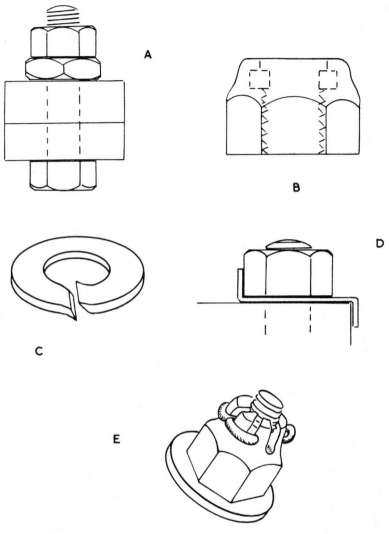

Fig. 16-9. A nut can be locked with another nut (A), with friction material (B), a spring washer (C), a tab washer (D), or a split pin (E).

Tubular or box wrenches (Fig. 16-10D) fit over a bolt head or nut completely, so there is little risk of slipping. They can be long to reach awkward situations.

For most work with nuts and bolts, the modern alternative to separate wrenches for a great many applications is a socket set. This is a boxed outfit containing sockets that are like closed versions of ring wrenches on square extensions. The square extension fits a variety of levers and turning devices, including a lever with ratchet that turns either way, a brace-action handle, extensions, and a universal joint. The square part is standard and usually ⅜ inch or ½ inch. A set might contain sockets for more than one range of nuts, and any others needed can be bought. Sockets are of no use if a nut can only be turned from the side. Open-ended wrenches are still needed if the shop is to be fully equipped.

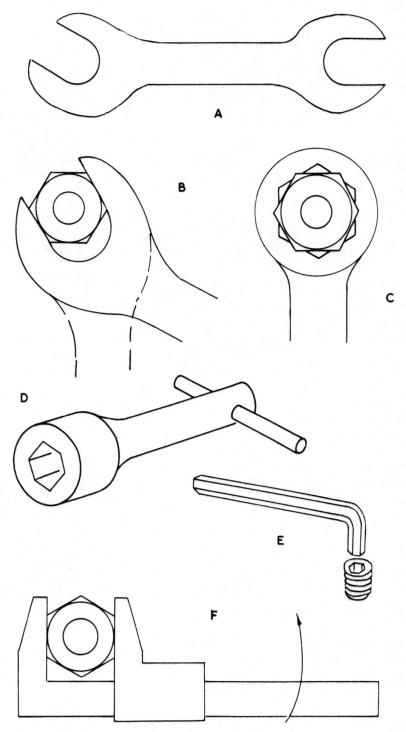

Fig. 16-10. A wrench can be open-ended (A,B) ring (C) or box (D). A screw can be turned with an Allen key (E) or an adjustable wrench can be used (F).

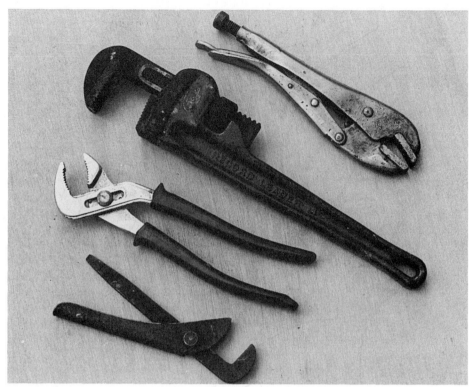

Fig. 16-11. Two plier-action wrenches, a large one with screw adjustment and a lock-on type.

In many machine assemblies, it is important to achieve the right degree of tightness. A torque wrench is a self-contained wrench (one that takes a socket). It can be adjusted so when a set degree of tightness is obtained, it slips.

Some small screws without heads, called grub screws, are used to secure parts. One type has hexagonal sockets in the top. The size of the socket varies according to the size of the screw, and a set of Allen keys or wrenches (Fig. 16-10E) should be obtained. These are bent pieces of hardened hexagonal steel rod. A set of nine should suit most needs, although there are also metric sizes for foreign cars and machinery.

Modern machinery, including such things as refrigerators and dish washers, call for maintenance tools with cranked and bent handles. Such tools can be obtained from obsolete equipment; many wrenches that have general uses can be acquired from these sources.

Any engineer who claims to be proud of his craft does not like adjustable wrenches, although he might have one or more for gripping round or awkward shapes. An adjustable wrench cannot usually be set so exactly it fits like a one-size wrench. When it is used, it tends to round off the corners of the nut or bolt head. For the same reason, an engineer does not like pliers or wrenches that work on the plier principle and do not keep the jaws parallel (Fig. 16-11). They slip and round the corners of a nut. There might be occasions when none of the stock wrenches will fit a nut that has to be turned, and an adjustable wrench has to be used. Make use it turns in the direction that pulls against the root of the rigid jaw (Fig. 16-10F).

17

Soldering and Brazing

The best method of joining two pieces of iron and steel, when the method is appropriate, is a blacksmith's weld. If the two pieces are being worked on the anvil at red heat, higher heating that allows them to be hammered together is the obvious way of joining them. The ability to make a blacksmith's weld is an accomplishment, and those who consider themselves metalworking craftsmen should not use any other method when that is the technique that will get the best results.

However, there are many situations where steel parts have to be joined and it would be unsatisfactory to raise them to welding temperature. There are also the problems of joining other metals to themselves and to each other. Blacksmith's welds are only appropriate to iron and steel.

In some assemblies, it is satisfactory to rivet or bolt parts together through drilled holes. There are other joining methods that actually fuse the metals together in a manner related to the smith's weld. These methods use a lower and more localized temperature, and a filler metal that is run into the joint and bonded to the surfaces.

There are two methods, also known as welding, that can be done with an oxy-acetylene flame or by using electricity. Both produce a very high heat in a very small space. A filler rod and the surface to be joined can be melted together without the adjoining parts becoming very hot. However, both methods require fairly elaborate equipment, and the occasional welder might not be justified in obtaining it.

Other methods are called soldering and brazing. They are done at lower temperatures and use much simpler equipment. The simplest method is soldering, often described as "soft" soldering. The joint is not very strong, but there is ample strength for many purposes and it is particularly good for electrical work. A soldered joint makes a through route for electricity that cannot be affected by corrosion as a screwed or sprung joint might. "Hard" soldering and brazing are similar techniques and the names might sometimes be used interchangeably. Brazing uses a higher temperature and makes the strongest joint—sometimes as strong as a welded joint. Hard soldering can also be called silver soldering. It is done in the same way, but the temperature used and the resulting strength are less than with brazing.

The melting points of the metals being joined have to be considered. Brass will melt at brazing temperatures. Some metals are more amenable to one method than another. Of the common metals and alloys, aluminum does not lend itself to the methods that are easily used with other metals.

Soft solder is an alloy of lead and tin. Sometimes there are small quantities of other metals, but a lead/tin alloy is all that is needed for normal joints. The melting point of the alloy is considerably lower than that of either of the metals alone. This applies to nearly all alloys. The proportions of lead and tin affect the melting point and the characteristics of the solder. A high proportion of lead allows the solder to remain plastic much long. This property was important when much plumbing was done with lead pipes. The plumber "wiped" a joint while the solder was soft enough to be molded into shape. is sold as tinner's solder or electrician's solder. It might be in a bar up to ¼ inch thick, or more like a wire about ¹⁄₁₆ inch in diameter. The lowest melting point is made with proportions of two parts tin to one part lead (181°C). A small amount of bismuth added will make the melting point even lower. General-purpose solder has about equal parts of lead and tin.

Soldering is done by heating the solder and the surfaces to be joined. Heat causes oxidization, which prevents a proper flow of the solder. It stays in little globules instead of spreading over the metal. The surfaces have to be kept from the air by melting flux over them, and the flux also assists the flow of the solder.

FLUX

Prepared fluxes can be bought, either as pastes or liquids. Where practical, fluxes should be washed off. For electrical work, this is usually impossible and the flux has to be left on the work. Electrician's flux is a resin, which does not corrode, so it does no harm if left in place.

Other fluxes include tallow, used on lead, and sal ammoniac (ammonium chloride), once the usual flux for copper. A paste manufactured flux is more convenient for small joints, and a liquid manufactured flux is better for large areas. One type of electrician's solder is supplied as a tube with resin flux inside, which melts when heat is applied. There is no need to apply flux separately to small joints, such as the end of a wire to a contact point.

The comparatively low temperature needed to melt soft solder can be obtained with a gas flame of from a heated metal rod. Copper has a particular affinity for soft solder, and the tool used for heating small joints is a soldering bit (Fig. 17-1A and 17-2). The traditional type is heated with a flame, but most soldering bits today—particularly for electrical and other fine work—have electric heating elements enclosed (Fig. 17-1B). However, for stouter metal parts that will take heat rapidly, a soldering bit of considerable bulk to hold the required heat is necessary. This is better heated with a gas flame.

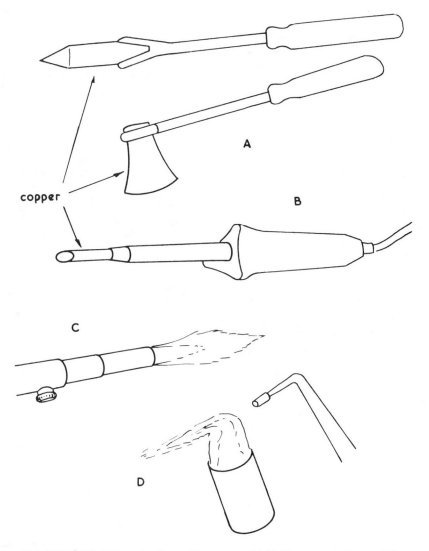

copper

A

B

C

D

Fig. 17-1. Soldering can be done with a copper bit (A,B) or a torch flame (C,D).

The alternative is to use a flame directly. This is described as sweating a joint. Direct heating of the work over a gas ring or a bunsen burner will melt solder, but it is better to have the flame under control so it can be directed where needed. A propane torch, burning gas and air, is convenient (Fig. 17-1C). For fine work, a mouth blowlamp can be used. The flame is produced by alcohol-soaked batting in a metal tubular container, and the blowpipe diverts the flame where needed (Fig. 17-1D). The flame from a torch or other device should be controllable so it can be anything from a little needle-like flame to a full blast.

Surfaces to be joined should be both mechanically and chemically clean. They can be scraped just before soldering to remove corrosion and get them bright. Flux will

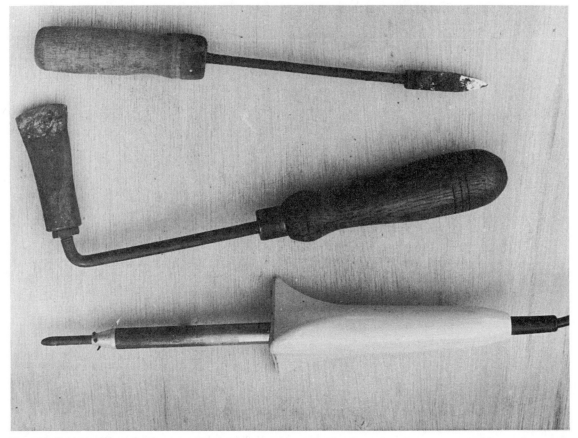

Fig. 17-2. Soldering "irons" with copper bits that have to be heated with a flame, have been superseded for most purposes by electrically heated bits.

deal with chemical cleaning. Solder will not flow on and bond to dirty surfaces. The stick of solder should also be cleaned by dipping it into flux just before using. If a soldering bit is being used, its end must also be cleaned and already *tinned* (coated with solder). To tin a bit, heat it with its own element or with a flame until solder melts when touched on the end. With a little practice you can judge the correct amount of heat by holding the bit a few inches from your cheek—a very heat-sensitive part of your body.

USING A BIT

Merely touching solder on the bit will result in the formation of gobules. Quickly rub the end of the bit on all faces with a file and dip its end in flux. Then touch the stick of solder on it. Solder will flow over the bit faces. It might help to put the solder on a piece of clean scrap metal and rub the bit on it. Once the bit has been tinned, further treatment should not be needed for a long time—unless the bit is very much overheated.

Each time the bit is heated, dip it very briefly into flux before use so that it comes clean to the work. If much soldering is to be done, it is better to keep a second container of flux in which to dip the bit and the stick of solder. Otherwise the working flux might become contaminated with dirt. Use a brush or a pointed piece of wood to apply flux to a joint.

As an example, a piece of sheet metal can have another flanged part joined to it (Fig. 17-3A). With brass, copper, or mild steel, rub the meeting surfaces bright with emery paper or scrape them with a knife blade. With tinplate, scraping would go through the very thin layer of tin, so merely wipe and let the flux clean it.

Heat the soldering bit sufficiently, dip it in flux, and melt a little solder on its end. "Tin" both surfaces. Have flux on them and slowly move the bit along them (Fig. 17-3B). As heat flows from the bit into the metal, solder will melt and flow from the bit. The metal has to get heat from the bit and be raised to the melting point of solder. If you

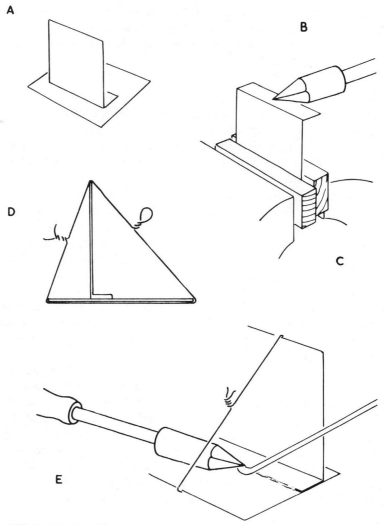

Fig. 17-3. Parts to be soldered are tinned with solder and wired together: (A) flange; (B) use flux and slowly move the bit; (C) use wood pads in the jaws; (D) twist the iron wire; (E) run the bit along the joint.

hold the metal in a vise, that will take heat away rapidly. Wood is a poor conductor, so if you want to grip the metal, put wood pads in the jaws (Fig. 17-3C). You can probably work with the metal resting on wood. Feed more solder onto the bit as you tin the surfaces. If necessary, reheat the bit to complete tinning.

To make the joint, put more flux in the joint and hold the parts together. A small piece of work can be held with pliers, although wiring is a good way of temporarily holding without clamps or other masses of metal taking heat away. Soft iron wire can be twisted (Fig. 17-3D). A second loop allows easier tensioning with pliers.

Run the hot bit along one side of the joint, and feed more solder onto it (Fig. 17-3E). Be careful not to melt too much. When the solder has melted through the joint you will see brightness on the other side. There is a shine or gloss to melted solder that is distinct from its solidified appearance. Watch this brightness as you move the bit along. Be careful not to move the parts while the solder is molten. After the heat has been withdrawn, watch the surface of the solder. The brightness will suddenly disappear. When this happens, the solder has set and the joint will not move. Allow it to cool. Water will cool it without affecting strength.

USING A FLAME

Melted solder will flow towards the hottest point, a properly used to sweat a joint. Put the solder on one side and apply heat to the other side of the joint. The idea is to draw the solder through. As an example, a tube can be mounted on a flat piece of sheet metal. If the finished article is to be a closed bowl, the bottom is made oversize and the surplus metal filed level after soldering.

For this sort of joint, there is no need for the surfaces to be tinned, but if larger areas are to be joined, tinning first is advisable. The surfaces should be mechanically clean, so rub them bright before assembly. Put the tube on the base and secure it with iron wire (Fig. 17-4A). Apply flux. It is possible to add solder by touching with the end of a bar of solder, but it is very easy to let too much melt. A safer way of getting the right amount is to put small pieces of solder in place before heating.

Solder is very ductile, and the end of a bar can be hammered to spread and thin it. Hammer the end so pieces can be cut off with snips (Fig. 17-4B), and put these around the inside of the joint (Fig. 17-4C). A useful tool for doing this is a spatula made from wire about $\frac{1}{8}$ inch in diameter, flattened at the end (Fig. 17-4D). For soldering with a flame, it helps to stand the work on a piece of asbestos.

Adjust a torch flame quite small and play it around the outside of the work. Keep the flame moving so that heating is fairly even. It is the end of the blue cone in the flame that is the hot part. Keep this in contact with the metal. The solder inside will melt and run into the joint. Once this happens, there will probably be enough heat in the metal to complete the joint. Hold the flame to one side, ready to apply it briefly if needed. Excessive overheating will burn off the flux and badly oxidize the metal, so the solder will not flow. If the silvery line of solder does not show through the outside of the joint all around, dab a little flux on with a brush. That should draw it through. If not, a quick heat might do it. Do not disturb the work until the solder has set.

SPELTER

Brazing is done with brass, although the particular mixture of copper and zinc intended

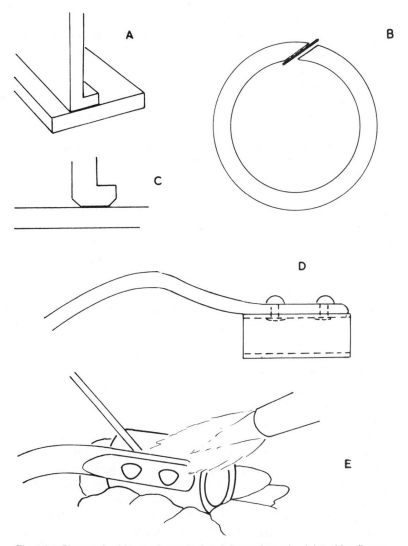

Fig. 17-4. Pieces of solder can be melted and drawn through a joint with a flame: (A) secure with wire; (B) hammer and cut pieces with snips; (C) position pieces on inside of the joint; (D) use a spatula made from wire.

for the work is called *spelter*. Silver solder is a mixture of copper, zinc, and a small amount of silver. The addition of silver lowers the melting point. Except for this, the joints are made in the same way. Spelter can be bought with different proportions of copper and zinc. Equal parts gives a melting point of about 550°C, three parts copper to two parts zinc gives about 620°C, and two parts copper to one part zinc melts at 700°C. Oddments of scrap brass can be used for brazing, but the melting point will not be known without a test. All of the heats are red-hot in any case. The differences in melting points do not matter, unless the joints are being made in metals that would melt themselves if heated too much, or there are two joints of the same material. If one can be made with spelter of a high melting point it should not be affected if the other joint is made carefully with spelter of a lower melting point. Brass is really the only critical metal, and joints can be less risky to make with silver solder than with spelter of the lowest melting point.

Spelter is supplied as stout wire or flat strips, and it can be granulated as a coarse powder. Silver solder is usually sold in flat sheets about $\frac{1}{32}$ inch thick. Because of the silver content, it is expensive and is usually purchased in small pieces by ounce weight. There are silver solders with different melting points. They are particularly suitable for copper and its alloys with zinc and tin. For mild steel, it is better to use spelter.

The flux used is borax, which is a white powder. When put on the metal and heated it effervesces, which can lift off pieces of spelter or silver solder. They can be pushed back with a long wire spatula. Borax dissolves oxides on the surface and melts to form a glassy layer, which prevents atmospheric oxygen from reaching it. It is possible to get rid of the moisture by roasting the borax and then pounding it to a powder. It can be made into a paste with a little water and granulated spelter, if that is how the spelter is to be applied.

Liquid brazing fluxes can be obtained. These are basically borax, but they do not bubble when heated. The hard, glassy flux can be chipped off after the joint has cooled. It can also be dissolved in a hot alum solution or removed in an acid pickle (see Chapter 18).

A joint is typically along a seam when sheet metal is rolled into a cylinder (Fig. 17-5A). It helps to file the joint so that it is slightly open on the inside (Fig. 17-5B). Use soft iron wire to tie the cylinder in shape. Heat to red. There will be no opportunity to adjust or alter things once brazing has been started, so get the assembly secure with wire that will not melt.

Support the piece with the joint downward. Small coke can be put under and around to both reflect heat inward and support the work. Pieces of asbestos can be used in a similar way—on the smith's hearth or in a metal tray of coke so that the flame is prevented from doing damage to anything nearby.

Use a gas torch. A self-contained propane torch is most convenient, but a kerosene torch could also be used. For a more powerful flame on large work, you might need a gas torch with air pressure provided by foot bellows or an electric blower.

Put flux along the joint. Cut small pieces of spelter or silver solder and put them in the flux (Fig. 17-5C). Have a spatula ready to push down any that rise away from the joint (Fig. 17-5D). Alternatively, use only flux in the joint and have a length of spelter wire or rod ready to touch on the joint when it is hot enough. If this is the method chosen, warm the spelter rod in the side of the flame so it does not go cold into the joint.

Play the flame at first around the outside of the metal, directing it occasionally at the joint. This will keep the flux down. Follow by heating into the cylinder (Fig. 17-5E)—swinging from side to side, rather than directly at the joint all the time. With silver solder, the first sign of redness should be enough to melt it. But for spelter, there will have to be more heat. If necessary, have the red-hot end of the spatula dipped in flux and ready, so it can be used to stroke the molten silver solder or spelter along the joint.

If the spelter is used as a wire to be touched on the joint, dip its end in flux and touch it on the joint when you think the heat is sufficient. Be careful not to melt too much. The molten spelter will usually run along the joint. If one part is obviously hotter than another, touch the cooler part of the joint.

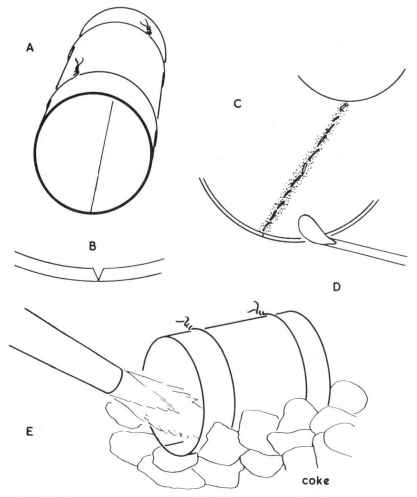

Fig. 17-5. For hard soldering a seam (A,B,C,D) the metal is wire (E) and supported with coke.

In either case, leave the work in place to cool until it is well below red heat, then it can be cooled in water. Quenching at red heat might crack spelter. If the work is dipped in an acid pickle to clean it and remove flux, remove any iron wire first. Otherwise it will cause discoloring of copper or brass.

When dealing with mild steel or anything of much bulk, you might have trouble raising enough heat. Metal away from the joint can draw away so much heat that it might be difficult to get the joint hot enough. Conserve heat as much as possible. Have the joint level and accessible, but support and surround the work with coke. The coke will get red hot during heating. This will be reflected back to the metal, preventing heat from being dispersed and directing it where it is wanted.

Mild steel should be bright. A joint cannot be made in the black condition that is usual with a smith's weld. File and rub with emery cloth or use a scratch brush. In a bad case, grind the surface. Coat joints with borax and braze in the way just described. Lap joints can be made by soft soldering (Fig. 17-6A). A ring from thicker material might have a piece of spelter coated with flux put between the meeting ends (Fig. 17-6B). There must be a slight space for spelter to flow. Soft solder will creep through an almost-tight joint and silver solder does not need much space. But for spelter, the joint must be open or filed to a V shape to give the molten metal an entry (Fig. 17-6C).

Brazing can supplement rivets. For instance, a tube might be riveted to a flattened bar for a garden tool (Fig. 17-6D). The rivets alone might not be strong enough to stand up to heavy use. Before riveting, clean the meeting surfaces bright. Close the rivets, but not quite as tightly as you might have done if they were to be the only fastenings.

Support the work with one side upward and horizontal, but apply flux underneath as well as on top (Fig. 17-5E). Heat and braze the parts, using enough spelter to run

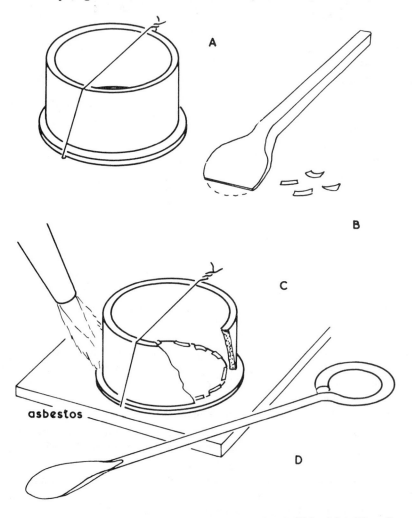

Fig. 17-6. Brazing is done with the metal heated to redness: (A) lap joint; (B) spelter coated with flux is placed between ends; (C) the joint must be open or filed to a V shape; (D) tube riveted to bar; (E) apply flux before heating and brazing.

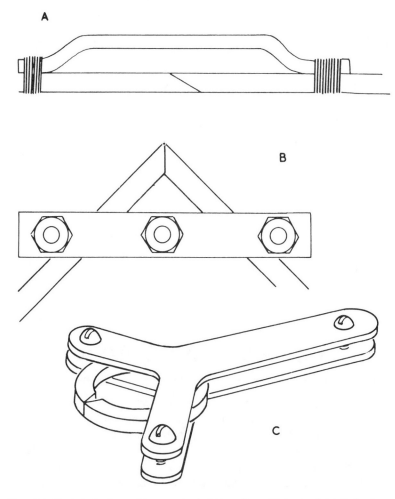

Fig. 17-7. Parts to be brazed have to be held together with improvised devices: (A) wire on a strut; (B) bolt parts; (C) use a Y-clamp.

through. After the joint has lost its redness, pick up the work with tongs and turn it over. The joint will probably be satisfactory on the far side, but if not, support it that way up and heat again with more spelter there.

Keeping parts together so they will not move or distort when heated to redness is sometimes a problem. Iron wire is useful. Even if it becomes brazed on, it can be filed off. Various clamping devices can be made, but they must stand up to heat. It is possible to wire on a strut to parts away from the flame (Fig. 17-7A). Strips of metal can be used with bolts through holes to hold parts together (Fig. 17-7B). For joining the ends of rings—which tend to open as they expand with heat—a Y-shaped clamping piece can be made (Fig. 17-7C). Nuts, bolts, or screws could be used in a tapped part.

18

Hollowing and Raising

The internal particles of metal can be made to flow. This is revealed in many operations in blacksmithing, where hammering will make steel longer and thinner or shorter and thicker. The whole mass of steel is still the same, but its shape is different. A blacksmith can work sheet steel to a compound curve while it is hot, but it is too rigid to permit this when it is cold. The metal is made to flow so its shape can be altered. Many other metals and alloys are sufficiently ductile when cold to allow compound curvature without heating.

Most of the non-ferrous metals and alloys can be shaped by heating, although some intended mainly for machining will be too crystaline and brittle. Metals and alloys that have been produced by rolling into sheet form can be worked to compound curves. The process is called *raising* by some craftsmen, whatever the method of shaping. Others talk of *hollowing* when the shape is obtained by deepening the middle of a disc and *raising* by stretching its rim. Much shaping is a combination of the two processes.

Bowls and cups of most elaborate design have been made in gold and silver, but the cost of materials prohibits their use by the average craftsman. Similar work can be done with less valuable metals.

Copper is particularly suitable because it can be made into quite deep compound shapes, and its finished appearance when polished is very attractive. Sheet brass is less ductile, but brass with a high copper content can be made into bowls and similar items. The copper and tin alloy, called *gilding metal* in sheet form, will shape almost as much and as easily as copper alone. It polishes to a rich golden color and can be made harder

310

than copper. Aluminum can also be shaped, but not to the same extent as copper, and the fact that it cannot be brazed or hard-soldered limits what can be made of it.

Copper and its alloys can be plated, so the finished work can be coated with nickel, chromium, or silver to prevent corrosion and give a rich appearance.

All of these non-ferrous metals work-harden. Because the process of raising involves a considerable amount of heavy hammering, it might be necessary to anneal a piece of work many times before obtaining the shape you want. Consequently, a propane torch or something similar should be available. The metal could be put on the coke in a blacksmith's hearth or there could be a special hearth for annealing. A suitable form is a sheet steel box about 18 inches square and at least 4 inches deep. This should be almost full of coke, or pieces of asbestos could be used. What is needed is something that will not allow heat through, but will conserve it around the metal.

The annealed metal can be cooled in water, then scoured clean with a damp cloth and pumice or domestic scouring powder. Dry it before continuing to work. If much beaten work is to be done, it is better to cool the metal in an acid pickle. This will quench and clean at one time. Acid baths have been mentioned, but for frequent use while annealing copper, brass, and gilding metal during raising, a sulfuric acid pickle made in the following way is suitable.

Use an earthenware container. Have a wooden lid that is kept on except when metal is being dipped. Locate it in the open air or in a well-ventilated area. Do not breathe the fumes when metal is dipped, and do not let the fumes reach tools because they will become corroded. Use a proportion of one part sulfuric acid to six or seven parts of water, and always pour the acid slowly into the water. **Caution: Never pour water into acid**. It will spurt dangerously.

Do not let iron or steel go into the acid. This means that smith's tongs or pliers cannot be used for dipping. Apart from corroding them, the steel affects the acid so stains occur on the metal being dipped, and these are difficult to scour off. It is possible to buy brass tongs, or they can be made from copper rod that is worked cold. Otherwise they are similar to smith's tongs made from steel.

Another way of making them is to use brass sheet that is about ⅛ inch thick. Cut two similar parts (Fig. 18-1A) and silver solder jaws to them (Fig. 18-1B). Use a copper or brass rivet. After dipping metal in acid, wash the tongs as well as the metal in water. Use plenty of water on spilled acid. Avoid getting acid on skin or clothes. If there is an accident, dilute quickly with plenty of water.

There are two stages of the work. In the first stage, the metal has to be kept as soft as possible for as long as possible during shaping. The number of times work has to stop for annealing is kept to a minimum. In the second stage, work-hardening is deliberate to strengthen the finished article. Wooden tools are considered to work-harden less than steel ones, so most craftsmen prefer to do the early work with mallets and keep steel hammers for the final work, called planishing. However, it is possible to hollow and raise with steel hammers, and special ones are made for this. The difference in the degree of work-hardening between wood and steel is slight.

TOOLS

The main wooden hollowing tool is a bossing or doming mallet (Figs. 18-2A and 18-3).

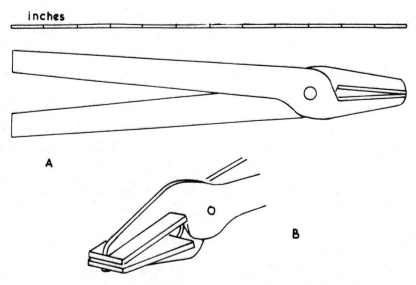

inches

A

B

Fig. 18-1. Brass tongs (A,B) for dipping acid can be made from sheet.

The head is close-grained, heavy hardwood and the handle is usually cane, although it could be an ordinary hammer handle. For flat work, there is a similarly made tinner's mallet (Fig. 18-2B). For raising, one end of the tinman's mallet head can be given a shape similar to a cross peen on a hammer (Fig. 18-2C) or a special mallet could be made from flat-sectioned wood (Fig. 18-2D).

If hollowing is to be done with a steel hammer, the special hammer is made with two ball peens on a head longer than a normal hammer. It is sold as a hollowing hammer, in weights between 1 and 3 pounds, but much hollowing can be done with an ordinary ball peen hammer.

Hollowing can be done over a sandbag. This is leather of stout canvas filled with fine sand (Fig. 18-2E). Strong stitching is needed to stand up to heavy pounding. Much hollowing can be done on wood. For a small hollow such as a spoon, all that is needed is a hole in the end grain of a piece of wood (Fig. 18-2F). For a larger bowl shape, a hollow can be gouged out of the end of a log (Fig. 18-2G). It does not have to be a perfectly symmetrical hollow. A tray with a flat rim can be worked over an edge. A block of wood can be shaped to grip in a vise (Figs. 18-2H and 18-4). If much hollowing is to be done, it is worthwhile having a section of tree trunk standing on the floor and about 30 inches high so that the hollows in it are at bench height.

To make a bowl that has a fairly regular curve, but that is not necessarily a hemisphere, cut a disc with snips. A thickness between 16 and 20 gauge is suitable. Thinner metal can be difficult to keep in shape for a first attempt and thicker metal might require considerable work to get the shape. Remove sharpness around the edge with a file so as not to cut your hands. Some copper is soft enough in the sheet for shaping to commence, but usually it is advisable to anneal before starting work.

Position yourself so you can swing the bossing mallet or hollowing hammer over the sandbag or the hollowed wood. You will be moving the metal about, but you have to continue hitting over the same part of the support. At first, there is a tendency to

312

Fig. 18-2. Sheet metal is hollowed with mallets. The material is held on wood blocks or a sandbag: (A) doming mallet; (B) tinner's mallet; (C) shaped tinner's mallet; (D) mallet made from flat-sectioned wood; (E) canvas filled with fine sand; (F) hole used for hollowing; (G) a log is used for hollowing; (H) a shaped block of wood.

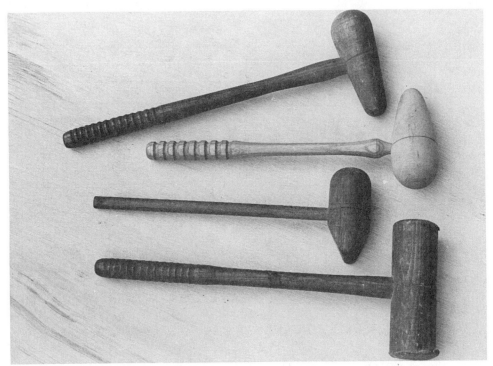

Fig. 18-3. Two bossing mallets, a combined doming and raising mallet, and a plain mallet.

Fig. 18-4. A tray with a flat rim, with the mallet and wood block used for hollowing it.

follow the metal with the blows. Spread your legs so you do not sway and keep your elbow close to your side as the pivot point. At first it might help to draw a number of pencil circles on the disc (Fig. 18-5A).

Start near the center, using the large end of the bossing mallet. Pull the disc around slightly between blows, holding its edge at the far side. Try to arrange the blows to overlap and follow increasingly large circles. At first the edge will wrinkle, but this will be corrected as the overlapping blows move outwards to the rim. Tilt the bowl so the part you are hitting is level (Fig. 18-5B).

You will find that by the time you have gotten this far the metal will be quite hard and hits on it do not have anything like the effect they did when you started. This is a sign that the metal should be annealed again. Immediately after annealing—copper in particular—the metal is very ductile, and that is when you can get the greatest effect.

It is usual to work by eye. Hold the bowl up and look across it from several directions. At first it is unlikely to have the same cross-section all around; it might have flatter parts of the section where you do not want them. A conical shape is common (Fig. 18-5C). To put this right, tilt the bowl more when working around the flatter parts. Concentrate on getting the bowl as deep as you want it, then work around to get the curves correct. Watch that the bowl keeps its shape when viewed from above. Draw a circle on a piece of wood and invert the bowl over it. It is unlikely the rim will be level. Slight undulations are possible and do not matter at this stage. If there are large differences between parts, they will have to be corrected by more work with the mallet. As you get the circular shape correct, the uneven edge should improve as well—unless earlier hammering was very erratic.

Another bowl shape has its central area almost flat and its rim curled in (Fig. 18-5D). A deeper bowl can also have a curled-in edge (Fig. 18-5E). There are many possible curves, and it is worthwhile looking at classical items such as Greek architecture to see what curves are pleasing. A section that is part of a circle might be acceptable, but a curve that starts almost flat and gets increasingly tighter towards the rim might be considered more attractive (Fig. 18-5F). A card template can be cut as a guide to the shape to be hollowed, but it is unlikely that the final shape will match it exactly. What is important is that what you have in the finished bowl should be a pleasing curve. If it is an increasing or decreasing curve in its section, be careful that no part comes out of sequence by curving too much or too little.

To make the curled-in edge, use the small end of the bossing mallet or a similar end of a hollowing hammer. Work over a hole (Fig. 18-5G). Make several courses of blows around and tilt the work as the curve develops (Fig. 18-5H). It should be possible to get all the curl needed in this way. If the edge wrinkles, finish it on a sandbag or on a shallow hollow in the wood instead of a hole. If the curl is to turn in much, final shaping might have to be over a round stake.

This is a steel rod with a rounded top. A bought one might have a head larger than the stem and be something like a ball peen. Its bottom either fits in the hardie hole of the anvil, into a hole in a tree trunk, or can be held in a vise (Fig. 18-5J). The end of a round rod could be ground to shape. In both cases, the part on which the bowl will rest should be finished smooth. Any marks on it would be reproduced in the bowl. Use a tinman's mallet to close the rim over this mushroom stake, working around a little at a time to get an even shape (Fig. 18-5K).

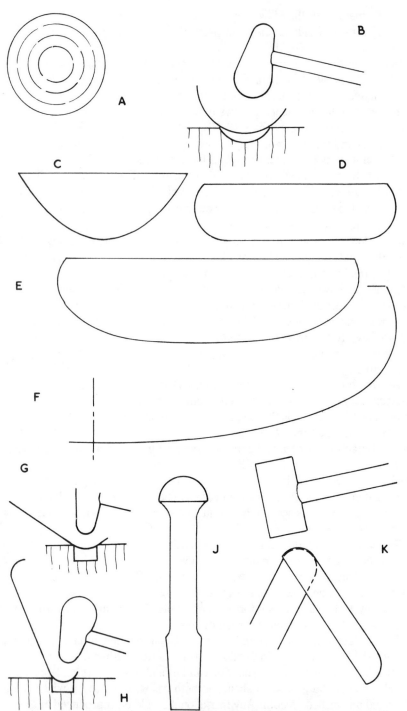

Fig. 18-5. The edge of a hollowed bowl can be turned in over a stake: (A) pencil drawn circles; (B) tilt the bowl; (C) a conical shape; (D) curled rim; (E) a deeper bowl; (F) a flat curve; (G) use a bossing mallet; (H) develop the curve; (J) at the bottom might fit into a hardie hole; (K) use a tinman's mallet.

A bowl or tray with a flat rim is something like a curled edge inside a border. Draw the circle where the hollow is to come. If the rim is to be round, it is helpful to drive in two nails as guides—whether hollowing is to be over the edge of a piece of wood or a shaped block (Fig. 18-6A). If the outer edge is not to be parallel with the hollow, you will have to estimate the hollowing position in relation to the wooden edge. After the first course of blows, the angle can be seen and corrected in further series of hits. A round hollow in an octagonal or other polygonal rim looks attractive.

Start hollowing with light blows (Fig. 18-6B). The first time around you are mainly feeling the accuracy of the positioning of the blows. Follow with more blows that bring the angle to near the marked circle (Fig. 18-6C). When the outline is established, make more courses from this toward the flat bottom to get a sufficient depth. There will have

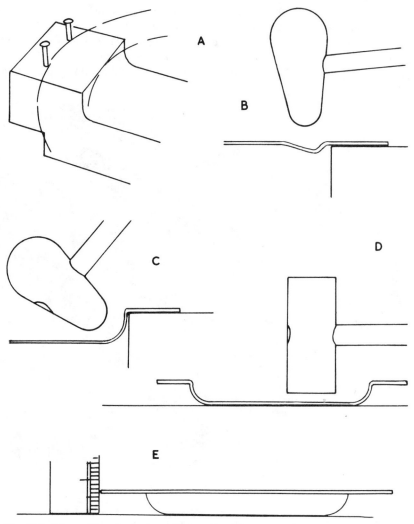

Fig. 18-6. A tray with a rim is shaped over a wood edge (A,B,C) and its base flattened level (D.E).

to be some flattening blows on the bottom to maintain shape (Fig. 18-6D). When doing this, check the flatness of the rim and the regular height all around (Fig. 18-6E).

Anneal as necessary when you find your blows are having little effect. Continuing too long could crack the metal, which becomes crystaline and brittle as it becomes hard.

PLANISHING

After a bowl or tray has been hollowed to a satisfactory shape, it might be hard from hammering, or it might be soft if the final work came just after annealing. This has to be followed by planishing, which is careful hammering all over. It is done to get the metal uniformly hard and strong, and to decorate it. The work finishes with little overlapping facets that polish to reflect the light and give the work the characteristic hammered, hand-wrought appearance.

Planishing hammers are mostly light, 1 to 1½ pounds, and with long springy handles (Fig. 18-7). Most work is done with a flat-faced hammer head on a curved surface (Fig. 18-8A), but for a flat or near-flat surface the face is domed (Fig. 18-8B). The faces or peens can be round or square. The hammer face must be absolutely smooth and highly polished. Ordinary hammer faces become damaged and would not do for planishing, but

Fig. 18-7. Planishing hammers, including an adapted ball peen hammer and a small smith-made one.

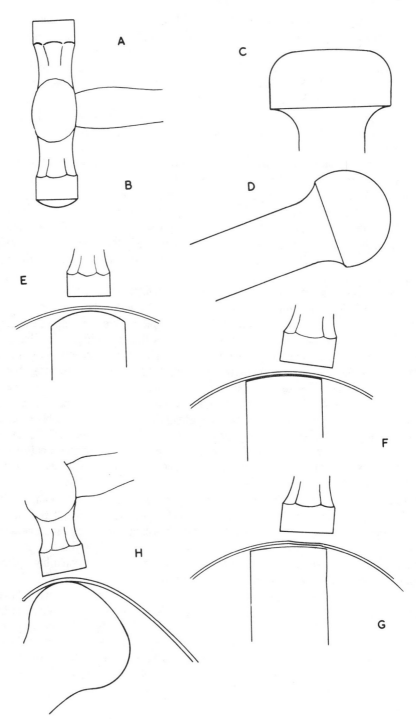

Fig. 18-8. Planishing is done with polished hammers and stakes: (A) flat-faced hammer; (B) this face is domed; (C) rounded edges; (D) curled-in rim; (E) pinch the metal; (F) bowl curve; (G) flattened; (H) tilt the stake.

a new hammer might be polished and kept for planishing. Do not use a planishing hammer for anything else, and it is advisable to store planishing hammers with their faces wrapped in cloth soaked in oil.

Planishing is done over a stake. For bowls, this is a rounded top and could be the mushroom stake (Fig. 18-5D). The curve of the stake should be less than the curve of the bowl. How much less is not critical, but a very much smaller curve makes planishing difficult because there is less tolerance for a slightly misdirected blow.

For a tray or anything else nearly flat, the stake should have a near-flat center and rounded edges (Fig. 18-8C). For a curled-in rim, a rod could be forged to grip in the vise (Fig. 18-8D). Stakes can be made with mild steel, but they will not last long if not case-hardened. Stake surfaces should be as smooth and polished as the hammer faces, and they should be given similar protection in storage.

Planishing consists of pinching the metal between the hammer and the stake (Fig. 18-8E). The problem is to get it right every time because the bowl is pulled around just enough for each hammer mark to overlap the previous one in that course and the marks in the previous course. Start with the bowl scoured clean. It might help to see the effect if it is polished as well.

Position yourself so you have a light in front of you, then each facet left from the hammer should reflect the light and show where it is. As with hollowing, arrange your stance so you pivot your arm and hammer to get the blows over the top of the stake. Start at the center of the bowl and planish in circles that get bigger. If a blow falls incorrectly, you might be able to disguise its mark by planishing correctly over it again. If you have hit a long way out and distorted the bowl, go to the sandbag and use a bossing mallet to correct the shape before you continue planishing.

As you continue on a bowl that has a tighter curve towards the rim, you will have to tilt the stake. Inside the bowl, the stake is marking the metal with every blow outside. If the curve of the top of the stake conforms to the bowl curve, there will be no mark (Fig. 18-8F). Even worse, if the stake curve is flatter than that of the bowl, you will flatten the shape (Fig. 18-8G). Tilting the stake allows you to planish over a suitable curve (Fig. 18-8H).

With a flat-bottomed tray the central area is planished with a domed hammer (Fig. 18-9A). As the curve is reached, change to a flat-faced hammer and tilt the stake so you work on its curved edge (Fig. 18-9B). Some planishing hammers have one square face, and this is easier to use close to the angle (Fig. 18-9C). For the flat rim, use a domed hammer over a flat straight-edged stake (Fig. 18-9D). This could be a piece of flat polished bar extending from one side of the vise.

When any piece of work has been planished, its edge will almost certainly have to be trued. If it is a tray with a flat rim, the outer edges can be filed straight, cleaned with emery cloth and then polished with the surfaces. The edge of a bowl can have exceptional high spots rubbed level with a file, but leveling the edge is best done by inverting the bowl on a piece of coarse emery paper attached to a flat board. Rub the bowl on this until it is leveled all around. Follow with a finer grit, then round the edge with the emery paper in your hand.

ASSEMBLY

A flat-bottomed tray or bowl will stand without any support, but a bowl with a rounded

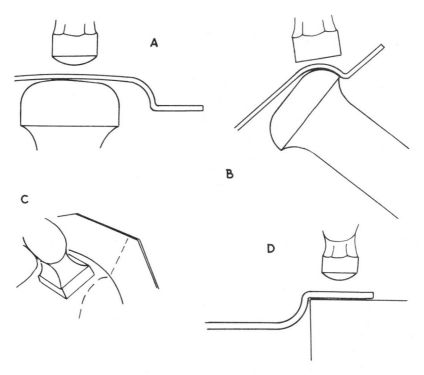

Fig. 18-9. The metal has to be trapped between hammer and stake (A,B) for correct planishing (C,D).

bottom needs feet or some other base so it will stand level. Some silverware designs have quite elaborate supports and these designs can be reproduced in copper or its alloys. A simple ring shows how a base can be added.

The base ring can be made from a solid bar. For a bowl about 4 inches across it might be ¼- × -⅛-inch section, or proportionately bigger for a larger bowl (Fig. 18-10A). To match the curve without having to file the top of the ring, it should slope outward so the first step after annealing the bar is to bend it to the curve of the bowl at the point it will touch. A piece of card or scrap metal can be made into a template (Fig. 18-10B). The theoretical length of bar needed is π d, or about 3.14 times the diameter. If you cut it to a little more than three times the diameter, that will do. The ring will stretch slightly during making up. Bend the bar edgewise to the template. The beak of the anvil is convenient to work on with a mallet, otherwise, have a thick round rod in the vise (Fig. 18-10C).

Having achieved the shape in that direction, wrap the bar in a circle around the beak or rod. File the meeting ends slightly open on the inside (Fig. 18-10D) and braze or silver solder them. True the shape of the ring with a mallet over the beak or a rod. Try it on the bowl. If necessary, use a half-round file to correct any unevenness of the top edge. Stand the bowl on the ring and move it about until the rim is level all around. With a scriber, mark where the ring comes.

Tie the ring on with iron wire, then sweat it on with soft solder. Be careful not to overheat. Heat that will melt soft solder will not be enough to anneal the copper and

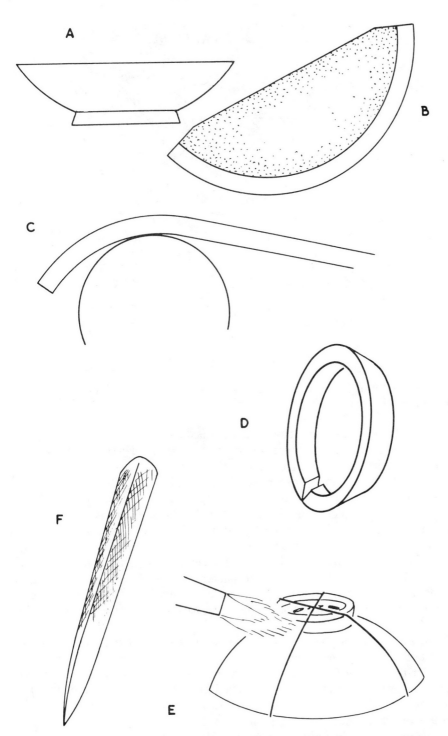

Fig. 18-10. A base for a bowl can be made from a strip brazed and soldered on: (A) bowl; (B) template; (C) bend the bar edgewise; (D) file the ends; (E) heat gently; (F) scraper.

undo the hardening achieved by planishing. Put flux around the joint and have small pieces of solder inside the ring while heating gently outside (Fig. 18-10E). Stop heating as soon as the solder melts. If it does not run everywhere in the joint, touch the gaps with a brush dipped in flux. If there is obviously not enough solder, touch the end of a stick on the inside of the joint. Do this very briefly or too much solder will melt and run where you do not want it.

A useful tool for removing excess solder is a scraper made from the end of an old triangular file, ground smooth to a point (Fig. 18-10F). Use it sideways across the unwanted solder until you are through to the metal, then rub with fine abrasive paper before polishing.

The underside of the ring will need leveling. It can be rubbed up and down a flat file while being turned, or it can be rubbed with a circular action on a piece of emery paper.

A small tray with a flat rim can have pieces put on to make it into an ashtray (Fig. 18-11A). A suitable mold for shaping the pieces can be made by drilling about a ¾-inch-diameter hole across a piece of hardwood, then cutting it in half (Fig. 18-11B).

Cut the cigarette holders (Fig. 18-11C) with rounded or beveled corners. They could be left smooth or planished while flat with a domed hammer on a flat stake. Smooth the

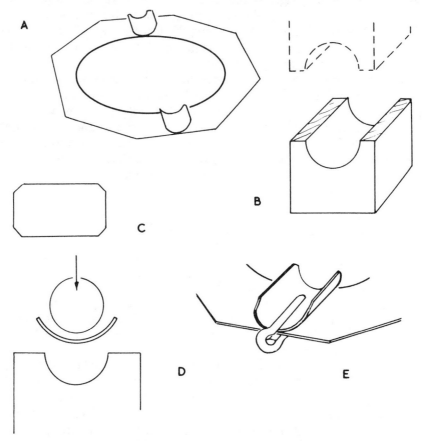

Fig. 18-11. Cigarette holders can be soldered to the rim of a tray: (A) tray; (B) mold; (C) cigarette holders; (D) tap the holders in the molds; (E) clamps.

edges and shape the pieces by using a piece of wood rod to tap them into the mold (Fig. 8-11D), with the planished side on top.

Sweat the holders to the tray rim with soft solder. Split pins sprung open make suitable clamps (Fig. 18-11E). Very little solder is needed. Put a small piece of flux at one side and heat the other side gently until the solder runs through.

All of the shaping described so far is hollowing, done mostly from the inside. Raising is stretching the metal mostly from the outside, and is used to make items that are much deeper than a bowl. By careful work, it is possible to start with a disc and finish with a cup or vase much deeper than it is across (Fig. 18-12A).

The first step is to hollow the disc in the same way as if making a bowl, except the center area can be left flat if that is what you want (Fig. 18-12B). Work the bowl to a reasonable depth, but there is no need to go more than the metal wants to go.

Raising is done with the mallet shaped like a cross peen or with a raising hammer— which is like a cross peen hammer, but with a longer head to give sufficient reach. The hammer can make more progress with each blow, but it rapidly hardens the metal. The mallet might be slower, but annealing stops should be less frequent.

Use a stake with a domed top and tilt it in the vise. Start by working around just above what will be the base (Fig. 18-12C). Make a course above this, but not closely adjoining it (Fig. 18-12D). Make one or more courses above this until you are hitting around the rim (Fig. 18-12E). On the way, it is probable that the edge will start wrinkling. Keep this in check. Have a piece of leather on the bench and use a bossing mallet to knock out any wrinkles over this (Fig. 18-12F).

Anneal the work and go back to the start again. Make courses around the metal. Work between the previous courses and be careful to deal with wrinkles as they occur. What you are doing is stretching the metal upward, but at the same time you have to reduce the circumference of the rim considerably in the process. The lower part will get to shape first, but you will have to work progressively upward with many annealings to get the top to the shape you want. A flared vase looks good, and curving the section outwards toward the rim simplifies the final stages of raising.

BUILT-UP WORK

Raising is a slow process, although the results are very satisfying to the maker. A very similar result can be attained by building up the work.

Vase

Built-up work allows the production of shapes that would be impossible by raising, such as a vase with a narrower top than bottom (Fig. 18-13A). The body is made from flat sheet rolled around and brazed or silver soldered. Then the bottom is added. The techniques are described in Chapter 17.

Draw a full-size side view of the vase. Extend the side lines until they meet. Use this as the center for compasses in order to get the developed shape needed to make the conical body. Step off three times around the curve, allow a little extra (Fig. 18-13B).

Cut a piece of copper or gliding metal to this shape. Anneal it and wrap it around the beak of the anvil or a rod in the vise. File the meeting edges straight and slightly open on the inside. Wire the cone and braze the joint, then the bottom can be silver

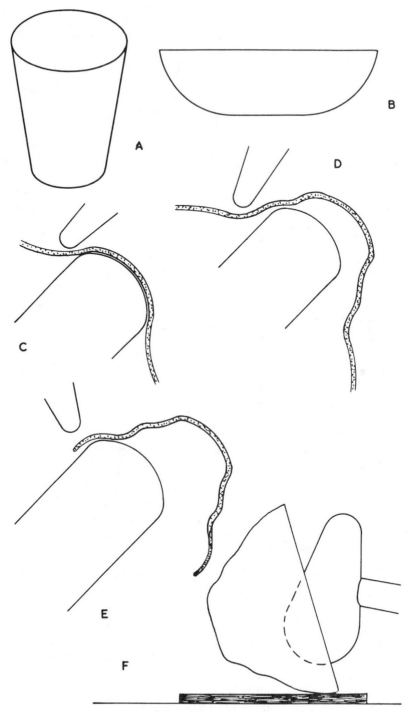

Fig. 18-12. Use a hammer or mallet to make a deep shape: (A) hollow the disc; (B) the center area is left flat; (C) work just above the base; (D) make a course; (E) make a course until you are hitting against the rim; (F) use a bossing mallet.

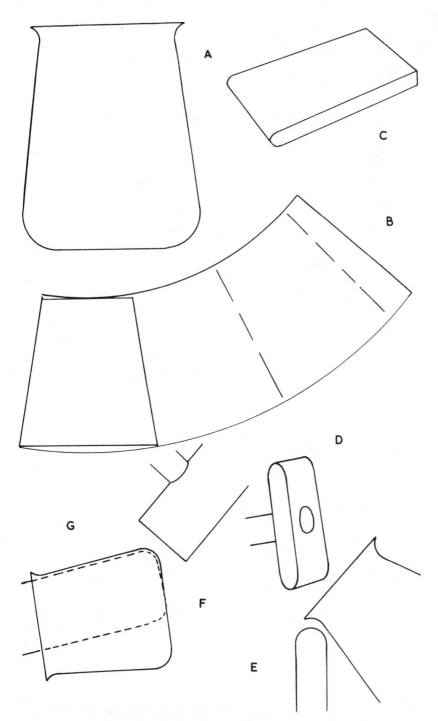

Fig. 18-13. Instead of raising, a deep shape can be built up: (A) vase; (B) step off three times; (C) round straight top; (D) creasing hammer; (E) flare evenly; (F) use a stake to round; (G) use a mallet to turn in the edge.

soldered. Alternatively, silver solder this joint and use soft solder for the bottom. Either are satisfactory (Fig. 17-5).

After joining and cleaning true the circular shape, rub the top and bottom level on emery paper, if necessary. Flare the top outward. Use a stake with a rounded straight top (Fig. 18-13C). Make it from steel bar. Grind and polish the curve of the top. A piece of mild steel should be satisfactory for occasional use. An old flat or hand file can be broken to a few inches long and the teeth ground off toward the end, then the rounding ground and polished. This little stake is used with a creasing hammer, which is like a cross peen hammer in both directions (Fig. 18-13D). A normal cross peen hammer could be used, but a creasing hammer with a broad flatter curve is more suitable. It could be forged from a length of bar about 1- × -⅜-inch section.

Hold the vase tilted over the stake and hammer around to flare the top. Use light blows and watch that the flaring is even (Fig. 18-13E). The silver soldered or brazed joint should flare with the adjoining metal without trouble, but see that it is not built up thickly. If necessary, file it level inside. Any amount of flaring should be possible, but a small amount should be adequate.

At the other end, use a stake with rounding to match what you want (Fig. 18-13F). Have this in the vise and work around with a mallet to turn in the edge (Fig. 18-13G). Level the bottom by rubbing it on emery paper.

If the seam has been brazed and the bottom is to be attached with silver solder, go ahead and make the joint. Cut a disc slightly larger than the bottom of the tubular part and wire it on (Fig. 18-14A). Put borax and pieces of silver solder inside and heat outside to melt and draw through the solder. Be careful not to overheat, or the brazing of the seam might be melted as well.

If the bottom is to be attached with soft solder, planish the conical part now. Deal with the turned-in bottom over the stake it was shaped on, and the body of the vase over the smooth top (Fig. 18-14B). Use a domed planishing hammer. Take care to make the planishing marks overlap and go close to the flared top without getting so close as to damage it. When this has been done, wire on the base disc and sweat the joint with soft solder—using no more heat than necessary.

In either case, file the edge of the disc to match the curve of the vase (Fig. 18-14C). Rub this smooth and polish the joint. Figure 18-15 shows finished vases.

There could be punched decoration around the top. The pattern shown in Fig. 18-14D is made with two punches. One is a piece of steel rod filed to a half-moon shape on the end (Fig. 18-14E). The other is made by drilling a small shallow hole in the end of the rod, then filing to make almost a knife edge around it (Fig. 18-14F). Draw a pencil line around the vase as a guide. Punch the overlapping half-moon marks about three-fourths of the way around, working over a supporting rod in the vise. Then check the remaining space and adjust the last few marks accordingly. A variation, using the same two punches and another straightline one, has a continuous line with leaves and berries (Fig. 18-14G).

Jug or Pitcher

An example of further building up is a jug (Figs. 18-16 and 18-17). Suggested sizes are shown (Fig. 18-18) with most parts made of 18 or 20 gauge copper, brass, or gilding metal. The example has the top copper contrasting with the other parts gilding metal.

Make the body (Fig. 18-18A) in a similar way to that of the small vase by developing

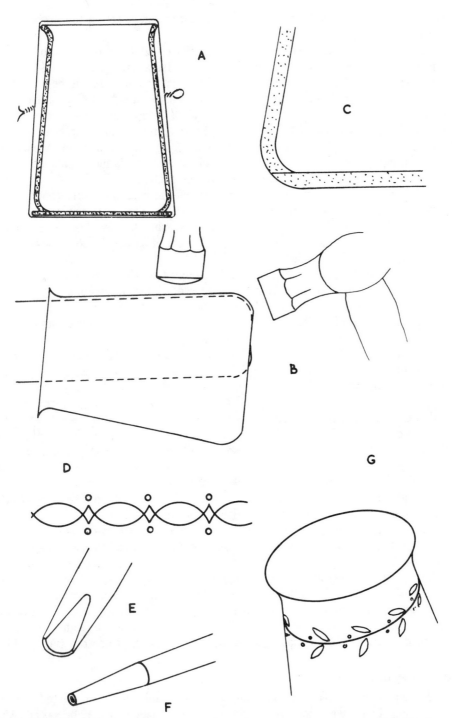

Fig. 18-14. The bottom is soldered to a vase which can be decorated by punching: (A) wire the disc; (B) shape over a stake; (C) file to match the disc; (D) punched decoration; (E) file to shape; (F) drill a shallow hole: (G) leaf and berry decoration.

Fig. 18-15. Two vases made as described and one with the cone the other way.

the shape (Fig. 18-13B), then form it circular and silver solder the edges as described in Chapter 17. Planish all over and true the top and bottom edges.

Cut a disc of sheet metal for the bottom (Fig. 18-18B) to press inside the body. Make a ring of ⅛-inch square strip (Fig. 18-18C) with its ends silver soldered, the same size as the disc. Use soft solder to join the ring to the disc. With the body inverted, press the bottom into place, with the meeting surfaces cleaned and fluxed. Use a small flame to heat just to melt the solder. Have a piece of solder ready to touch on to add more. The joint must be filled, but avoid an excess of solder. Scrape the joint clean and level it if necessary.

Use a half-round file inside the top edge of the body to bring it to a thin edge (Fig. 18-18D). Make sure this end is as near a true circle as you can get it.

The top (Fig. 18-18E) has to be developed as part of a cone, with its apex low in the body (Fig. 18-18F). The joint is along the lower side. Half a development around

Fig. 18-16. A jug or pitcher made of copper and gilding metal.

a centerline on the long side can be drawn and turned over for the full piece (Fig. 18-19). Draw the inner curve to the distance F–G and the outer curve to the distance F–H (Fig. 18-19A). Mark around the development a distance equal to half the circumference.

Above the side view draw a semi-circle and step off the radius to divide the circumference into six spaces. Divide the development into the same number. Project from the semi-circle and draw lines towards the center (Fig. 18-18J). Put matching lines on the development (Fig. 18-19B) and number them. On the development lines, mark the distances of the points on the rim from the center on the side view. Draw a curve through those points (Fig. 18-19C) to get the outer shape. The inner shape is part of a circle.

Make the top. Try it in place in the body before silver soldering. Allow for it expanding slightly when it is planished. If it is too small it can be stretched by hammering, but if

Fig. 18-17. The base of the jug is let in.

it is made too big it cannot be reduced except by cutting and joining again. It should press into a close fit in the body, where it is soft soldered.

The handle could be a strip of thicker metal about ⅝ inch wide, but it is shown made of the same thickness as the other parts, with the edges folded in (Fig. 18-18K). Fold a piece slightly longer than needed, then shape the handle so the parts to be in contact with the body are in line (Fig. 18-18L). Cut and round the ends, then hollow them to fit closely. Solder them on.

Clean by dipping in an acid bath, wash thoroughly, then polish all over.

Bowl with Wired Rim

Another form of decoration is a ring of twisted wire, often put around the top of a bowl

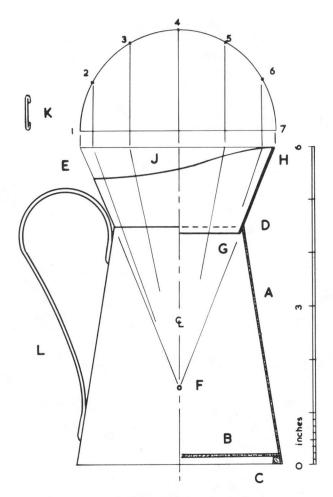

Fig. 18-18. Suggested sizes for the jug.

or cup (Figs. 18-20 and 18-21A). A doubled piece of wire somewhat more than twice the distance around the object should be annealed just before twisting. Grip the two ends in a vise and hold the loop with a hook in the chuck of a hand drill. Pull back on the hand drill while turning the handle to twist the wire (Fig. 18-21B). The action of twisting hardens the metal rapidly. If a tight twist is wanted, it might be necessary to anneal the wire again to get the closest twist.

Cut the meeting ends diagonally (Fig. 18-21C) so that the joint is less obvious than if it was cut straight across. Make the ring too small because it is easily stretched. If it is too big it cannot be made smaller, except by cutting a section out and joining again. Silver solder the ends. Lightly tap around the ring with a mallet over the beak or a rod until it has stretched almost enough to press into position. It is unwise to stretch it absolutely to size and then try it in place. This might be enough to further stretch it

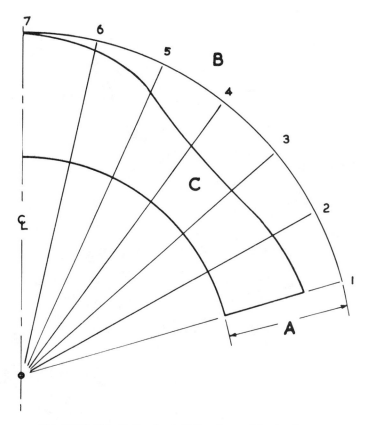

Fig. 18-19. How to develop half the shape of the jug top.

oversize before fitting. A variation on leaving the wire round in section to use a hammer on the wire so the outside is flattened.

Have the wire and the edge clean, then put the ring in place. Hold it with split pins at fairly close intervals (Fig. 18-21D). Put flux all around with a brush, and have the brush ready to add more if necessary. Stand the bowl with its top downward, preferably on a sheet of asbestos, or support it with something inside so the rim is held clear of the bench. Have a stick of solder prepared by flattening so that quite a thin edge can touch on the wire. Putting pieces of solder in place on the wire will not work, unless it is very thick wire.

Heat around the edge by fanning the flame and swinging it across the wire. Do not concentrate it on one spot at first. When there is an overall warmth, work on a shorter part and touch the end of the stick of solder in the joint (Fig. 18-21E). As soon as it flows, withdraw the stick. Coax what has melted along with the flux brush to spread the solder as far as possible. Move along to a new part and do the same until the full circuit has been done. Look for gaps under the wires and fill them with solder. Working in this way, it should be possible to get the wire attached with very little surplus solder left to be scraped off. When the joint has set, remove the split pins and clean the bowl in acid pickle. Scour it clean, dry it, and polish it.

Fig. 18-20. This bowl has a twisted wire ring soldered around its rim.

POLISHING

Getting a bright shine on the non-ferrous metals involves a process of breaking down the surface with finer and finer abrasives until the scratches produced are so fine that the eye sees the metal as perfectly smooth.

Finish any filed edge with a fine file, using a draw filing action, moving sideways. The scratches left by this process can be rubbed away with emery paper or other abrasive. Two grades should be enough, but make sure the coarser grade really does remove file marks, and that the finer grade removes the marks of the coarser grade. Do not let the emery paper rub the planished surface.

Spelter and silver solder will polish with the metal, and silver solder will finish almost the same color as gilding metal and not show much on copper. The brass color of spelter is slightly more obvious. However, make sure there are no projections at the joints because polishing will highlight them. Rub them down with the tip of a file, followed by emery paper. Soft solder will not polish. Any that has gone where it should not must be scraped away to expose the metal underneath.

A planished surface is already fairly smooth, due to the compacting action with hammer and stake. Use pumice powder or domestic scouring powder on a damp cloth

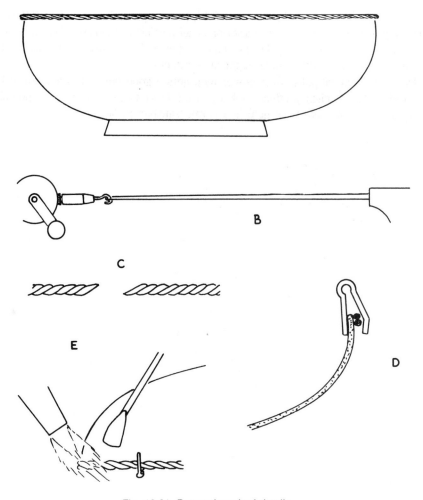

Fig. 18-21. Decorative wired details.

to remove stains, flux residue, and anything else on the surface. Wash off and thoroughly dry the metal.

It should be possible to get a good shine by hand polishing using a liquid or paste metal polish on a soft cloth. The first polishing will require plenty of rubbing and might take some time. For the finest finish, start with a polish intended for brass. Then finish with one sold for silver. An alternative to liquid polish is batting impregnated with polish.

A faster and more effective first treatment is to use a power polisher. Have a polishing mop made of many discs of cloth that can be driven at a sufficient speed and that is well charged with a suitable compound. It is the polishing compound that does the work, so recharge the mop as necessary. Hold the bowl or vase downwards so that it it not able to catch and be pulled from your hands. Be careful that an edge is not brought upward to the mop, for the same reason.

Power polishing is, as the name implies, powerful. On the main areas, treat the metal lightly. Heavy pressure could remove much of the appearance of planishing. Where solder has been scraped or an edge has been filed, heavier pressure will finish off the effect of scraping and remove abrasive marks or small particles of solder. Final polishing is best done with a mop without polishing compound on it. Do not use a mop that has been used on steel or the softer metal might be scratched.

Although an initial polish on a power mop gets a good finish, too much of it later would reduce the planishing effect. Upkeep of the finish is better done by hand polishing. A suitable protective treatment is a spray transparent lacquer.

19

Casting

An alternative to forging and fabricating metal is to melt it and run it into a mold. When metal is extracted from ore it is run into molds, then the blocks are further worked during manufacture to form the bars and sheets we use. If sufficient heat is available, most metals and alloys can be melted again and poured into molds of any shape. It is the amount of heat necessary that limits the choice of metals that can be cast in a small shop.

If some decorative ironwork is examined, much of it will be found to be a combination of forged and cast iron. Castings are used where an animal or human face has to be included, or where there are floral representations too complicated for forging. The gate to a medieval castle might have the coat of arms of the owner as a centerpiece cast to shape. Many small decorations, such as a cast-iron flower finial come at the end of a forged bar. Cast iron of this type is rather brittle, but used for decoration without fine detail, this does not matter. In the industrial production of cast iron and steel, there are techniques that overcome any tendency to brittleness and other faults. Many steel tools start as castings. Casting is also valuable where weight is important. Anything bulky, and therefore heavy, is almost certainly cast.

Unfortunately, the heat required to melt iron and steel is more than can be achieved in a blacksmith's shop. The end of a bar might be heated enough to melt away, but what is required is enough heat to melt a quantity of metal in a container to a state where it is fully liquid and can be poured. The heat limit restricts the casting done in a small shop to those metals and alloys with low melting points.

Lead is the metal in general use with the lowest melting point. This is a good choice for practice castings. It does not cast with very sharp angles, but if it is alloyed with

Table 19-1. Melting Points.

Metal	Degrees Fahrenheit	Degrees Celsius
Lead	621	327
Zinc	787	419
Antimony	1166	630
Aluminum	1214	660
Brass	1650	900
Iron	2768	1520

antimony it becomes printers' type metal and will cast sharply. Proportions are four parts lead to one part antimony. Old printing type could be used. Aluminum has about twice the melting temperature of lead, but that heat should be possible using a blacksmith's hearth. Some fires might only melt brass. Zinc is not readily available, but if it can be obtained, it can be alloyed with lead and antimony to make a good casting metal that is within the heat range of a smith's shop. A suitable proportion is 14 parts lead, five parts zinc and one part antimony. Typical melting points are shown in Table 19-1.

Most metals and alloys shrink as they cool. This will have to be allowed for in making a casting. A shrinkage of about ⅛ inch per foot is probable. An alloy containing antimony keeps its size or expands slightly on cooling.

Lead and type metal can be melted in an iron container. A ladle could be used for small quantities, but a handled iron pot with a spout is needed for larger quantities. Metals that require a higher temperature should only be melted in a crucible, which is made of fireclay or plumbago. Special long tongs with jaws are used to embrace the crucible. Obviously, molten metal has to be handled with great care, and early experience is best gained with lead or its alloys melted in a ladle. If a metal runs where it should not, smother it with sand. Never pour water on it.

Metal can be melted repeatedly. Old castings can be melted to make new things. Cutting or breaking into small pieces will speed melting. Once there is some molten metal, anything solid lowered into it will soon melt. Impurities will rise to the surface and this *dross* should be skimmed off with a small ladle before pouring. When metal is poured, do not break the flow.

Casting is done in a mold; sometimes the whole process is described as molding. For metal casting, the mold is usually made of sand. Sea sand or builders' sand is not really suitable, although you can experiment with whatever sand is available. The best material is sold as foundry sand or green sand, which has the right proportions of clay and silica to give a good bond combined with ventilation. It is used slightly damp. Having it too wet could be dangerous when the moisture comes into contact with the hot metal. A mixture with five percent water is about right. To test for the right amount of moisture, squeeze a handful of sand tightly. It should keep the shape of your hand when released. If much sand adheres to your hand, it is too wet.

SINGLE MOLD

For most casting, the mold has to be in two parts. But some simple things that have

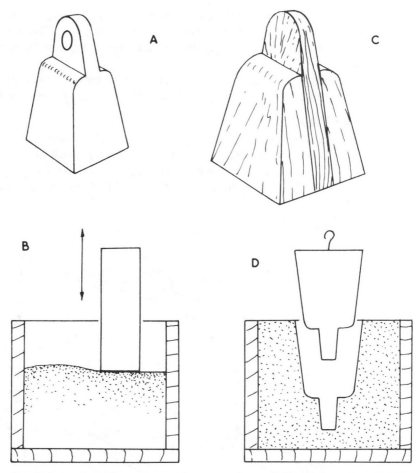

Fig. 19-1. A weight (A) can be cast from a wooden mold (C) in a box of sand (B,D).

a flat part pointing upward can be made in a single mold. An example is a lead block to be used as a weight (Fig. 19-1A). In a simple example, the hole is not cast, but is drilled or punched afterward.

Use any wooden box that is big enough to hold enough sand and stout enough not to burst when the sand is rammed tight. Put sand in the box and ram it down a little at a time with a flat-ended piece of wood (Fig. 19-1B) or even the handle of a hammer.

Make a wooden pattern of the weight. It must be tapered so that it can be withdrawn from the sand. This applies to the narrow part for the hole as well as the main body. It could be cut from solid wood or built up (Fig. 19-1C). If a lathe is available, a round pattern can be turned. Finish the surface smooth. It does not matter what kind of wood is used. For general patternmaking in industry, pine and mahogany are used. For this weight, the wood can be used as it is. When a pattern is to be used many times, it is usual to seal its surface with shellac or varnish.

Scoop out some sand from the middle of the box and press the pattern in. It helps to put a screw eye in its base so it can be withdrawn (Fig. 19-1D). Ram the sand tight around the pattern and level its top. When you are certain it is closely packed, withdraw the pattern and examine the mold. Pour lead in until it is level and let it cool. Then remove some sand so that you can lift it out. Punch or drill the hole. File or hammer the bottom level.

This is the basic method that can be used for the simplest castings. For most casting, the mold is made in two parts even when one surface of the finished work is to be flat.

FLAT-FACED CASTINGS

Molding is done in flasks, which are boxes open top and bottom, and arranged to fit against each other. In production work, the flasks are cast iron. However, small work can be done in wooden flasks. The lower one is called a drag and the other is the cope or top part.

Wooden boxes can be made in identical sizes (Fig. 19-2A). Pieces across the end

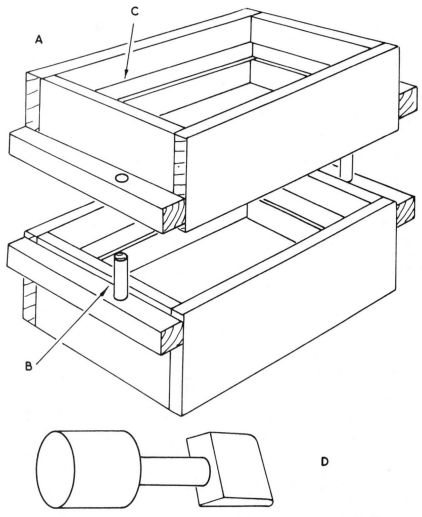

Fig. 19-2. A wooden flask for casting can be made as two open boxes: (A) identical size boxes; (B) dowels; (C) grooves; (D) a narrow tapered end.

act as handles and provide positions for locating dowels that stand up from the drag and engage easily in holes in the top part (Fig. 19-2B). So that the parts cannot be reversed in relation to each other, have the dowels off-center so that they will not match the other way. It will help to have grooves on the insides of the box to provide a key to grip the sand (Fig. 19-2C). Sizes will depend on the work to be done, but the wood should be thick enough to remain stiff and the corner joints should be strong.

Although green sand is used in the flask, there has to be another sand to sprinkle between the meeting surfaces to prevent them from bonding together. The parting sand is used dry and can be bought as such, but brick dust can also be used. It is sprinkled through a fine sieve or riddle (mesh about 1/16 inch) over the sand in the drag, and sometimes on the pattern before it is put in.

A rammer is a sort of straight-ended mallet that can be wood or iron. A narrow tapered end will get into smaller spaces (Fig. 19-2D). Have a trowel available for dealing with sand.

If the object to be made has a flat face and the rest of the shape can be tapered to withdraw from the sand, the whole shape can be arranged in one half of the flask. The weight previously described could be made in this way; a stepped pedestal would be another example. Make a pattern and include a slight taper to all edges. Surfaces can be flat because they do not affect withdrawal (Fig. 19-3A).

Put the pattern on a flat board and have the drag face downward around it. Sprinkle facing sand through the sieve on the board and pattern. Put in green sand with the trowel and press it down at intervals with the rammer (Fig. 19-3B). Make sure the whole box is filled. See that sand is forced into the corners. Fill to overflowing, then scrape the surface level with a straight-edged piece of wood.

Lift and turn the drag over. Put the top part in place, and sprinkle facing sand in. Stand a tapered rod slightly to one side of the pattern so that the metal can be poured in (Fig. 19-3C). This is called a gate stick and can be wood or metal. It could be round, a tapered square, or octagonal. Fill the top part with sand, ramming it tight in the same way as the drag, then scrape its top level.

Ease out the gate stick, tapping it gently at the side to loosen it. The top of the hole left can be made into a funnel shape for ease in pouring metal.

Lift away the top part and put it aside, face up. Cut a small channel from the gate stick position to the pattern, to serve as a runner for the molten metal when it is poured. A piece of sheet metal folded into a deep scoop or gouge will cut the runner (Fig. 19-3D).

To get the pattern out, enter the point of a screw in it, so that it can be used as a handle. There will almost certainly be a few flaws in the mold where sand has fallen or broken away. Bellows can be used to blow away loose sand. If repairs have to be made, there are molders' tools that are used like small trowels for pressing sand into place. They can be made by a smith and are bars with opposite ends formed into small trowel shapes (Fig. 19-4).

If the work is small, all that has to be done now is to put the parts of the flask back together and pour the metal. There will be enough ventilation in the sand to carry the air away, but the pouring metal will put pressure on the whole mold, so the top part should be weighted or attached to the drag to prevent it from lifting. For a clean casting, the inside of the mold can be dusted with graphite.

If the work is larger, it is advisable to provide some escape for air as the metal is

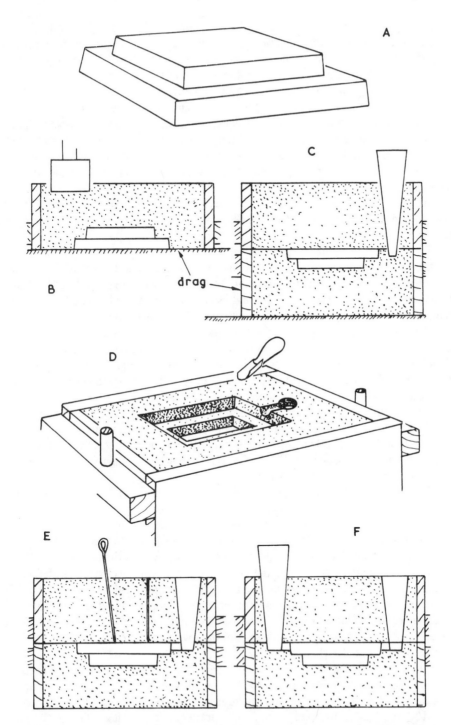

Fig. 19-3. A flat pattern (A) goes into one part and is covered with sand in the other part (B). Then the sand is cut to allow pouring molten metal (C). A deep scoop (D) will cut the metal. A pointed wire (E) allows air to escape or you can use a riser (F).

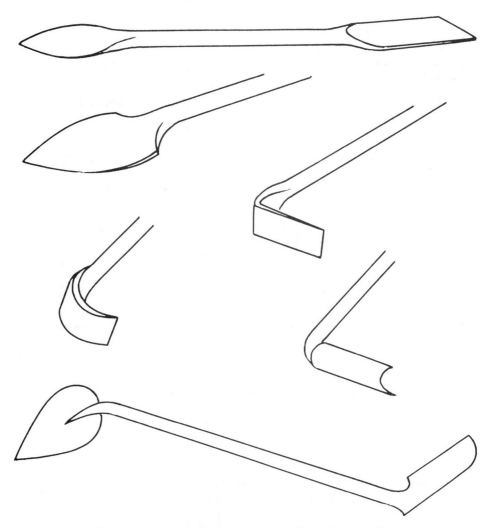

Fig. 19-4. Small steel hand tools are used to correct a mold.

poured in. This can be done while the pattern is still in place by pushing in a pointed wire pricker at several places until it is felt pressing against the pattern (Fig. 19-3E). For a very large casting, it might be better to provide a hole called a *riser*. A riser is really a repeat of the gate stick hole at the side remote from it (Fig. 19-3F). Excess metal that has run off that way or into ventilating holes will have to be cut off after the casting is removed.

SYMMETRICAL CASTINGS

Many things that have to be cast could not be made in one half of the flask because it would be impossible to withdraw the pattern. Many castings have a cylindrical form. The only way they can be cast is to have half in each part of the flask so that the curves are into the sand, which should not be disturbed when the pattern is removed.

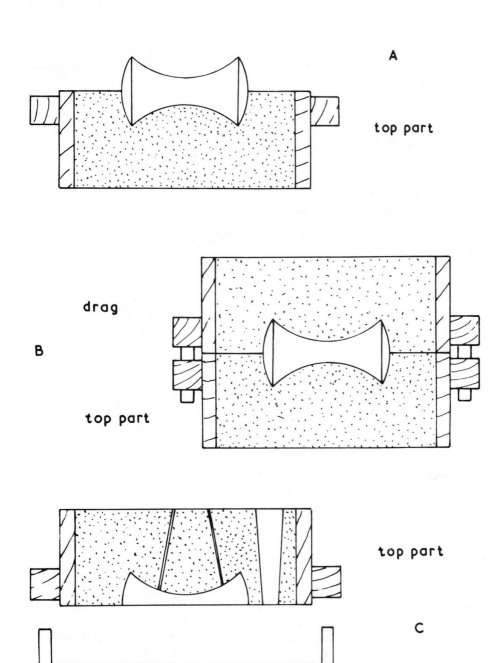

A

top part

drag

B

top part

top part

C

drag

Fig. 19-5. A symmetrical item is arranged in both parts of a flask.

To get a tight pack of sand in each part when a solid symmetrical pattern is being used, preparation has to start with a temporary filling of the top part of the flask. Place the top part with the side that will be toward the drag upward, and fill it with sand. Pack it reasonably tightly and press the pattern halfway into it (Fig. 19-5A). If it is a big pattern, cut out some of the sand first and finish the sand surface level.

Put the drag on and sprinkle on parting sand. Fill the drag and ram the sand tightly. Scrape it level (Fig. 19-5B). Turn over the flask to bring the drag underneath. Separate the boxes carefully to leave the pattern in the drag. Knock out the sand from the top part. Put it back on the drag, sprinkle in parting sand, and repack the top part tightly. Then scrape it level. Having this extra stage is necessary because the first filling of the upper part cannot be done tightly enough.

With both parts of the flask properly packed, use the gate stick and make ventilating holes if they are needed. Then separate the parts and remove the pattern (Fig. 19-5C). Cut a runner and clean up the mold if necessary. Dust with graphite. Put the parts back together and pour the metal.

CORED CASTINGS

Many castings have to be made with holes through them. Sometimes holes are drilled, but it is helpful to cast the hole when the metal is poured. For many purposes, that is all that is needed. For more precision, the cast hole can be opened to size. To make a hole, there has to be a core arranged in the mold so that the metal flows around it and the core can be removed from the casting after it has set.

Suppose a cylindrical casting is required with a hole through that will be machined to make a bearing (Fig. 19-6A). A core must be made longer than the final length of the casting so that it can be supported in the molded sand. This is built up in a core

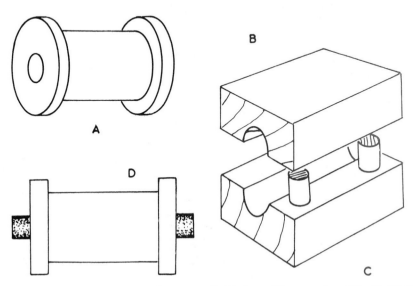

Fig. 19-6. A hollow casting requires a core that is formed in a core box: (A) cylindrical casting; (B) two-part mold; (C) dowels are used to position the parts; (D) core prints are used to make patterns.

box, which is a two-part mold, into which the sand mixture can be packed (Fig. 19-6B). Make it from wood, with half the diameter gouged from each part. Use dowels or other pegs to keep the two parts correctly located in relation to each other (Fig. 19-6C).

The core will go into the sand so it is supported outside the main hollows left by the pattern. To allow for this, the pattern is given core prints (Fig. 19-6D) that are the diameter of the core and that extend far enough to make the recesses in the sand. In pattern making, it is usual to stain the core prints so that they are a different color from the main pattern, to indicate that they are not part of the final shape. Of course, the overall length across the core prints should be the same as the length of the core.

Glossary

abrasive—A natural or artificial substance used for grinding, polishing, buffing, lapping, or sandblasting. Commonly includes garnet, emery, corundum, diamond, aluminum oxide, and silicon carbide.

aging—In a metal or alloy, a change in properties that takes place slowly at room temperature and more rapidly at higher temperatures.

alloy—A substance having metallic properties, composed of one or more chemical elements, at least one of which is a metallic element.

alumel—A nickel-based alloy frequently used as a component of thermocouples.

angle iron—Now actually mild steel. Bars with 90° angle cross-section.

annealing—Heating and holding at a suitable temperature and then cooling at a suitable rate, usually for the purpose of reducing hardness, improving machinability, or achieving other desired properties.

anvil—Any heavy iron or steel device on which work is hammered.

arbor—Round part to hold another being worked on. A rotating shaft.

asbestos—Fire-resistant mineral material.

auger—A wood drill bit having its own handle, instead of fitting in a brace.

backing up—Upsetting by hammering end of work.

baking—Heating at a low temperature to remove gases.

base metal—The metal present in the highest proportion in an alloy. Brass, for example, is a copper-base alloy.

bastard—Intermediate file with teeth between coarse and fine.

beak or bick—Round conical pointed end of anvil. Also horn.

bell mouth—Spread end of tube.

belt grinding—Grinding with an abrasive belt.

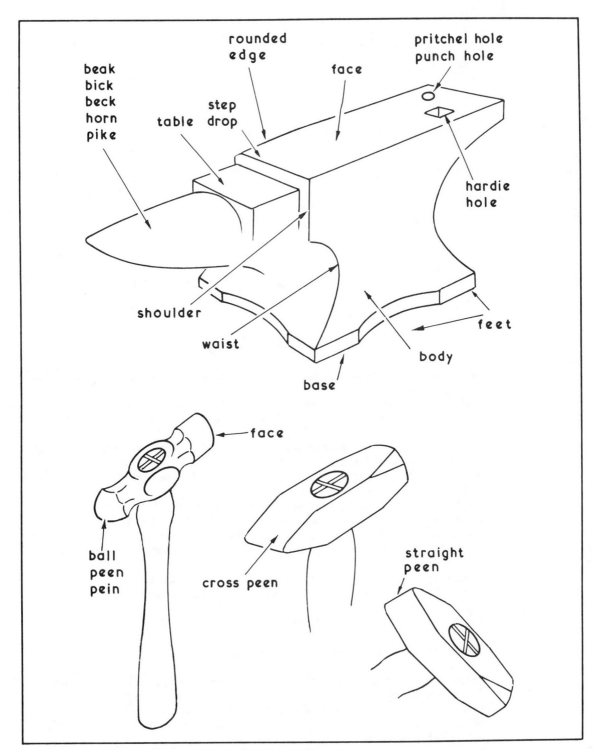

Fig. G-1. Names of the main parts of the anvil and hammers.

bentonite—A clay-like substance used as an ingredient in molding sands.

bevel—The cutting angle of a tool.

bick iron or bick horn—Light anvil for sheet metalwork.

binder—A material other than water added to molding sand to bind the particles together.

bit—Less common name for jaws of tongs.

bit or drill bit—Tool for making holes by cutting rather than punching.

blacksmith's vise—Alternative name for leg vise.

blasting—Cleaning or finishing metal by impingement with abrasive particles carried by gas or liquid.

blind riser—A riser that does not extend through the top of the mold.

blowhole—A hole in a casting caused by gas trapped during solidification.

body—Main part of anvil.

bolster—Block with hole to support work being punched. Also, wide woodworking or masonry chisel, or shoulder where the tang of a tool fits into a handle.

borax—Chemical used as welding or brazing flux.

boss—Center part of a wheel. In smithing, a locally raised part. Type of punch for raising sheet metal from the reverse side.

bossing mallet—Wooden mallet with egg-shaped head for shaping sheet metal.

bottom board—A flat board used to hold the flask when making molds (usually called molding board).

bottom fuller—Tool to fit in the hardie hole of anvil for drawing or shaping steel.

bottom swage—Tool to fit in hardie hole of anvil, having a grooved top surface.

brass—An alloy consisting mainly of copper (over 50 percent) and zinc, to which smaller amounts of other metals may be added.

brazing—Joining parts by flowing a thin layer of non-ferrous filler metal in the space between them. The term brazing is ordinarily used if the process is carried out above 800°F; below this temperature it is called soldering.

breeze—Alternative name for coke.

brine—Salt water used as a cooling bath.

brinnell hardness test—A test for the hardness of a material by forcing a hardened steel or carbide ball of specified diameter into it under a specified load.

bronze—A copper-based, tin alloy with or without other elements. Certain alloys without tin are sometimes referred to as bronzes. The term is rather loosely applied.

buffing—Developing a lustrous surface appearance by contacting the work with a rotating buffing wheel.

buffing wheel—Fabric, leather, or paper discs held together, usually by sewing, used to form wheels for grinding, polishing, or buffing.

bumping—Ramming sand into a mold by jarring or jolting.

burin—An engraving tool.

burnt-in sand—A casting defect caused by sand adhering to the surface of the casting.

burr—Turned over edge. Small rotary file.

butcher—Sett for cutting shoulder.

butt—End to end as in a butt weld.

butterfly nut—Nut to fit on bolt, with projections for hand tightening.

calipers—Tool with hinged curved jaws for checking thicknesses and diameters.

capillary attraction—A combination of forces that causes molten metals or other liquids to flow between closely spaced solid surfaces.

cape chisel—Narrow chisel for cutting grooves in metal.

carbide—A compound of carbon with one or more metallic elements.

carbide tip—Very hard tip to make a cutting edge, bonded to a steel tool.

carbonizing, carburizing—Alternative name for case-hardening.

carriage bolt—Bolt with shallow domed head and square neck to prevent turning in wood.

carriage screw—Similar to a carriage bolt, but with a wood screw end.

case-hardening—Applying a high-carbon surface to mild steel.

casting—(noun) An object obtained by solidification of a substance in a mold. (verb) Pouring into a mold to obtain an object of the desired shape.

casting shrinkage—The reduction in volume of a metal as it solidifies and cools.

casting stresses—Stresses set up in a casting, primarily caused by shrinkage.

catalyst—A substance that changes the rate of a reaction without itself undergoing any net change.

center punch—Pointed punch to make a dot in metal.

centrifugal casting—A casting made by pouring metal into a rotating mold.

chaplet—A metal support for holding cores in place in sand molds.

cheek—An intermediate section of a flask used between the cope and the drag when molding a shape requiring more than one parting line.

chill—A metal insert placed in a sand mold to increase the cooling rate at that point.

chisel—A tool for cutting wood or stone.

chromel—A nickel-chromium alloy used for thermocouples and heating elements.

clay—An earthy substance consisting mainly of hydrous aluminum silicate and used often in molding sands as a binder.

clinker—Waste product from burned coal.

coke—Substance resulting from heating coal to drive out elements producing yellow flame and smoke. Coke is smokeless and burns with a blue flame.

cold chisel—Tool which is hammered for cutting cold metal.

cold sett or sate—Handled chisel for cutting cold steel.

cold shut—A discontinuity in the surface of a casting as a result of two streams of molten metal failing to unite.

collar—Loop joining parts of scroll work.

cope—The upper or topmost section of a flask, mold, or pattern.

core—A formed section inserted inside a mold to shape the interior of a casting.

core blower—A machine for making foundry cores.

corrosion—Oxidization of surface of metal, such as rust on iron.

countersink—Beveled edge of hole. Tool for producing this.

coupler—Ring to slide on handles of tongs to lock them.

croning process—A shell molding process.

cross-cut chisel—Alternative name for cape chisel.

crowbar—Steel lever, usually with curved notched end.

crucible—A pot or vessel used for melting metal or other substances.

crush—A casting defect caused by partial displacement of the sand in a mold before the metal is poured.

cupping tool—Punching tool with hollowed end for forming a round head rivet. A lower one is a rivet set.

cut-off tools—Upper and lower tools for shearing rod with a hammer blow.

cut-off wheel—Thin rotating abrasive wheel for cutting hard steel.

cutting saddle—Plate to put over an anvil face to protect it when the part to be cut is too large for the table.

defect—A condition that impairs the usefulness of an object.

degasser (or **degasifier**)—A material added to molten metal to remove dissolved gases which otherwise might be trapped when the metal solidifies.

degassing—The act of removing dissolved gases from molten metals.

dendrite—A crystal with a branching tree-like pattern often seen in castings that have been very slowly cooled.

deoxidizer—A substance added to molten metal to remove dissolved oxygen.

die—Tool for cutting a screw thread on a rod or a tool for forming steel.

die casting—A casting process whereby molten metal is forced under pressure into the cavity of a metal mold.

dividers—Hinged pair of points for scratching a circle or comparing distances.

dowel—In smithing, a projecting locating part to fit into a hole in another piece.

draft—Taper on the surfaces of a pattern to allow it to be withdrawn from the mold.

drag—The bottom section of a mold, flask, or pattern.

drawing—The action of hammering to make iron longer and thinner.

drift—Tapered pin to drive through holes to pull them into line.

drill bit—Tool for making holes by cutting rather than punching. Also drill or bit.

drill press—A machine that uses bits to drill holes.

drop—A casting defect caused by sand dropping from the cope.

dross—The scum that forms on the surface of a molten metal due to oxidization or impurities rising to the surface.

dry sand mold—A mold made of sand and then dried.

ductility—The ability of a material to deform without fracturing.

dusting—Applying a powder such as graphite to a mold surface.

elasticity—The property of a material allowing it to regain its original shape after deformation.

emboss—Raise sheet metal with hammer, punch or boss from reverse side.

emery—An impure form of aluminum oxide used as an abrasive.

erosion—A casting defect caused by the scouring action of flowing metal.

etching—Eating into steel with acid, usually to mark a name.

eye—Ring shaped in the end of a rod.

eye bolt—Bolt with a flattened or shaped end with a hole through.

face—Working surface of anvil. Level machine part. The action of making a surface flat.

facing—Special sand placed in direct contact with the pattern to improve the surface finish of a casting.

faggot weld—End of rod turned back and welded close to itself.

ferrule—A tube or cap on a wooden handle to prevent it from splitting.

file—Tool with teeth, that are made with grooves cut across it.

fines—Sand grains substantially smaller than the predominate size in a sand mixture.

finish—In a metal, surface condition, quality, or appearance.

firebrick—Brick that withstands high temperatures.

fireclay—Clay that will not crack when fired.

fireplace tongs—For picking up coal.

flairing—Spreading the end of a tube.

flask—A metal or wood frame for making a sand mold.

flatter or flattie—Handled tool with broad flat face that can be put over an uneven hot surface and hammered to flatten it.

flux—Liquid or powder used to aid metal flow in welding, brazing, and soldering.

forge—A furnace for heating iron and steel.

forge, riveting—Portable forge with fan blower, originally intended for heating rivets for structural steelwork.

foundry—A place where castings are made.

fuller, bottom—Tool to fit in hardie hole of anvil for drawing or shaping steel.

fuller, top—A similar handled tool used with it.

gagger—A piece of metal used to reinforce or support the sand in a mold.

galvanized iron—Iron coated with zinc as protection against rust.

gas pocket—A cavity in a casting caused by trapped gas.

gassing—Evolution of gasses from a metal during solidification.

gate—The portion of the runner where molten metal enters the mold cavity.

gated pattern—A pattern that includes the gate in the mold.

gauge—Size, particularly thicknesses and sizes of rods, by number or letter to a recognized scheme or code.

grain refiner—A substance added to molten metal to attain a finer grain structure in the casting.

green coal—Unburned coal.

grinding—Removing stock from work by use of a grinding wheel.

grinding wheel—A circular cutting tool made of abrasive grains bonded together.

grit size—The nominal size of abrasive particles according to the number of openings per lineal inch in a screen through which the particles will pass.

hacksaw—Metal-cutting hand saw with blade tensioned in a frame.

hardie or hardy—Tool that fits in the hardie hole of the anvil with an edge for cutting steel.

hardie hole—Square hole in heel of anvil.

heading plate—Thick steel plate with tapered holes to take rods on which thickened heads can be formed.

heat treatment—Heating steel to alter its character, including annealing, hardening, tempering, and normalizing.

heel—Opposite end of anvil to beak. Also tail.

high-carbon steel—Steel with sufficient carbon to permit hardening and tempering. Steel with 0.2 percent carbon.

hold-down or hold-fast—Device of angular form driven into an anvil hole so its other arm holds down work on the anvil face.

holding furnace—A small furnace in which molten metal is transferred and held until ready to pour.

hollow ground—A concave bevel on a cutting tool.

honing—Sharpening or smoothing with a fine abrasive stone.

hook rule—Rule for measuring from a hooked end over the edge of hot steel.

horn—Alternative name for beak of anvil.

horse power—Unit for stating power produced or needed.

hot chisel—Tool which is hammered to cut hot metal.

hot sett or sate—Handled chisel for cutting hot steel.

hot tear—A fracture form in a casting during solidification because the casting is restrained from shrinking for some reason.

ingate—Same as gate.

ingot—A casting used for remelting.

insert—A removable portion of a mold.

investing casting—Casting metal into a mold made by surrounding (investing) an expendable pattern, usually wax with a refractory slurry which sets, after which the pattern is melted out. Also called "lost wax" casting.

investment compound—A mixture of refractory filler, binder, and liquid used to make molds for investment casting.

jacket—A wood or metal form slipped over a sand mold for support, especially during pouring.

jaws—Gripping surfaces of tongs or vise.

jig—A device to guide tools, particularly in repetition work.

joggle—An offset double bend in a bar.

jump up—Alternative name for upset.

ladle—A receptacle for transferring or pouring metal.

lapping—Using a grinding compound between two surfaces to rub them to match each other.

lathe—Machine for revolving wood or metal so a tool can make it round.

leaf spring—Flat steel long spring usually in graduated sets, as used in automobile suspensions.

leg vise—Vise to attach to bench with leg to floor.

loam—A molding material consisting of sand, silt, and clay used for making very large castings.

lost wax process—Investment casting in which a wax pattern is used.

low-carbon steel—Steel that cannot be tempered. Carbon content less than 0.2 percent.

machinist's vise—Vise to mount on top of bench.

mall or maul—Large mallet.

malleable—Capable of being shaped.

mallet—Type of hammer with wood, rawhide, or plastic head.

mallet, bossing—With eggshaped wooden head for shaping sheet metal.

mallet, tinman's—With cylindrical wooden head for sheet metal work.

mandril or manrel—Iron block on which parts are shaped, particularly a round cone for shaping rings.

match plate—A plate of metal or other material on which are mounted patterns to facilitate molding operations.

melting point—The temperature at which a pure metal, compound, or eutectic changes from a solid to a liquid.

metallurgy—The science and technology of metals.

mild steel—Low-carbon steel that cannot be tempered.

milling tool—Rotating cutter.

misrun—A defective casting not fully formed, caused by solidification of the metal before the mold cavity is filled.

mold—A form of sand, metal, or other material that contains a cavity into which molten metal is poured to form a casting.

molding machine—A machine used for making molds by mechanically compacting sand around a pattern.

mold wash—An emulsion of various materials used to coat the surfaces of a mold cavity.

monkey—Hollow punch for truing shoulder of a swaged tenon.

mulling—Mixing sand and clay by a rubbing or rolling action.

nail beader—Heading tool with a raised face.

nail set or sett—Punch with flat end for driving nail head below surface.

neutral flame—A gas flame in which there is neither an excess of fuel nor air.

normalize—Reduce internal stresses after working by heating and allowing to cool slowly, in the same way as annealing.

offset—Double bend to alter alignment of bar.

oxidation or oxidization—Colored spectrum that forms on polished steel as it heats. Used as a guide for tempering heats of tool steel.

oxidizing flame—A flame with an excess of air (or oxygen).

parting dust—A composition used to facilitate the separation of the pattern in sand molding and prevent sticking of the sand at the junction of the cope and drag.

parting line—A plane on a pattern corresponding to the separation between the cope and drag.

patina—Colored oxidation on metal surfaces, due to long exposure to air, particularly on bronze. It can be simulated by chemical action.

pattern—A form of wood, metal, or other material around which molding material is placed to make a mold.

peen or pein or pane—The shaped end of a hammer head.

peen, ball—Hemispherical knob.

peen, cross—Narrow rounded wedge shape across the head.

peen, straight—Similar to cross peen, but in line with handle.

peening—Hollowing with ball peen hammer.

permanent mold—A metal mold used repeatedly for the production of castings.

pickling—Removing surface oxides from metals by chemical action.

pig—An ingot.

pigtail—Alternative name for scroll.

pintle—Single fixed hinge pin.

pipe—A central cavity formed in a casting during solidification.

plaster molding—Molding where a slurry of gypsum (plaster of Paris) is formed around a pattern, allowed to harden, and thoroughly dried.

pliers—Small gripping tool with tongs action.

plumbago—A high-quality graphite powder.

poker—Tool for moving coal in fire.

porosity—In a metal, fine holes or pores; in a sand, degree of permeability to gases.

post vise—Alternative name for leg vise.

pouring—Transferring molten metal from a ladle or crucible to a mold.

pouring basin—A basin or funnel on top of a mold to receive the molten metal.

precision casting—A metal casting of accurate, reproducible dimensions.

precoat—A special refractory coating applied to wax patterns in investment casting.

pressure casting—Making castings with pressure on the molten metal as in die casting.

pritchel hole—Round hole in the tail of an anvil.

pritchel or punch—Tool intended to be hit with a hammer to make a dent or hole.

pyrometer—A device for measuring temperatures above the range of thermometers.

quench—Too cool hot steel in a liquid.

quenching bath—The liquid into which hot steel is dipped to cool it quickly.

rabbling—Stirring molten metal with a tool.

rake—Poker with bent flattened end for pulling coal in fire.

ramming—Packing sand into a compact mass.

rasp—A coarse, file-type tool with teeth individually raised.

reducing flame—A gas flame produced with excess fuel.

refining—Light hammering to finish a surface.

refractory—A material with a very high melting point suitable for use in molds and furnace linings.

reins—Handles of tongs.

resinoid wheel—A grinding wheel bonded with synthetic resins.

riddle—A sand sieve used in a foundry.

riser—A reservoir of molten metal attached to a casting to provide additional metal required as a result of shrinkage during solidification.

riveting forge—Small portable forge.

rivet set or sett—Tool with hollow for supporting or forming a round-head rivet. An upper one is called a cupping tool.

rout—Cut grooves or hollows.

router—Hand or power tool for cutting grooves and hollows.

rule—Measuring tool, not "ruler." Can be brass.

rule, hook—Handled measuring rule with hooked end.

runner—A channel through which molten metal flows, usually the portion connecting the sprue with the gate.

runout—The accidental escape of molten metal from a mold.

rust—Corrosion on iron or steel.

saddle, cutting—Plate to put over an anvil face to protect it when the part to be cut is too large for the table. Shaped piece over which steel is curved.

sag—A casting defect caused by insufficient strength of the sand.

sand—A granular material from the disintegration of rocks. Foundry sands are mostly pure silicon dioxide. Molding sands contain clay.

sate—Alternative name for sett.

scab—A casting defect where a thin layer of metal separates from the casting.

scarf—Beveled end ready for welding.

scarf collar—Loop used to hold parts of scroll work together.

scrap—Discarded metal that may be reclaimed by melting.

scribe or scriber—Hard sharp steel point for scratching metal.

scroll—Decorative spiral bend.

scroll forks—Double pinned tools for pulling curves around.

scroll iron or tool—Pattern around which a scroll is shaped.

scroll wrench—Double pronged hand tool for curving.

sea coal—Finely divided coal sometimes added to molding sands.

semipermanent mold—A metal mold in which sand cores are used.

seating—Preparing a surface onto which another has to fit.

second man—Support for long work.

set or sett—A hammer-like head on a wood handle, hit with a hammer to shape steel.

set screw—Screw used to draw parts together.

shank—The neck or part of the tool between the handle and the blade.

shell molding—Croning process. Forming molds from thermosetting resin-bonded sand mixtures brought into contact with a hot pattern.

shift—Casting defect caused by mismatch of the cope and drag.

shot—Small spherical pieces of metal.

shoulder—A thickened part of a rod against which another part may rest. On an anvil, the side of the face next to the table.

shovel—Scoop for coal.

shrinkage cavity—A void left in a casting as a result of shrinkage.

shrinkage cracks—Hot tears in a casting due to shrinkage.

shrinkage rule—A measuring rule with expanded graduations to compensate for shrinkage of a casting as it cools.

shrinkhead—Same as riser.

silver brazing—Brazing with silver-based alloys.

skim gate—A gate designed to prevent passage of slag into the mold.

skimmer—A spoon-shaped tool for removing dross from the surface of a molten metal.

skull—The solidified metal or dross left on walls of a crucible when the molten metal is poured out.

slag—Non-burning waste from coal.

slag inclusion—Slag or dross trapped in a solidified casting.

sledge—A large two-handed hammer.

slush casting—A hollow casting, usually made of low-melting metal. After the desired thickness has solidified on the walls of the mold, the balance of the molten metal is poured out.

snagging—Free hand grinding of castings to remove flashings, etc.

snap flask—A flask hinged at one corner so that it can be quickly separated from the mold.

solidification shrinkage—The decrease in volume of a metal when it solidifies.

spatula—A bar with a flattened end, for use with plaster, paint, flux, etc.

spectrum—The rainbow range of colored oxides on heated polished steel.

spring steel—High-carbon steel, similar to tool steel.

spring swage—Top and bottom swages linked with a spring handle.

sprue—The channel that connects the pouring basin with the runner. Sometimes the definition includes all gates, risers, and runners.

stainless steel—Steel alloyed with other metals to resist corrosion.

stake—Shaped block used an an anvil for sheet metalwork.

stake vise—Alternative name for leg vise.

steel—Alloy of iron and carbon.

steel plate—Sheet metal over 3/16 inch thick.

steel sheet—Thinner steel sheets.

step—Top edge of anvil face next to table.

stock—Supply of steel. The body of a tool. One head of a lathe.

stress raiser or stress riser—Changes in contour of a part which introduce localization of stress.

strop—Leather strap used in final stages of tool sharpening.

swage block—Large block with many hollows and holes.

swage, bottom—Grooved tool that fits into hardie hole of anvil.

swage, spring—Top and bottom swages linked with a spring handle.

swage, top—Handled grooved tool used over the bottom swage.

table—On an anvil, the flat part between the face and the beak.

tail—Opposite end of anvil to beak. Also heel.

tang—Part of a tool that is driven into a handle.

tap—Tool for cutting a screw thread in a hole.

tarnish—Surface discoloration of a metal caused by formation of an oxide film.

temper—Reduce fully hardened steel to a suitable hardness for a particular use.

template—Pattern used for marking around to transfer an outline.

tenon—Projecting lug on one part to fit into a hole in another part.

tensile strength—The ratio of the maximum load a bar of metal can withstand to the original cross-sectional area.

thermocouple—A device for measuring temperature, consisting of two dissimilar metals which produce a voltage or current roughly proportional to the differences in temperature of the hot and cold ends.

tines—Prongs, as on a fork.

tinman's mallet—Mallet with wooden cylindrical head for sheet metalwork.

tinplate—Thin sheet steel coated with tin, as used for cans.

tinsnips—Shears for cutting sheet metal.

tolerance—The permissible variation in size of a part.

tongs—Long-handled plier-type tool for holding metal.

tongs, bow—With gap in jaws behind meeting points.

tongs, close-mouthed—With jaws that meet when closed.

tongs, fireplace—For picking up coal.

tongs, flat-jawed—With flat gripping surfaces.

tongs, open-mouthed—With jaws that do not meet when closed.

top fuller—Handled tool, used with bottom fuller for drawing or shaping steel.

top swage—Handled tool with grooved surface to match bottom swage.

traveler—Handled wheel to measure curves by counting revolutions.

tripoli—Abrasive compound used for buffing.

tumbling—Turning work piece, as when making square end on rod.

tuyere or twee iron—Nozzle through which blast of air enters fire.

uphand sledge—Sledge hammer of moderate weight, not used with a full swing.

upsetting—Making steel shorter and thicker. Reverse of drawing down.

veiner or veining tool—V-shaped wood carving tool.

vent—A small opening in a mold for the escape of gases.

vise or vice—Two-jawed device with tightening screw. Fixed to bench and used for holding work.

vise, blacksmith's—Vise with leg, post, or stake to floor.

visegrip pliers—Self-locking pliers.

vise, machinists—Vise to mount on top of bench.

waist—Narrow part of anvil body.

wash—A coating sometimes applied to the cavity of a mold.

weld—Fuse two pieces of metal together with heat.

wildness—A condition whereby molten metal releases so much gas that it becomes violently agitated.

wing nut—Alternative name for butterfly nut.

wrench—Any tool for levering or twisting.

wrought iron—Iron with little or no carbon, produced by a puddling process.

Index